C. Currier's Lith. E. Valois, lith. 33 Spruce St N.Y.

WEST COLLEGE.

1790.

A

HISTORY

OF

WILLIAMS COLLEGE.

BY

REV. CALVIN DURFEE.

"Ask now of the days that are past." — DEUT. iv. 32.

BOSTON:
A. WILLIAMS AND COMPANY,
100 WASHINGTON STREET.
1860.

University Press, Cambridge:
Printed by Welch, Bigelow, and Company.

TO

DAVID DUDLEY FIELD, LL.D.,

NEW YORK,

This Volume,

PREPARED AND PUBLISHED

TO PRESERVE THE HISTORY OF OUR ALMA MATER,

TO PERPETUATE THE MEMORY OF GOOD MEN,

TO EXHIBIT THE DEALINGS OF PROVIDENCE, AND EXALT THE RICHES OF DIVINE GRACE,

Is Dedicated,

WITH VERY PLEASANT REMEMBRANCES,

BY HIS FRIEND AND CLASSMATE,

CALVIN DURFEE.

PREFACE.

In the year 1802 there appeared in the Massachusetts Historical Collections (Vol. VIII.) an article, entitled, "Historical Sketch of Colonel Williams and of Williams College," of which Dr. Fitch is the reputed author. In 1828 Dr. Griffin preached a sermon at the dedication of the Chapel, in which he traced "the dispensations of Providence toward this College." Additional facts and statements have since appeared in the History of Berkshire County, and in Holland's History of Western Massachusetts. In 1841 Professor Albert Hopkins published, in the American Quarterly Register, an account of "Revivals of Religion in Williams College." A memoir of Dr. Fitch appeared in the same work shortly after. In 1843, at the semi-centennial celebration, the addresses of Dr. Hopkins and Dr. Robbins were rich in historical records and facts respecting the College. In 1847 S. H. Davis and D. A. Wells, then of the Senior Class, published a pamphlet, entitled, "Sketches of Williams College." The discourse of Dr. Hopkins in commemoration of Mr. Lawrence, delivered February 21, 1853, contains an account of his donations to the College. In 1855 the annual address before the Society of Alumni, by the Hon. Joseph White, was commemorative of the life and services of Colonel Williams. The author has made a free use of these valuable works whenever he has found them to his purpose. Still the present work is not a reprint; on the contrary, many of the materials, which are deeply interesting to the sons of Williams, have been derived from other sources, — from pamphlets, College catalogues, unpublished letters, living individuals, — and the College records have been carefully examined. The first chapter was furnished by Mr. White. The chapters containing the religious history of the College (except that which relates to Dr. Moore's administration) were prepared by Professor Albert Hopkins. The chapter containing a sketch of the buildings, libraries, and apparatus was mostly furnished by Professor Tatlock. And the last chapter, with some slight alterations and additions, is taken from the pamphlet of Davis and Wells.

As the operations of the American Board had their origin on this spot, and as so many young men have here been educated for the missionary service, Williams College has received the appropriate title of "The Missionary College." And as it has been repeatedly visited with the special influences of the Divine Spirit, a large space has been assigned to its religious history.

No one will consider the sketches of the Presidents as adequate memoirs; but for the purposes of a work of this kind, they are supposed to be all that would be expected or required. And the history of the College would be incomplete without some account of the men who have presided over it.

In recording the history of the efforts which were made to effect the removal of the College, the writer was fully aware of the difficulty and delicacy of the task. To do full justice to all the actors in that scene, on the one hand, and avoid all injustice, on the other, was certainly his desire and aim. And if there has been a failure here, no one will regret it more sincerely than the writer himself. He has not consciously colored the subject with any opinions of his own. He felt, in the language of a friend, "that he was acting the part of a historian, without any point to carry, fallacy to expose, or rebuke to inflict. Providence kindly interposed in that dark hour to save the College from what seemed to be her impending fate; and she needs no darker background than the memory of that gloomy period on which to exhibit her present beautiful and majestic proportions."

To the general reader it may not appear necessary or important that there should be so much particularity as to certain facts and dates, or that so much should be recorded respecting individuals. But it is the manifest duty of a college to record and remember the virtues and labors of those who have contributed to its existence and prosperity; and on this account a more extended notice has been given of individuals in this work than is usual in general history. *Indeed, biography is history.*

The history of a college is little else than the biography of individuals; and antiquarians are constantly calling for names and dates; and a work of this kind is intended to be a book of reference; and minute facts and dates, though of no great moment in themselves, sometimes have an importance on account of their connection with things of common interest.

The author begs permission to acknowledge his indebtedness and to express his gratitude to those individuals who have aided him in the preparation of this work. Especially are his thanks due to Governor Washburn, not merely for his invaluable Introduction, but for his judicious criticisms and friendly suggestions on the work in general.

The work has cost the author more time, and been extended much farther, than was originally intended or anticipated. Still it falls far short of reaching his own ideal of what such a history should be. He has not reached the standard at which he aimed. He sensibly feels that the College deserves a far more worthy memorial. He has this consolation, however, that he has done what he could towards accomplishing a work which ought to have been undertaken by an abler hand. Imperfect as the work still is, the author ventures to solicit for it the favorable consideration of the Alumni and friends of the College.

C. D.

WILLIAMSTOWN, January 1, 1860.

CONTENTS.

CHAPTER X.

CHAPTER XI.

CHAPTER XII.

CHAPTER XIII.

CHAPTER XIV.

CHAPTER XV.

CHAPTER XVI.

CHAPTER XVII.

APPENDIX.

HISTORY

OF

WILLIAMS COLLLGE.

INTRODUCTION.

Dear Sir: —

I thank you for the opportunity you have furnished me of examining the manuscript of your History of Williams College in advance of its publication. I have read it with interest and pleasure, and, in common with every alumnus and friend of the College, am under obligation for the successful effort you have made to gather up, for preservation, so many incidents and events connected with its origin and progress.

No man of generous emotions can read the narrative which you have there presented, without admiring the self-sacrificing courage and resolution with which her friends and patrons have borne her on, in her hours of weakness, through the difficulties and adversities which have beset her way. While to her sons the memories and associations of the past which are there awakened, and with so many of which they have held personal relations, are scarcely less sacred than those which cluster around the home of one's childhood.

For myself, though I pretend to no peculiar sensitiveness of organization or feeling, Williams College has had a strong hold upon my affections ever since I left her halls, nearly half a century ago. Like every other college, she has had an inner and an outer life, like that of which every individual is conscious in his own experience.

The outer life of a college is what the world sees in the character of its officers, in its public exhibitions, its usual habits of order, and the general direction which its alumni take in life from the impulse they receive while there. Oxford and Cambridge each stamp characteristics upon their students which are well understood and easily distinguishable in England. The character of this outer life may be affected by a variety of circumstances which are merely aids or hinderances in the system of instruction which is there pursued, — its library, its apparatus for illustration, its methods of teaching, its associations with other institutions, and the more or less direct manner in which the current revolutions in the sentiments and opinions of the world around it are made to bear upon it.

But whatever may be the causes which give to an institution its character as the world sees it, there is an inner life to every one of these, upon which much of its failure or success depends, which lies behind the ordinary principles of action, and can only be fully understood by one who has shared in and experienced it. It is something independent of the text-books studied, the recitations required, or the strictness and punctuality with which the formulas of discipline are enforced. It is shared in by officer as well as student, and often acts upon and through the official guardians and almoners of the College.

In the case of Williams College, it has, in the latter respect, been highly favored from the first. It long enjoyed the best wishes, wise counsels, and active zeal of such men, to speak of the dead only, as Drs. West and Hyde and Shepherd, and the Hon. Daniel Noble.

But the inner life of the College has been affected, more than by anything else, by the relations which have always existed between its immediate officers of government and instruction and its students. It has been felt in the moral, social, and intellectual character of the institution.

This has been more the relation of a parent to a child, than of the head or usher of a school to its pupil. The number of students has been such that every teacher has personally known and been known by them all, and both have felt that reciprocal interest in each other which grows out of such a knowledge and familiarity. Government has not, therefore, been felt, like that of the state, only when it lays its heavy hand upon some offender against its laws. Its parental care and solicitude, with which it has constantly watched over the student here, have often stood between him and evil, and given to college life, as such, a character upon the unconscious influence of which, the success of its sons has often depended, far more than upon the teachings of the recitation or lecture room.

Another circumstance which has exerted a decided influence upon the inner life of the College, has been the religious element, to which you have properly assigned a considerable space in your work. If it did not make young men religious, it served to create a respect for the religious sentiments and experiences of others, and to prevent their subsiding into cold indifference towards religion as a personal matter.

Besides, the proportion of the prominent scholars there who have espoused a system of belief which recognizes the need of a living faith, as well as a purer morality, has tended to give dignity and attraction to a life of piety among their thoughtless and otherwise reckless associates. It has been something widely different from cant, and has shown itself, not merely in the great numbers of those who have entered the ministry, and especially the missionary field, but in the general prevailing tone of sentiment among the great body of the alumni.

Another circumstance which, in my judgment, enters most intimately into the inner life of this College, is the grand and lovely scenery by which it is surrounded. I have not space in which to attempt, even, to analyze how these mountains and this valley — summer with its robe of green, and autumn with its gorgeous hues — enter into the education of the heart and intellect of the young men who resort hither. I appeal to any one who has spent a college life among these scenes, whether there is not something to which the memory recurs in after life, beyond the recollection, however vivid, of mere localities, and whether on revisiting them he has not felt a chord of sympathy touched within him, which no ordinary law of association has been able to awaken. As a part of the process of education, it was beautifully alluded to by President Hopkins in his address on the occasion of consecrating the Mission Park; and I doubt if there was an alumnus present who did not recognize the force of the allusion.

I might add, that the varied character of the natural scenery of the region around Williams College renders it a peculiarly favorable locality for the pursuit of natural science, which has been successfully cultivated here for more than forty years. In this department, the College may justly claim a high rank and an honorable history.

An attention to natural science was aroused here by the efforts of Amos Eaton, of the Class of 1799, who, if not the pioneer, was an early laborer in that field, and was surpassed by no one in zeal and successful effort to excite and diffuse a taste for its pursuit in our country. And in this he found an earnest coadjutor in Professor Dewey.

There were few books upon the subject accessible to the student at that day, and in 1816 he published a Botanical Dictionary, which he had translated from the French of Richard. The following winter he came to Williamstown, and delivered a course of lectures upon mineralogy, which was followed by one on botany. To aid his students in pursuing the latter, he prepared a *Manual of Botany*, which was published by his Class in April of that year, — a copy of which is before me. Among his students was one who has since attained higher honors and distinctions, as a naturalist, than his teacher, and still holds an eminent rank, especially among the geologists of our country. The names of Eaton and Emmons are among those of her sons, of whom the College may be justly proud for their services and eminence in the department of Natural History.

The efforts of Mr. Eaton inaugurated a new branch of science among those taught in the College, the fruits of which are seen in the erection of Jackson Hall, and the rich store of treasures it contains.

And nowhere has Nature provided a more varied, and at the same time accessible, field for study and observation than here. Valley and mountain, meadow and forest, invite the student of her mysteries to an ever renewed and never exhausted store of materials. Well do I remember the zeal and delight with which many of the classes, in my day, engaged in this study. Every glen and lonely valley were sought out and explored for the flower that nestled in spring by the brook-side, or reared its head in the gaudier hues of summer. Every gray old cliff and rocky bed of the streams that come leaping down the mountain's side were searched with novel and curious interest. And if the student brought back little of useful practical knowledge, he gathered the priceless fruits of invigorated health and fresher spirits with which to engage in the more serious labors of the course.

But I am in danger of forgetting the purpose with which I sat down, while thus giving way to speculations and suggestions like these, as I contemplate the moral condition and local influences of the College. You wished only that I would jot down such personal reminiscences as might be suggested by a perusal of your History. These, you are aware, go back through a large portion of the recorded life of our Alma Mater.

I entered the Junior Class in 1815. She was then twenty-two years of age. She now rejoices in the laurels of sixty-seven. It was the commencement of Dr. Moore's administration, whom I accompanied from Dartmouth. Conflicting opinions have been entertained respecting his efforts to have the College removed; and though it was an unfortunate measure both for the College and himself, I am unwilling to ascribe his conduct to any improper motives. When he was invited to become its President, it was represented to him, by one who spoke in behalf of the trustees, that it would without doubt be removed; and that the only question was in which, of several towns named, the institution should be located. And to understand the question of its removal in its true light, it should be remembered what the condition of the College then was, especially in the matter of access to it.

It is difficult at this day to make one understand the perfect isolation of the spot. During my residence in College, nothing in the form of stage-coach or vehicle for public communication ever entered the town. Once a week, a solitary messenger, generally on horseback, came over the Florida Mountain, bringing us our newspapers and letters from Boston and the eastern parts of the State. Once in a week a Mr. Green came up from the south, generally in a one-horse wagon, bringing the county newspapers printed at Stockbridge and Pittsfield. And by some similar mode, and at like intervals, we heard from Troy and Albany. With the exception of these, not a ripple of the commotions that disturbed the world outside of these barriers of hills and mountains, ever reached the unruffled calm of our valley life. Nor was that all. It was scarcely less difficult to reach the place by private than by public conveyance, except by one's own means of transit. My home, you are aware, was near the centre of the State.* And as my resources were too limited to make use of a private conveyance, I was compelled to rely upon stage and chance. My route was by stage to Pittsfield, and thence by a providential team or carriage, the remainder of my journey.

---

* Leicester.

I have often smiled as I have recalled with what persevering assiduity I waylaid every man who passed by the hotel, in order to find some one who would consent to take as a passenger a luckless wight in pursuit of an education under such difficulties. I think I am warranted in saying that I made that passage in every form and shape of team and vehicle, generally a loaded one, which the ingenuity of man had, up to that time, ever constructed. My bones ache at the mere recollection!

Those who came from "Parson Hallock's," so graphically described in the sketch you have given of the remarks of Judge Dewey, and other localities upon and over the mountain, between there and the Connecticut River, were generally fortunate enough to find their way singly by means of one-horse wagons, or in larger groups in some more capacious farm-wagon fitted and furnished for the occasion. It was, at best, a most primitive mode of conveyance, and probably will not often be repeated, until the day of railroads shall have passed by.

While such was the difficulty of access to the College, it presented little, to the eye of one who visited it for the first time, to reward the struggle it had cost him. When I joined it, it had two buildings, and, I think, fifty-eight students, with two professors and two tutors. The East College was a fine, plain imposing structure, four stories in height, built of brick. Not one of its lower rooms was occupied, and a part only of its other stories. Not one of the rooms or passage-ways was painted. No one of the rooms was papered, or ever had a carpet upon it. And I do not believe the entire furniture of any one room, excepting perhaps the bed, could have cost, or would have sold for, five dollars. I have before me a bill of the furniture of the Senior recitation-room in 1816, *including the locks upon the doors*, and find it amounts to $ 7.26. And from the best sources to which I can refer, I do not think the expenses of a student in College could have ordinarily exceeded two hundred dollars a year, all told.

The southeast corner room on the second story contained the whole philosophical apparatus of the College, and there was no crowding or want of space for its several parts. In the yard of the East College was a small wooden building, in which Professor Dewey, with most admirable diligence and ingenuity, had fitted up his chemical laboratory, and gave his lectures and illustrations upon chemistry, to the students.

The West College contained the Chapel, which occupied the second and third stories of the south end of the building. In the upper half was a gallery which was accessible from the third story. The lower body of the Chapel was reached through the second story. It had on one side a stage. The desk rose a little above this, and stood against the west wall, while the professors and tutors occupied elevated seats upon the same side of the Chapel, looking down upon the students, who sat as quietly as they could upon hard, long benches across the other end of the Chapel. The rooms in that College generally were much inferior to those in the East one, though furnished in similar style.

The only water we had to use, was drawn from a spring at the foot of the hill, south f the East College. And to that, every student from both Colleges repaired with his pail as his necessities required. The consequence was, it must be confessed, there was no excessive use of that element of comfort and neatness.

And yet it was not from the poverty of the students that the style of their rooms and their surroundings was thus humble and poverty-stricken. It was borrowed from the traditionary habits and fashion of the institution. It had grown up in a sequestered spot with limited means, while many of the early students had resorted to it because of its cheap education, and there was next to nothing to awaken any rivalry in the style of dress, furniture, or living, or even to arouse a comparison between these and what may have prevailed in other colleges.

The amusements of the students, a subject fraught with so many difficulties and dangers in most colleges, were simple and few. There was always a pleasant, social relation and intercourse between them and many of the families of the town. And a ball once or twice a year, — Commencement Ball being one, — and an occasional ride to Pownal, or "The Cave" in Adams, or "The South Part," constituted the principal portion of the fashionable dissipation of time in which they indulged. I do not mean to say that there were not occasions when hilarity among the students became boisterous and assumed a grosser form. Everybody at that day drank, and, so be, it excited the animal spirits, it mattered not much what the liquor was. Some kept this in their rooms, and indulged in its use in their convivial meetings without concealment or disgrace.

As I look back upon the history of the past, there are few things more obvious in the management of colleges than this most favorable change in the matter of intoxicating drinks. Not only must it be vastly more easy to sustain an orderly government than formerly, but, what is of far greater importance, it must be incomparably easier for a student to sustain his own self-respect in the prosecution of his collegiate course. And yet, so far as my own observation extended, there was nothing like a prevailing vice of drunkenness in College. There may have been times when one or more individuals may have been overcome on these convivial occasions. But it never was regarded as a thing to be emulated, or calculated to win favor. And I do not now recall a single instance where a student carried from the College a habit of intemperance, acquired there, into the walks of after life.

There is one source of satisfaction in recurring

to the early as well as the later history of our Alma Mater, and that is the character which her students have somehow acquired and exemplified in active life. It, at least, shows that, if the training they have received there did not develop and strengthen their qualities as men and as scholars, it did not crush out or dwarf the intellects and common sense of those who resorted thither for an education.

I might test this by taking the Triennial Catalogue of her Alumni, and tracing them, some into one field of usefulness and honor, and some into another, and finding the estimate in which they have been held within their several spheres. As I thus run my eye along its pages, I see the name of Mills, of the Class of 1797, an able jurist and advocate, and a distinguished Senator in Congress; Williams, of the Class of 1800, Chief Justice and Governor of Vermont; Bradish, of the Class of 1804, Lieutenant-Governor of New York; Howe of the same Class, the learned jurist, whose early promise, in the place he held upon the bench, is still remembered with affectionate regret; Buel, of the Class of 1805; Betts, of the Class of 1806, the able Judge of the United States District Court of New York; Professor Dewey, of the same Class; Morell, of 1807, once Chief Justice of Michigan; Kellogg, of 1810, Judge of the Supreme Court of Vermont; Edwards, of the same Class, late President of Andover Theological Seminary, — a strong, energetic man, whose life was full of active usefulness and benevolence; Maynard, of the same Class, who, in founding a law school in Hamilton College, did but justice to the character of a profession which he illustrated and adorned; Judge Dewey, of 1811, who enjoys a well-earned reputation in the place he still holds on the bench of our Supreme Court; Page, of 1812, a Judge of the Supreme Court of New York; and Ashley, of 1813, late a Senator in Congress. Burbank, of the Class of 1797, the first President of our Association of the Alumni, and Childs, of the Class of 1802, the founder and President of the Berkshire Medical Institution, might be named among others of her Alumni who have dignified and adorned the medical profession. I might go on, but space forbids; though, as I turn away, my eye rests upon the Class of 1819, and the names of Brigham, of the American Bible Society; Hallock, of the American Tract Society; Hallock, of the Journal of Commerce; and Richards, late Secretary of State of the Sandwich Islands, — out of a class of thirteen. She has produced useful men, if she may not boast eminent scholars.

And even in the field of scholarship and Belles-Lettres, there are names enough to show that hers is not merely a training for homely, every-day usefulness and duty. I have only to mention Talcott, of the Class of 1809, once Attorney-General of New York, the brilliant and accomplished orator, the profound lawyer, the beautiful and refined scholar, who, though dying at the age of forty-six, stood in the very first rank among the great names that have illustrated the Bar of New York; Dewey, of the Class of 1814, the profound thinker, and eminent writer and pulpit orator; Jonas King, of the Class of 1816, whose reputation is not limited to Greece alone; and Porter and Barnard, of the Class of 1818, — to come no nearer the present time, — the first cut down in his early promise of development, the other known alike in the departments of letters, of politics, and diplomacy. Nor ought I to omit the name of Bryant, one of the finest poets of his age, who, though not a graduate of any college, gave evidence and an earnest of his rare genius while a member of this.

I have not selected these names with any view to an invidious distinction. I have taken them at a casual glance, from an aggregate scarcely, if at all, exceeding five hundred of its earliest Alumni, when, as I have remarked, its means were small, and large numbers of its students had shared, to a limited extent only, the advantages of previous educational training.

But not to dwell longer upon any of the real or supposed causes which have exhibited themselves in the inner or outer life of the College, or the moral or intellectual training of its scholars, the facts mentioned in your History justify the assumption that it has kept pace, in some things, with institutions apparently much more favorably situated.

If Williams College was the first to publish an

Annual Catalogue of her students, the first to form an association of her Alumni, the first to found and maintain an Observatory, on this continent, and the first to inaugurate scientific expeditions, as you have stated, it was but the outward manifestation of an active, pervading spirit, which has been quietly and unobtrusively at work there, ever since the germ of a literary institution was planted in the forest on the pleasant banks of the Hoosac.

Of the changes and struggles through which the College has passed since 1815, your pages are too full to warrant my attempting to add anything. No friend of the institution or of the cause of sound learning can have witnessed these without much interest and solicitude. They have at least served to test who its true friends were. And, what must strike with much force the mind of every man who recalls its history, friends have always sprung up at the very moment when their aid was most needed. I have no doubt the associated interest of the Alumni, which has been kept alive by their annual meeting, has had a decided effect in awakening and stimulating a generous sympathy in behalf of the College. I have never attended a meeting of that body when I have not witnessed manifestations of renewed affection for our Alma Mater, and a warmer zeal to stand by and sustain her.

Dr. Griffin, with his broad benevolence and varied experience, brought to the institution his whole heart, and gave to it his untiring zeal. He found there an elevated standard of scholarship, which Dr. Moore had done much to introduce and establish. And in his successor the College has had an officer in every way competent to sustain whatever of reputation it had attained under any former administration.

Of Dr. Hopkins delicacy forbids me to speak as I would, though I might only utter a common sentiment, and I therefore forbear. Under his administration the College has attained a rank in numbers and influence and prosperity, which its most sanguine friends could not have anticipated in 1815.

But it has ceased to be extravagant to look forward to almost any extent of influence or height of prosperity in her future history. Names have become associated with Williams College whose fame, like that of its founder, will be as lasting as the hills that encircle the lovely valley in which it stands. Lawrence, in what he did and gave for her, was worthily acting out his own noble nature; and Jackson has inscribed his name upon tablets there which time can never efface; and the recent donation of Morris will be held in grateful remembrance through all coming ages. And who can doubt that the same kind Providence which has never failed to sustain her in her hours of utmost need, will raise up other noble and generous hearts to minister to her wants, and to make her, as she has been, worthy to take her place among her sister institutions in the land, and to keep pace with these in their onward and upward progress?

Again thanking you for the perusal of your sheets, and asking pardon for the length to which these desultory thoughts and reminiscences have been extended,

I am, very respectfully,

Your obedient servant,

EMORY WASHBURN.

REV. CALVIN DURFEE.

HISTORY OF WILLIAMS COLLEGE.

CHAPTER I.

BIOGRAPHICAL SKETCH OF COL. EPHRAIM WILLIAMS.

As Williams College owes its origin and name to Colonel Ephraim Williams, it is obvious that no apology will be needed for placing on these pages a brief sketch of the life and services of its founder.

EPHRAIM WILLIAMS was a descendant, in the third generation, from the Puritan, Robert Williams, who is supposed to have removed from Norwich, in England, and settled in Roxbury. He was admitted freeman in 1638, and died at an advanced age, September 1, 1693. He left three sons, — Samuel, Isaac, and Stephen, — through whom, says John Farmer, he became the "common ancestor of the divines, civilians, and warriors of his name, who have honored the country of their birth."

Captain Isaac Williams, second son of Robert, was born in 1638, and removed, while yet a young man, to Cambridge Village, afterwards the town of Newton. He was chosen deacon of the church in that town, when it was first constituted, in 1664. He died in 1707, leaving his homestead and the larger part of his property to his youngest son, Ephraim Williams, the father of the subject of this memoir.

Colonel Ephraim Williams, senior, was born at Newton, October 21, 1691. He married Elizabeth Jackson, the daughter and eldest child of Abraham Jackson, himself the only son of John Jackson, who was the first settler of Newton. Ephraim, who was their eldest son, was born at Newton, on the 24th day of February, 1715. Soon after the birth of a second son, February 24, 1718, the mother died. The two children, Ephraim and Thomas, were immediately taken by their grandfather, Abraham Jackson, to his own home. He adopted and "brought them up under the paternal roof of his own mansion, and gave them a good education for the time." At his death in 1740, he left them two hundred pounds, saying that "he had already spent considerable sums for their bringing up and education."

Abraham Jackson was a man of the Puritan stamp, distinguished for his intelligence, integrity, and devotion to the public good. During a long life, he was a most useful citizen, and an honorable man. In 1706, we find him associated with Isaac Williams on the first school committee of Newton. Of his liberality the records of the town furnish one most interesting proof. On the 14th of May, 1701, he gave one acre of land, "for the setting the school-house upon, and the enlarging the burying-place, and the convenience of the training-place." A beautiful example, doubtless, of the spirit of his inculcations upon his youthful charge, and fully justifying the historian when he says: "It is quite apparent that the first sprouts of Williams College were germinated in the family of Abraham Jackson,* the son of the first settler of Newton."

As he approached the age of manhood, young Williams found scope for his enterprise and love of adventure upon the ocean. He made several voyages across the Atlantic, visiting England, Spain, and Holland. In these voyages, and in his intercourse with general society, he acquired those accomplishments of manner, and that knowledge of human character, together with a fund of general information, which well prepared him for his future career. He continued this mode of life until about the age of twenty-five.

In the year 1739, his father had removed, with his family, to the Indian town of Stockbridge. His family was one of the four English families designated by the Provincial government to settle in that place, in aid of the mission to the Stockbridge Indians, which had just been commenced by the Rev. John Sargeant. At the earnest solicitation of his father, the son now abandoned a seafaring life, and removed to Stockbridge. Here he purchased large tracts of land, and resided for several years, an active and useful citizen of the infant

* Great-grandfather of Nathan Jackson, of New York.

settlement; and often its agent at the General Court. But the time had arrived for his entrance upon more responsible duties.

On the 29th of March, 1744, Great Britain declared war against France and Spain. It was proclaimed in Boston in June. "At the declaration of war," says General Hoyt, "many Indians who had been active in the former war, and who resided about the frontiers on the Connecticut, suddenly left their stations, and repaired to Canada to join the hostile tribes in that quarter, — often firing upon the houses of the frontier settlers as they commenced their march." "Perfectly acquainted with the topography of the country, they were employed during the war, not only on predatory excursions of their own, but as guides to other and more distant Indians."

To guard against these invasions, the Provincial government authorized the construction of a cordon of small forts and block-houses across the highlands, from Fort Dummer on the Connecticut to the valley of the Hoosac at the base of Saddle Mountain. Principal among these were Fort Shirley, in Heath, Pelham, in Rowe, and Fort Massachusetts. There were also block-houses in Bernardston and Coleraine, and small works at Pontoosuck, Stockbridge, and Sheffield. Forts Shirley, Pelham, and Massachusetts were erected in the summer of 1744, under the superintendence of Ephraim Williams, Jr., who had received a captain's commission, and was intrusted with the command of the line of defences upon the northern frontiers west of the Connecticut. His headquarters were at Fort Massachusetts. His superior officer, as well as personal friend, was John Stoddard, of Northampton, Colonel of the Hampshire regiment. Thus was Williams first made acquainted with the valley of the Hoosac, destined to the end of life to be the theatre of his labors, and the object of his cares and affectionate regards.

In this exposed position, — pushed far into the wilderness, — on a beautiful meadow in Adams, Williams and his hardy companions erected their fort of logs, surrounded with pickets of squared timbers driven into the ground so as to form a continuous fence, mounted with a few iron guns, or swivels, and defensible against musketry alone. The garrison at this time numbered fifty men, while a less number served for the other and smaller works.

Being now thirty years of age, with vigorous health, bold, active, and vigilant, Captain Williams shared fully with his men the privations and dangers of the service, and exerted his best powers in defence of the frontiers.

In the spring of 1746, he enlisted a company and joined the forces which had assembled at Albany, with the view of proceeding to Canada, by the way of Lake Champlain. The projected invasion of Canada was abandoned. The troops were withdrawn for the defence of Boston; and Captain Williams returned to his command on the frontiers. Fort Massachusetts was rebuilt and garrisoned with one hundred men. As heretofore, it continued to be the object of frequent attacks.

A single instance, as related by General Hoyt, may be given. On the 2d of August, 1748, four men being fired upon at some distance from the fort, Captain Williams sallied with thirty men. After driving the enemy about forty rods, a party of fifty Indians in ambuscade suddenly fired, and endeavored to cut off his retreat. By a quick movement he regained the fort, with one man killed, and two wounded. At once a large body of three hundred Indians and thirty French advanced and opened their fire upon the fort. After sustaining a sharp fire from the garrison for two hours, the enemy drew off with their killed and wounded.

Peace was declared at Aix-la-Chapelle, October 18, 1748. The war closed in the Colonies the following summer. From this time, Captain Williams resided on the Connecticut, at Hatfield, and with his brother Thomas, at Deerfield.

With a rising reputation as an officer, with great dignity of person and manners, he found ready admission into the highest circles of rank and influence, and numbered among his intimate friends and associates the leading men in the county, — such men as John Worthington of Springfield, Joseph Hawley of Northampton, Oliver Partridge and Israel Williams of Hatfield, and Jonathan Ashley, the minister at Deerfield, — men who had no superiors in the Province.

But he did not forget the valley of the Hoosac and his companions in arms. Much of his thought and effort was devoted to them. Mainly through his influence with its leading men, the General Court on the 18th of April, 1749, appointed a committee, consisting of Colonels Dwight and Choate and Oliver Partridge, Esq., "to survey and lay out two townships on Hoosac River, each of the contents of six miles square, in the best of the land, and in as regular form as may be, joining them together; and return a correct plat of said townships; and also to return the course and distance of said towns from Fort Massachusetts."

Captain Williams remained at Boston during the session of 1749–50, urging forward the settlement of the new townships. As the result of these efforts, a committee was ordered, on the 17th of January, 1750, to lay out the West township into sixty-three contiguous home lots of from thirteen to fourteen acres, — each lot being entitled to one sixty-third part of the township. After reserving one lot for the first settled minister, one for the support of the ministry, and a third for the support of schools, the committee were directed to dispose of the remaining sixty lots to actual settlers, for £6 16*s.* 6*d.* each, and upon the usual conditions. The committee are also directed "to grant as many lots to the soldiers of the garrison of Fort Massachusetts as they should think proper."

On the 16th of February, also, a grant of one hundred and ninety acres of land, in the East township, was made to Williams himself, on the condition that "he erect and finish for service, within two years, a good grist-mill and saw-mill on the North Branch of the Hoosac River, and keep the same in good repair for twenty years." The mills were erected, and Williams became owner of the large meadow upon which the fort was built.

The committee proceeded without delay to the work of settling the West township. Sixty-three lots, fourteen rods wide, were laid out on a broad street running from Green River to Hemlock Brook, and sixty of them disposed of to purchasers by lot. Of these lots, more than one half were taken by the officers and soldiers of Fort Massachusetts, Captain Williams himself drawing lots number eight and ten. Several of the proprietors removed their families, and commenced the work of settlement immediately.

Thus it appears that these sister towns, in the upper valley of the Hoosac, are the foster-children of Fort Massachusetts, and may look to Ephraim Williams as their founder.

But the progress of improvement was soon to be stayed. The peace was indeed but a cessation of arms. The combatants ceased to fight for want of breath. Mutually exhausted, they were glad to adjourn the inevitable contest for supremacy in the New World, till there should be renewed strength and more auspicious circumstances. And already the indications of the approaching contest began to multiply.

The English Colonists justly complained, that their French neighbors had, in violation of the treaty, not only refused to abandon their forts at Crown Point and at Niagara, but had also increased their defences at these points, and erected new works on Lake Erie; and, moreover, had used untiring diligence in extending their influence among the Indian tribes, and in connecting the Mississippi and Ohio Rivers with the Lakes by a line of fortified posts. These complaints and remonstrances of the English Colonists were unheeded, and it was evident that the final struggle could not be long delayed.

Meanwhile the Indian allies had already scented the coming war, and in the spring and summer of 1754 commenced hostilities on the frontiers of Pennsylvania and New England.

Immediate measures of defence were adopted. Forts Dummer and Massachusetts were strengthened, and their garrisons increased. Between them a series of stockades was renewed on the line of the Deerfield, instead of Forts Shirley and Pelham; while at the West, additional works were built at New Framlingham, now Lanesborough, and at West Hoosac, now Williamstown. As in the previous war, the command was intrusted to Ephraim Williams, who now held a Major's commission in the second Hampshire regiment, which was commanded by Israel Williams of Hatfield.

The Colonies determined to prosecute the war, thus commenced, with their utmost vigor, and upon an extensive scale. The plan adopted embraced three principal expeditions, to be conducted simultaneously in the following spring.

On the 18th of February, 1755, the General Court of Massachusetts resolved to raise five thousand men for the war. They empowered Governor Shirley to enlist twelve hundred men for the Crown Point expedition, whenever the other Provinces should agree to raise their respective proportions, as determined by the Congress at Albany. The proposition of Massachusetts was assented to by the sister Colonies. Shirley issued his proclamation on the 26th of March. The troops were enlisted in three regiments of four hundred each, and commanded severally by Timothy Ruggles, of Worcester; Moses Titcomb, of Essex; and Ephraim Williams, of Hampshire. Colonel Williams and his staff received their commissions on the 29th of March.

The expedition was popular, and the regiments were speedily filled. That of Williams comprised ten companies. His own company was commanded by John Burke, of Bernardston. On his staff were Seth Pomeroy, of Northampton, Lieutenant-Colonel; Noah Ashley, of Westfield, Major; Thomas Williams, of Deerfield, Surgeon; and Perez Marsh, of Dalton, Surgeon's Mate. William Williams, of Connecticut, one of the signers of the Declaration of Independence, was his Aid;

and the venerable Stephen Williams, of Longmeadow, was Chaplain.

The regiments — known as the "new levies" — were ordered to rendezvous at Albany. They encamped on the eastern bank of the Hudson near the last days of June. Early in July, the little army commenced its march up the east bank of the Hudson; and the main body, with forty pieces of cannon and a small party of Indians, arrived at the head of Lake George on the 29th of August. At the southern extremity of this peaceful water — resting in solitary beauty in its rough casket of mountain and forest, but soon to be dyed with the blood of many a fearful encounter — Johnson cleared the ground and formed his encampment, and waited for the arrival of his transports and stores.

On Sabbath morning, the 7th of September, some Indian scouts came into camp with the intelligence that they had discovered the trail of a large army, marching in three columns from South Bay towards the Hudson. Instantly a council was called, which resulted in an order to Colonel Williams to "build a picketed fort sufficient for a hundred men." Williams immediately commenced clearing the ground, and preparing the materials for the fort.

The army reported to Johnson proved to be a strong force of French regular troops, Canadians, and Indians, under the command of M. de Dieskau, a German Baron, who had recently arrived in

Canada with the commission of Commander-in-Chief of the French forces in North America. At Montreal, the Baron was persuaded to relinquish his purpose of attacking Oswego, and to proceed down Lake Champlain in quest of Johnson, of whose approach he had received information. Landing at South Bay, he advanced through the woods towards Fort Lyman — since named Fort Edward — on the Hudson, and arrived in its vicinity on the evening of the 7th. Deterred from attacking the fort by the fears of his Indians, he encamped for the night, with the design of proceeding in the morning on Johnson's track to the lake.

A party of wagoners who had deserted, two of whom had been captured by the enemy, returned to the camp at midnight, and reported Dieskau's position. Johnson waited till morning, and then called another council. Hendrick, the Mohawk chieftain, was invited to attend. It was agreed to send one thousand provincials and two hundred Indians in search of the enemy. Johnson at first proposed a smaller number, and asked the opinion of Hendrick. He replied, "If they are to fight, they are too few; if they are to be killed, they are too many." When the general proposed to divide them into three parties, the old chief, putting three sticks together, said, "These you cannot break; take them one by one, and you will break them easily." The party was not divided.

Colonel Williams was appointed to the command, and led the van of five hundred men, composed of his own regiment and volunteers from the other regiments of Massachusetts. Lieutenant-Colonel Whiting, of New Haven, Connecticut, a brave officer who had done good service at Louisbourg, was second in command, and brought up the rear.

It was a calm, bright morning of the 8th of September. The sun poured his unclouded splendors upon the still lake and the wooded hills, yet untouched by the autumnal frosts, when the brave Provincials filed from their rude camp into the road.

The route of Williams led up a deep ravine, having the French Mountain on the left, and a range of hills with a less elevation and a more gradual rise on the right. Having proceeded two miles, he halted for Whiting and Hendrick, who were at some distance in the rear. Flanking parties were thrown into the woods; and while in this position, a herd of frighted deer rushed down the valley between the men, but excited no suspicions.

Hendrick, mounted on a small horse, came up and took the lead with his Mohawks. The road soon left the bottom of the ravine, and gradually led up the hill-side on the right. The ground became rough and steep, and was covered with thick woods. At the distance of another mile, and already within Dieskau's ambuscade on the hill, Hendrick said to Colonel Williams, "I scent

Indians!" Williams halted his front rank for a few moments, to allow his files, which were stretched along the road, to close up. Hendrick continued to advance until he was deep within the ambuscade, when he was accosted, doubtless by a friendly Iroquois. "Whence come you?" said he. "From the Mohawks." "Whence come *you?*" "Montreal," was the reply.

At the same moment, two Indians on the left, perceiving the hesitation of the English, discharged their pieces; when suddenly the deep valley below rung with the terrific yells of the Abenakis and Canadians, who opened a heavy fire upon the Mohawks and the front of Williams's column. The Mohawks stood their ground and fought bravely, until Hendrick fell, shot through the back, when they were thrown into confusion. The dying chief, with an Indian's pride, spent his latest breath in lamentations, lest such a death might leave a stain upon his memory.

Williams, comprehending his position at a glance, ordered his men to take to the woods, and gain the eminence on their right. No sooner was this movement commenced, than a murderous volley from the Iroquois on the hill, strewed the ground with the dying and dead. Williams, who was standing upon or by the side of a large rock near the road, received a bullet through the head, and fell dead upon the spot. John Morse, late of Washington, in Berkshire County, was standing by his side, and was covered with the blood of his dying commander. With the aid of a comrade, he safely concealed the body from the scalping-knife of the advancing Indians.

The fight now became general. From the hill above and the ravine below, with discordant cries, the enemy pressed upon the astonished Provincials, whose ranks, encumbered with the retreating Mohawks, crowded the road. Colonel Whiting pressed forward to support the front, which was now desperately engaged with the enemy on either side. Here the conflict was severest. The Provincials did not yield the ground without a fierce struggle. Most of the slain fell at this spot. Here the enemy lost M. St. Pierre, their brave and renowned Indian leader. Finding himself nearly surrounded by superior numbers, who had command of the ground, and his men rapidly falling around him, Whiting wisely ordered a retreat.

The Provincials withdrew from the hill, and made a stand in the rear of Bloody Pond, — thus named by this day's baptism, — and held the enemy in check for some time. Forced again to retreat, they kept up a galling fire upon their pursuers, from behind rocks and trees, till they were met by a reinforcement of three hundred men, sent out to cover their retreat. They entered the camp at eleven o'clock, and took their places, and shared with their comrades the subsequent conflicts of the day. Thus closed the fatal fray, known to our fathers as "the bloody morning scout."

Colonel Williams was not mutilated. He was

carried by his mourning comrades to the height of land some fifteen or twenty rods in a southeasterly direction from the rock where he fell, and buried at the foot of a "huge pine beside the old military road." On the rough hill-side, beneath the forest shades, his remains have rested without a memorial, and "undisturbed until about twenty years ago, when his nephew, Dr. William H. Williams, of Raleigh, N. C., disinterred and carried off the skull." The ancient pine has fallen, and nothing but the stump remains. Yet two descendants of the parent tree, of vigorous growth, have sprung from its roots, and still shade the place of burial.

The rock upon which he fell still stands by the ancient road. It is an irregular quadrangle, and about seven feet in height. On this rock the Alumni of Williams College have erected a marble monument, twelve feet high, with appropriate inscriptions, and surrounded it with a substantial iron fence. Long may it stand, to tell the passer-by the brief story of the life and our regard for the memory of EPHRAIM WILLIAMS!

When about departing from Deerfield to join the army, Colonel Williams requested his brother Thomas to aid him in drafting a will, — giving no intimations, however, of his intentions in respect to the disposition of his property. From motives of delicacy the request was declined, and the matter was dropped. At Fort Massachusetts, he again met his old companions in arms, and gave them his last words of counsel and encouragement. Tradition informs us that, at the parting interview, some slight expressions fell from his lips of the purpose to leave to them, in the event of his death, more substantial tokens of his regard. At Albany he was reminded by illness of the uncertainty of life, and of his cherished purpose yet unfulfilled. His will was made and executed on the 22d of July, John Worthington and Israel Williams being appointed executors. After appropriate bequests in small amounts to relatives and personal friends, the will proceeds as follows: —

"It is my will and pleasure, that all of the residue of my real estate, not otherwise disposed of, be sold by my executors, or the survivor of them, within five years after an established peace, (which a good God soon grant!) according to their discretion; and that the same be put out at interest on good security; and that the interest money yearly arising therefrom, and the interest arising from my just debts due to me, and not otherwise disposed of, be improved by said executors, and by such as they shall appoint trustees for the charity aforesaid after them, for the support and maintenance of a free school in the township west of Fort Massachusetts (commonly called West Township) forever; provided said township fall within the jurisdiction of the Province of Massachusetts Bay, and continue under that jurisdiction; and provided also the Governor of said Province, with the Assembly of said Province, shall (when a suitable number of inhabitants are settled there) incorporate the same into a town by the name of Williamstown; and if the interest of such moneys be more than sufficient for such a purpose, that which remains be improved, as aforesaid, for the support of a like school in the East Township, in which said fort now stands; but in case the aforesaid provisos are not complied with, viz. if said West Township fall not within said Massachusetts Province, or do not continue under that jurisdiction, or if it shall be incorporated by any other name than that above mentioned, then my will is, that the interest of said moneys be applied to some other public beneficial and charitable purpose by my executors, as above directed, respecting other parts of my estate, according to their discretion and good judgment."

After no inconsiderable search, little has been found from the pen of Colonel Williams which reveals his principles of action, and his views upon the great subjects of life, duty, and destiny. For whatever is known of these, as well as of his personal appearance, habits, and manners, we are indebted to the impressions which he made upon his contemporaries, as revealed in the scanty notices of the times, and in the few traditions which yet linger amongst us.

From these we learn that his "person was large and fleshy," his countenance benignant, and his presence commanding; that he loved, and excelled in, the rough games and feats of agility and strength so common in his day, and often engaged in them with his soldiers during the intervals of duty; that his "address was easy, his manners simple and conciliating;" that he loved books, and the society of literary men, "and often lamented the want of a liberal education;" that to these endowments were added the higher qualities of mind, — quick and clear perceptions, a solid judgment, a lofty courage, and an unwavering constancy in scenes of danger, and that military genius which needed only a fitting opportunity to place him in the highest walks of his profession. He knew both how to command and how to conciliate the affections of his men. "He was greatly beloved by them while living, and lamented when dead." And finally, in the language of Colonel Worthington, who knew him well, "Humanity made a most striking trait in his character, and universal benevolence was his ruling passion." He truly adds, "His memory will always be dear."

Colonel Williams was never married. He died in the forty-first year of his age; cut down in the pride and strength of his manhood, in the midst of his useful and brilliant career, and at a juncture when broader fields, inviting to still higher achievements, were opening before him. He fell in the first campaign of that remarkable war which drove the French power from the banks of the St. Lawrence, and changed the destiny of this continent forever, — that war which opened the way, and hastened the advance, and educated the heroes of the Revolution. With equal abilities, with a larger experience, and a superior position to any of these, — the favorite of the people, and the idol of the army, — what might not have been witnessed in his career, had his life been prolonged to the allotted age of man?

But his work was done! Doubtless, in the eye of Him who sees all and disposes of all, it was *well* done! And at the close of one hundred years from his death, and in the clear light of what has already been accomplished by his dying bequest, shall we not also respond, "His work was well done!"

Nay, as Williams himself sat in his sick-chamber at Albany, and laid aside the pen with which he had made sure his last act of good-will to his old neighbors and friends in the Hoosac valley, and contemplated its beneficent results in the higher intelligence and well-being of their posterity in the future, could the veil have been lifted, and his eye have run down the line of the coming years till it rested on these times, and marked the results as they now stand revealed to us, — could he have seen the little hamlet of eleven settlers give place to the populous village, and the broad cultivated town, and the frontier which he had defended so well stretching onwards to the Lakes, across the western valley to the Pacific shore, — could he have beheld the free school expanding into the college, and bestowing a liberal culture upon sixty-five generations of generous youth, sending them forth each successive year equipped to do the work of men

"In the world's broad field of battle," —

could he have caught a glimpse of the maple grove, and the haystack beside it, and the uplifted hands of those youthful heroes of a new crusade, pleading for a fresh baptism upon the churches, and have seen the swift messengers of peace running to all lands, and publishing salvation, and the darkness lifting, and the day breaking, and heard the morning song, — would he not also, with a full heart, have exclaimed: —

"It is well! The ways of God are justified. I see there is a higher prize! I see there is a brighter glory! It is well. Though my sun go down at noon; though I fall in the first shock of battle, and others lead on to victory and win the soldier's prize; though my poor body sleep long years in the deep woods, and no kindly tear fall, and no friendly foot press the spot; — yet I shall not be forgotten. The men of other ages and far-off lands shall repeat my name with a blessing: it shall live with Mills on the ocean, with Hall on the 'burning strand;' the monumental marble shall speak it; and the sweet valley which I love, and the everlasting mountains around, shall guard and preserve it forever!"

In an address delivered before the Adelphic Union Society of Williams College in 1837, by Governor Everett, he personifies Colonel Williams in the following graphic language: —

"My friends (we may conceive he would say to a group of settlers gathered around old Fort Massachusetts, on some fit occasion, not long before his marching toward the place of rendezvous), — my friends, your hardships I am aware are great. I have witnessed — I have shared them. The hardships incident to opening a new country are always severe. They are heightened in our case by the constant danger in which we live from the savage enemy. At present we are rather encamped than settled. We live in block-houses; we lie upon our arms by night; and, like the Jews who returned to build Jerusalem, we go to work by day with implements of husbandry in one hand, and the weapons of war in the other. Nor is this the worst. We have been bred up in the populous settlement on the coast, where the school-house and the church are found at the centre of every village. Here, as yet, we can have neither. I know these things weigh upon you. You look on the dark and impenetrable forests in which you have made an opening, and contrast it with the pleasant villages where you were born and passed your early years, — where your parents are yet living, or where they have gone to their rest; and you cannot suppress a painful emotion. You are more especially, as I perceive, somewhat disheartened at the present moment of impending war. But, my friends, let not your spirits sink. The prospect is overcast; but brighter days will come. In vision I can plainly foresee them. The forest disappears; the cornfield, the pasture, takes its place. The hill-sides are spotted with flocks, the music of the water-wheel sounds in accord with the dashing stream. Your little groups of log-cabins swell into prosperous villages. Schools and churches spring up in the waste; institutions for learning arise; and, in what is now a wide solitude, libraries and cabinets unfold their treasures, and observatories point their tubes to the heavens. I tell you that not all the united powers of all the French and Indians on the St. Lawrence — no, not if backed by all the powers of darkness, which seem at times in league with them, to infest this howling wilderness — will long prevent the valleys of the Hoosac and the Housatonic from becoming the abode of industry, abundance, and refinement. A century will not pass before the voice of domestic wisdom, and fireside inspiration from the vales of Berkshire, will be heard throughout America and Europe. As for the contest impending, I am sure we shall conquer; if I mistake not, it is the first of a series of events of unutterable moment to all America, and even to mankind. Before it closes, the banner of St. George will float, I am sure, over Diamond Rock; and the extension of the British power over the whole continent will be but the first act of a great drama whose catastrophe I but dimly foresee.

"I speak of what concerns the whole country: the fortune of individuals is wrapt in the uncertain future. For myself, I must own that I feel a foreboding at my heart, which I cannot throw off. I can only say, if my hour is come, (and I think it is not distant,) I am prepared. I have been able to do but little; but if Providence has no further work for me to perform, I am ready to be discharged from the warfare. It is my purpose, before I am taken from you, to make a disposition of my property for the benefit of this infant community. My heart's desire is, that, in the picture of its future prospects which I behold in mental view, the last and best of earthly blessings shall not be wanting. I shall deem my life not spent in vain, though it be cut off to-morrow, if at its close I shall be accepted as the humble instrument of promoting the great cause of education.

"My friends, as I am soon to join the army, we meet, many of us, perhaps for the last time. I am a solitary branch; I can be spared. I have no wife to feel my loss, no children to follow me to the grave. Should I fall by the tomahawk, or in front of honorable battle, — on the shores of the stormy lake, or in the infested woods, — this poor body may want even a friendly hand to protect it from insult; but I must take the chances of a soldier's life. When I am gone, you will find some proof that my last thoughts were with the settlers of Fort Massachusetts; and perhaps, at some future day, should my desire to serve you and your children not be disappointed, my humble name will not be forgotten in the public assembly, and posterity will bestow a tear on the memory of Ephraim Williams."

CHAPTER II.

THE FREE SCHOOL.—ORGANIZATION OF THE COLLEGE.

THE property of Colonel Williams, at the time of his death, consisted chiefly in notes and bonds, and in lands in Hampshire and Berkshire Counties. John Worthington, Esq. of Springfield, and Israel Williams, Esq. of Hatfield, the executors of the will, sold the lands, and loaned the moneys arising from the sales. The yearly interest was again loaned, and thus the fund was annually growing under their faithful care, from the death of Colonel Williams, in 1755, till 1785. They then applied to the Legislature for an act enabling them to fulfil the benevolent intention of the testator. An act was accordingly passed, incorporating William Williams, Theodore Sedgwick, Woodbridge Little, John Bacon, Thompson J. Skinner, Israel Jones, and David Noble, Esquires, the Rev. Seth Swift, and the Rev. Daniel Collins, Trustees of the donation of Ephraim Williams, for maintaining a Free School in Williamstown.

The trustees held their first meeting at Pittsfield, on the 24th day of April, 1785. William Williams was elected President, and Rev. Seth Swift, Treasurer. Finding the funds which were now transferred to the treasurer by the executors insufficient to erect a building for the school, a committee, consisting of Messrs David Noble, Israel Jones, and Thompson J. Skinner, was appointed to procure such assistance in materials and funds for a house as they may be able to obtain from the people in Williamstown and elsewhere. "And as the present fund of the Corporation will be insufficient to effect an object of extensive usefulness in instructing the rising generation, and as it is probable that many persons may be disposed generously to contribute to the execution of the intention of the donor, it is therefore ordered that the said committee receive such contributions as may be made for that purpose, and that they prepare and circulate subscriptions therefor."

"Resolved, That it is the sense of this committee that the intention of Ephraim Williams, Esq., in that clause of his last will and testament which respects the maintenance of a Free School in Williamstown, and the trust reposed in them by the Legislature, will be most fully and properly executed by employing the whole donation in that town.

"Resolved, That it is the sense of this Corporation that the Free School in Williamstown be open and free, for the use and benefit of the inhabitants of that town, and the free citizens of the American States indiscriminately, under such rules and orders as may be hereafter established.

"Further, Resolved, That it is the sense of the Corporation that it will best coincide with the liberal views of the donor, and the intention of the Legislature, to admit no pupil into the Free School in Williamstown not having been previously taught to read English well."

At the next meeting of the Corporation, held at Williamstown, August 3, 1785, it was voted "that the house for the use of the Free School in Williamstown be erected in the northerly part of the town, upon the eminence south of Mr. William Hosford's house, or upon the eminence farther east, in the northwest corner of Captain Isaac Searl's lot, opposite the old lime-kiln, as the Corporation shall hereafter determine; and further, that it be constructed of brick, and be of the following dimensions, viz. fifty-six feet in length, and forty-two in breadth, from outside to outside, and twenty-one feet in height, with a bevel roof." And Thompson J. Skinner, Israel Jones, and David Noble were appointed a committee, to "provide the materials and erect the building as soon as may be."

At a meeting of the Trustees, held at Pittsfield, April 24, 1786, the following Resolve was passed: "That Theodore Sedgwick, Simeon Strong, and Caleb Strong, Esquires, be requested to appear at the Supreme Judicial Court, to be holden at Northampton, within and for the County of Hampshire, on the last Monday of April current, to make and answer to the memorials of the towns of Williamstown and Adams, presented by their respective agents at the last Supreme Judicial Court, holden at Great Barrington, in the County of Berkshire, on the first day of October last, respecting the proceedings of this Corporation." The College records furnish no report of the doings of this committee, nor does it appear from the records that there was any meeting of the Corporation in the year 1787.

There was evidently some difficulty and delay attending the erection of the proposed edifice. This may be fairly inferred from the following vote, which was passed May 1, 1788. "Voted, That the subscriptions already had and obtained for the purpose of erecting the house for the use of the Free School in Williamstown, be vacated and of no effect; and that at their next meeting the Corporation will attend to any subscriptions or proposals which may be then offered and made respecting the erecting said house, on one of the two eminences mentioned in their resolve passed at their meeting held in August, 1785, or any other place in the town of Williamstown."

At a meeting of the Trustees, held August 19, 1788, it was voted, that "the house for the use of the Free School in Williamstown be constructed of brick, and be of the following dimensions, viz. seventy-two feet in length, and forty feet in breadth, from inside to inside, three stories in height, with four stacks of chimneys and a bevel roof; that said house be erected on the eminence east of the meeting-house, and south of Mr. William Hosford's dwelling-house, on the south side of the highway; — provided the sum of five hundred pounds be paid, or secured to be paid, to the said Corporation, for the use of the said school, by Thompson J. Skinner, Esq., and others, as expressed in a certain instrument, subscribed by the said Skinner and others, bearing date August 16, 1788, now in the hands of the clerk of said Corporation, reference thereto being had; — and, also, provided that the said subscribers shall level and prepare the ground on the said eminence, in such a manner as the said Corporation shall judge proper for the accommodation of the said house; — provided, also, that Captain Lemuel Stewart shall make and execute to the said Corporation a good and sufficient deed of the whole of a certain piece of land," which is fully described in the records; — "provided, also, the said subscribers shall, by the fifteenth day of November next, procure a good well, which shall at all times afford a sufficient quantity of water for all necessary uses." At this meeting the Corporation voted to prefer a petition to the General Court, at their next session, for the grant of a lottery to enable them to raise the sum of twelve hundred pounds, for the purpose of erecting the proposed building; and the President of the Board, John Bacon, and Woodbridge Little, Esquires, to present this petition with the signature of the President. Theodore Sedgwick, Thompson J. Skinner, and Woodbridge Little, Esquires, were appointed a committee to prepare the scheme for said lottery, and procure the tickets to be printed, provided the lottery be granted. It was granted, and the avails of it amounted to £1,037 18*s.* 2*d.*

At a meeting of the Trustees, held at Williamstown, May 26, 1790, the following action was had. "Taking into consideration the importance and necessity of erecting without delay the building intended for the use of said school; and Colonel Skinner having this day engaged to sink the well already begun, and partly dug, on the western eminence where the house was ordered, on certain conditions, to be placed, and to level the said western eminence sufficient to accommodate the building, — do resolve, that the committee appointed to superintend and direct in the erection of said building shall proceed to set up said building, on said eminence, without delay, the conditions mentioned in the former vote of the Corporation not having been performed notwithstanding."

At a meeting of the Trustees held in Williamstown, October 26, 1790, we find that "Whereas, the Trustees, on the 19th of August, 1788, did vote, order, and direct that the house for the use of the Free School should be built and erected of the following dimensions, viz. seventy-two feet in length, and forty feet in breadth, and three stories high, with four stacks of chimneys, and bevel roof; and whereas the committee appointed for that purpose, by advice of several Trustees, and from considerations of utility, have erected the said building of the following dimensions, viz. eighty-two feet in length, forty-two in width, four stories high, with a bevel roof; the Trustees do approve of the conduct of the committee in the premises, and do hereby ratify and confirm the same to all intents and purposes, so that it shall have the same effect as if the said building had been erected of the dimensions prescribed by the previous order and vote." This building (now the old West College) was completed in 1790.

Messrs. Williams, Bacon, and Swift were appointed, at this meeting of the Board, a committee "to provide a schoolmaster of good moral character, and suitably qualified to instruct in reading and writing the English language, and in arithmetic. And the said committee were further authorized and directed to employ, as soon as may be after the building is completed, an instructor,"— whose qualifications are thus described: "A man of a good moral character; of the Protestant religion; well acquainted with the English and learned languages, the liberal arts and sciences; apt to teach, with talents to command the respect of his pupils; of mild disposition, and of elegant and accomplished manners." The committee, thus instructed, procured the services of the Rev. Ebenezer Fitch.

At the same meeting the Corporation adopted a seal, which was used for some years after the school had become a college. Its device was a teacher surrounded by three pupils, with books in their hands, and the motto, "E. LIBERALITATE E. WILLIAMS, ARMIGERI."

The Free School (so called agreeably to the will) was opened October 20, 1791, with Mr. Fitch as preceptor, and Mr. John Lester as assistant. There were two departments, a grammar school or academy, and an English free school. In the former, all the branches which composed the course of education in the colleges were taught, and a yearly tuition of thirty-five shillings was charged. The latter was chiefly composed of boys from the higher classes in the town schools, to whom gratuitous instruction was given in the common English branches.

The School opened with cheering prospects, and at once became quite popular. Young men in considerable numbers resorted to it from Massachusetts and the neighboring States, and some even from Canada. Its prospective reputation and usefulness strengthened the desire of the Trustees, "the people of Williamstown, and others, to effect more perfectly the object of the donor, to erect the School into a College." *

At a meeting of the Trustees, May 22, 1792, a petition was prepared and sanctioned to be sent to the General Court at its next session, asking for an act incorporating the School into a College. This petition is so worthy of the men who prepared and presented it, that we are sure our readers will wish to see it in their own language.

The Trustees of the donation of Ephraim Williams, Esq., for maintaining a Free School in Wil-

* History of Berkshire County, p. 167.

liamstown, "humbly show, that, partly out of the said donation, and partly by private subscriptions, and partly from the aid of a lottery, they have erected a large and convenient building within the said town of Williamstown, with lodging and study rooms sufficient to accommodate one hundred students, besides a common school-room sufficient for sixty scholars, a dining-room that will accommodate a hundred persons, a hall for public academical purposes, a room for a library, apparatus, &c., the whole being nearly finished. About six months have elapsed since they opened an English and grammar school in said building; since that period they have had, from this and some of the neighboring States, upwards of sixty young gentlemen, who have entered the grammar school, and the number is almost daily increasing. Your memorialists further show, that there are several circumstances attending the Free School in Williamstown that are peculiarly favorable to a seminary of a more public and important nature. It is in a part of the country that abounds with a variety of the most substantial articles of provision, and, being remote from any public market, such articles of provision may always be afforded at a low price. This will naturally tend to lessen the expenses of instruction, and to render the means of a liberal education more easy, and bring them more within the power of the middling and lower classes of citizens. Williamstown, being an enclosed place, will not be exposed to those temptations and allurements which are peculiarly incident to seaport towns: a rational hope may therefore be indulged that it will prove favorable to the morals and literary improvement of youth who may reside there. Your memorialists ask leave further to observe, that Yale and Dartmouth Colleges are both of them nearer to the county of Berkshire than Cambridge. Most of the youths in the counties of Hampshire and Berkshire who obtain a liberal education are sent to one or the other of these colleges, by means of which large sums of money are annually sent out of this Commonwealth for the purposes of education. The southerly part of Berkshire is contiguous to Connecticut. The town of Williamstown is bordering upon the most fertile parts of the States of New York and Vermont. If, therefore, a college was instituted in that town, such is its local position that great numbers of youth would probably resort there from the adjacent States, for the purpose of obtaining a liberal education. This would furnish an opportunity of diffusing our best habits and manners among the citizens of our sister States. It would, at the same time, be a resource of wealth, and add to the influence and wealth of Massachusetts. There being already two colleges within the Commonwealth,* cannot, as we humbly conceive, be a reasonable objection against the addition of a third, especially as the interest of the last, from its local situation, cannot interfere with either of the former.

* Maine was then a part of Massachusetts.

The interests of the whole will perfectly coincide, and, like a threefold cord, mutually confirm and strengthen each other.

"The University of Cambridge will always be considered as the parent of the other two, and from them will derive an additional degree of lustre and renown. We hope that it is a laudable wish we indulge of seeing Massachusetts the Athens of the United States of America, to which young gentlemen, from any part of the Union, may resort for instruction in all the branches of useful and polite literature; and we cannot entertain the least doubt but that the object of our present memorial perfectly coincides with the object of such a wish. Your memorialists, therefore, humbly pray your Honors, that the Free School in Williamstown, may be incorporated into a College by the name of WILLIAMS HALL, and that the nurturing, liberal hand of the Legislature may be extended to it by a grant of lands in the easterly part of the Commonwealth, or in such other way as to your Honors may seem fit."

This petition was dated at Williamstown, May 22, 1792, and signed by William Williams, Theodore Sedgwick, Woodbridge Little, John Bacon, Thompson J. Skinner, Seth Swift, Daniel Collins, Israel Jones, and David Noble.

This application for a charter proved successful, and the act of incorporation, changing the Free School into a College, under the name of Williams College, was granted by the Legislature, June 22, 1793.

By this act, all the trustees of the Free School were made trustees of the College, and to them were added the Rev. Stephen West, D. D., Henry Van Schaack, Hon. Elijah Williams, and the President of the College for the time being. General Philip Schuyler, Hon. Stephen Van Rensselaer, and Rev. Job Swift were subsequently elected. The charter allowed the board to consist of seventeen members, including the President, empowered them to fill all vacancies; to confer the usual academic degrees and doctorates; and to hold property, "the annual income of which shall not exceed the sum of twenty thousand dollars."

By this act of incorporation, all the property, real and personal, belonging to the Free School, was transferred to and vested in the hands of the College Corporation, and a grant of four thousand dollars was made from the State treasury for the purchase of a library and philosophical apparatus.

"This act of the Legislature did not change the destination of the fund of the Free School (for that would necessarily imply an illegal exercise of power on the part of the Legislature), but it only extended the power and increased the capacity of the fund, so that it was still promotive of the views of the beneficent testator respecting his general object, namely, the dissemination of learning; and the particular one, the location at Williamstown. The Williamstown Free School Fund was at all times to be considered as the STOCK, planted and rooted in Williamstown, on which public and private munificence might, from time to time, be engrafted. This construction of the will of Colonel Williams harmonizes with the views of the original trustees of the fund, and is strengthened and confirmed by the fact, that none of the residuary legatees of Colonel Williams ever claimed those funds, or considered them as forfeited by any supposed illegal interference of the Legislature by the act of 1793."

The first meeting of the board was called by Mr. Skinner, August 6, 1793 (notice having been previously given in the Stockbridge paper). All the trustees were present. The meeting having been organized, Mr. Fitch was unanimously elected President, Rev. Stephen West, D. D., Vice-President, and Daniel Dewey, Secretary. A committee waited on Mr. Fitch, who attended, and signified his acceptance of the office. It was voted, that Commencement be on the first Wednesday of September. "That the Grammar School be connected with the College," and the Free School be discontinued. That Mr. Noah Linsley be appointed Tutor, with a salary of £65 per annum; and Mr. Nathaniel Steel, master of the Grammar School, with a salary of £60. "That the salary of the President be £140, and the Corporation provide him with a house." "That each person who applies for admission be able to accurately read, parse, and construe, to the satisfaction of the President and Tutor, Virgil's Æneid, Tully's Orations, and the Evangelists in Greek; or if he prefers to become acquainted with French, he must be able to read and pronounce, with a tolerable degree of accuracy and fluency, Hudson's French Scholar's Guide, Telemachus, or some other approved French author." "That Messrs. Skinner, Swift, and Noble be a committee to counsel the President." The thanks of the board were also voted to Mr. Noble for the present of a bell.

At a subsequent meeting, it was also voted, "That a public dinner be provided at the next Commencement, for the President, Trustees, and officers of the College, together with such other gentlemen as the President may invite." "That Mr. Elijah Dunbar be appointed senior Tutor." "That the Monitor be allowed for his services the sum of thirteen shillings, and in future an annual stipend, equal to one quarter's tuition."

Hon. Theodore Sedgwick was appointed Professor of Law and Civil Polity. A code of laws, not differing materially from those now in use, was prepared and accepted at this meeting.

CHAPTER III.

BIOGRAPHICAL SKETCH OF PRESIDENT FITCH.

The Rev. Ebenezer Fitch, D. D., the first President of Williams College, was a native of Norwich, Conn. His private journal, which he kept while in college, and which we have, contains the following record: "I was born at Norwich, Sept. 26, 1756, on Sabbath morning. Sicut parentes aiunt." Yet, by some strange mistake, it is stated in the history of Berkshire County, and on his tombstone in West Bloomfield, N. Y., that Dr. Fitch was a native of Canterbury, Conn. That he passed his childhood in Canterbury, there can be no doubt. But his birth unquestionably occurred at Norwich. His father was Dr. Jabez Fitch, a physician of considerable eminence. His mother was Lydia Huntington of Norwich. Both of his parents were the descendants of most worthy ancestors.

President Fitch was probably the subject of renewing grace in early life. Though he did not make a public profession of religion until a few years after he was graduated, still, in after life, he referred the date of his conversion to the period preceding his entrance into college, supposing it to have occurred when he was about fifteen years old. He was fitted for college by the Rev. Dr. James Cogswell, who was for a number of years a minister in Canterbury. While a member of college, he excelled in every department of study; and was highly esteemed for his blameless and gentlemanly deportment. From early life he was remarkably conscientious and diligent in the pursuit of learning, and in the cultivation of a well-balanced Christian character. In the early part of his college life he commenced keeping a journal, which he continued with a good degree of regularity until the close of his Senior year. For the greater part of the time he recorded the leading events of the day. It is much to be regretted, however, that during the last three months of his course it is kept in characters which we have been utterly unable to decipher.

From this journal, under date of July 16, 1775, we make the following extract: —

"As I have always had the ministry in view, I think it high time for me to attend more seriously and diligently to the things of everlasting importance. Considering, also, the importance of pursuing my studies with diligence, so that I may be prepared to be useful to my fellow-men, I have determined, by Divine assistance, to pursue the following course: —

"As the care of my soul is of the first importance, and yet the most likely to be neglected by me, I will, by the assistance of Divine grace, for the future be more attentive to my spiritual welfare. And, 1st. I will have stated seasons for prayer, reading the Scriptures, and practical authors; for meditating on what I read, and for self-examination. 2d. I will endeavor to maintain a sober, steady, and regular course of conduct. 3d. In my intercourse with friends I will make subjects of divinity themes of conversation in all cases when it can be done to mutual edification. 4th. I will aim so to behave towards my friends as to merit their regard and esteem; and will strive to banish all envious and jealous thoughts towards them, and towards all mankind.

"Respecting my studies, I resolve upon the following plan, which I shall alter, if I find upon trial it will be for my interest. And, 1st. I will rise at four in the morning, and will make it my first business to fix my thoughts upon the duties, trials, and temptations of the day, and will arm my mind with proper resolutions to discharge the duties of the day with diligence and alacrity, and guard, as far as I can, against temptation to sin and a waste of time. 2d. I will then begin the business of the day, and will endeavor to have finished my college studies for the day (having attended to them the evening previous) by noon. 3d. The afternoon shall be devoted to exercise, general reading, and whatever of necessary business may demand my attention. 4th. At the end of every month I will make out a plan of the studies which I propose to pursue the succeeding month. I will then divide these studies into separate portions for each week; and these studies shall be the chief employment of my afternoons."

The last term of his Senior year was spent in Wethersfield, under the instruction of Dr. Dwight, who was a Tutor in College at that time. The Commencement at Yale College, at which Dr. Fitch was graduated in the fall of 1777, owing to the distracted state of the country in consequence of the Revolutionary War, was attended by only a small audience. Probably not more than three or four orations were delivered. The Valedictory was pronounced by Dr. Fitch.

After receiving the honors of his Alma Mater, he passed about two years at New Haven as a resident graduate; and a part of a year he passed in Hanover, N. J., teaching an academy.

Mr. Fitch was admitted to his Master's degree, and appointed a Tutor in Yale College in the fall of 1780. This office he resigned in 1783. He then formed a mercantile connection with Henry Daggett, Esq., of New Haven; and in pursuing the business of the firm, he went to London in June, 1783, and returned the following winter with a large purchase of goods. Mr. Fitch not being acquainted with what is familiarly termed "the tricks in trade," nor with the state and wants of the country at that time, made a most unfortunate purchase. "The goods were of a quality and price, at least many of them, above the wants and habits of the citizens of Connecticut." The consequence was that he involved himself in pecuniary embarrassment, from which he did not extricate himself for a number of years. In 1786 he was a second time elected to the office of Instructor in Yale College, and officiated as senior Tutor and Librarian until 1791.

Mr. Fitch made a public profession of religion while a Tutor at New Haven,—connecting himself with the College Church; and was licensed to preach the same month, May, 1787. He was elected to the office of Preceptor of the Academy in Williamstown, Mass., in 1790; and, October 26, 1791, commenced teaching a school there, which immediately became prosperous.

In May, 1792, Mr. Fitch was married to Mrs. Mary Cogswell, the widow of his cousin and classmate, Samuel Cogswell, Esq., of Lansingburg, N. Y., who was accidentally shot dead, on a gunning party, by a friend and fellow-graduate of Yale College. By this marriage he became the father of eleven children, ten of whom were sons.

In June, 1793, the institution at Williamstown received from the General Court of Massachusetts a charter for a College. In August of that year Mr. Fitch was elected President.

The first Commencement at Williams College was on the first Wednesday in September, 1795. On the 17th day of June previous, President Fitch was ordained a minister of the Gospel, at Williamstown, by the Berkshire Association, with special reference to his station as head of the College.

The Rev. Ephraim Judson, of Sheffield, preached the sermon from 2 Timothy iv. 2: "*Preach the word.*" The Rev. Dr. West, of Stockbridge, gave the charge, and the Rev. Mr. Swift, of Williamstown, gave the right hand of fellowship.

President Fitch received the honorary degree of Doctor of Divinity from Harvard University, in September, 1800.

Dr. Fitch presided over Williams College with a good degree of ability and success twenty-two years. And, with the exception of Dr. Manning, of Brown University, what *first* President ever retained that station for so long a period in this country? He resigned his office, and became pastor of the Congregational Church in West Bloomfield, N. Y., where he was installed in the fall of 1815. In retiring at the age of sixty from a life of so much care, toil, and activity as his had been, he soon began to feel and exhibit the enfeebling effects of overtasked energies. He continued, however, to discharge the regular and arduous duties of a pastor for twelve years. He was then constrained, by reason of age and consequent infirmities, to withdraw from his stated public labors in the vineyard of his Lord. During his ministry in West Bloomfield, though his congregation was not large, and he in the evening of his days, still the admissions to that church averaged *sixteen* annually, — over one hundred and ninety in all. Not a year passed, while he ministered to that people, that some were not brought out of darkness into marvellous light, and confessed Christ before men.

After his dismission, Dr. Fitch continued to preach occasionally, till within a short time of his decease. He died suddenly, March 21, 1833.

The next Lord's day, his remains were conveyed to the church where he had so often and so faithfully held forth the word of life; and where an impressive and appropriate discourse was delivered by the Rev. Julius Steel, from Rom. viii. 28: "*We know that all things work together for good to them that love God.*"

While President Fitch was in Europe, he traced the origin and history of his ancestors back through many generations; he always kept an exact account of all the branches of his family settled in this country. After his decease, all his manuscripts fell into the hands of his son, the Rev. C. Fitch, then of Batavia, N. Y., whose house with its contents was soon after consumed by fire. His contemporaries, like himself, have nearly all passed away in the lapse of eighty-six years; so that very general incidents of his life only can now be recovered from oblivion. And in this connection it may with propriety be stated, that he never published any of the productions of his pen, with the exception of a Baccalaureate discourse, delivered September, 1799, a discourse at the funeral of Mrs. Alice Robinson, in 1811, and a missionary sermon at Hudson, N. Y., in 1814. He is likewise the reputed author of "Historical Sketches of

Col. Ephraim Williams and of Williams College," published in the Massachusetts Historical Collections, Vol. VIII. First Series. From a few scattered and necessarily imperfect sources must now be obtained all our information respecting this truly excellent man. In personal appearance Dr. Fitch was rather below than above the middling stature. His countenance was grave but pleasant, and by no means austere. His appearance and deportment were always gentlemanly and dignified; though sometimes, through his great modesty, not marked with perfect ease and elegance.

Dr. Fitch was well qualified, in most respects, to have the *instruction and guardianship* of young men. It would not, probably, be considered strictly correct to assert that he was, on the whole, pre-eminently qualified to stand at the head of a college. He possessed the talent of government, however, to that degree that he was revered and beloved by his numerous pupils. He showed himself to be their friend; and they in turn cheerfully reciprocated his friendship. He treated them as young gentlemen, and they rarely failed to be gentlemanly in return. "The instructor was forgotten in the friend and father." We have almost invariably heard those who were graduated at Williams College during his presidency speak of him in terms of high respect and veneration.

Few instructors have been more uniformly and gratefully remembered by their pupils. During his presidency he aided some young men in obtaining an education, probably beyond his pecuniary ability. One of these, the day after his graduation, on taking leave of the President, assured him, if ever he should become able to do so, he would remunerate him for his kindness and confidence. More than twenty years afterwards, when Dr. Fitch had retired from the stated duties of his profession, and was receiving no regular income, he had contracted some debts which he had not the means of paying, besides living in a house which he did not own. Unexpectedly to him there arrived at his dwelling, in West Bloomfield, one evening, an individual whom Dr. Fitch did not at first recognize. On inquiry, it was ascertained to be Gurdon Huntington Backus (a nephew of Mrs. Fitch), who was graduated at Williams College in 1806. He had been successful in his profession as a lawyer, in Baltimore, and had now come to redeem the pledge, given years before, that, if ever he should become able to do so, he would give his venerable friend and patron something better than thanks for his education. He paid off all Dr. Fitch's debts, presented him with a deed of the place where he lived, and two thousand dollars besides. "Cast thy bread on the waters, thou shalt find it after many days."

The following letter will close our sketch of this truly excellent and useful man: —

"LENOX, June 7, 1842.

"DEAR SIR: —

"I spent near seven years in Williamstown while Dr. Fitch was President, and a part of the time boarded in his family. During more than thirty years which have since elapsed, the acquaintance which I have had an opportunity to form with other men has not lessened the estimate which I then entertained of his character. Perhaps the most prominent qualities of his heart and disposition were purity and benevolence. As a natural consequence of the purity of his own intentions, he was very seldom suspicious of others; and his benevolent feelings were awakened whenever an object was presented adapted to their excitement; and his benevolence, when carried out in acts of kindness and charity, was limited only by the extent of his ability. As a scholar, his literary acquirements were highly respectable. His official duties in connection with College, and the many cares necessarily incident to the management of a numerous and dependent family, did not leave him sufficient leisure for extensive scientific investigations, or for becoming acquainted with the whole circle of general literature. As a teacher, he was faithful and communicative; and those students who were instructed by him during their Senior year will never forget the ability and interest with which he explained and illustrated the writings of Locke, Paley, and Vattel. As a Christian, he was sincere and devout; desirous of knowing his duty, and when ascertained, was ready, beyond most men, to perform it. As a preacher, he was more instructive than impressive, but none could faithfully listen to his sermons without improvement. Dr. Fitch labored assiduously for the interest of the College, over which he was called to preside, and for the moral and intellectual improvement of the young men who resorted to it for an education.

" Thus, my dear sir, I have thrown together a few thoughts, which occur to me respecting one of the most estimable men with whom I have ever been acquainted.

" With much regard, very respectfully yours,

"JAMES W. ROBBINS.

"TO CALVIN DURFEE."

CHAPTER IV.

ADMINISTRATION OF PRESIDENT FITCH. 1793-1815.

It is not only the work of the antiquarian, but the delight of the thoughtful, to trace the varied streams of civilization and culture to their small sources. The broad plain for its fertility is indebted to the distant spring upon the mountain-side; and we love to acknowledge the unity of the whole system of providential irrigation. We bow with reverence before the little fountain, as its waters leap among the rocks of the forest; for we know its mission, and respect its power for good. With such regard for the early efforts of educational organizations, we gratefully turn to Williams College in its "day of small things." It is not a smile, but a thankful ejaculation, that is excited as we behold good Dr. Fitch meeting his first class of four students, in the retired valley of the Hoosac. *There* were faith and zeal, pious purpose and prudent energy; and when did these virtues ever go unrewarded? Let us now proceed, and more particularly examine the record.

In October, 1793, Williams College was duly organized by the admission of three small classes.

President Fitch and Tutors Linsley and Dunbar constituted the first Faculty. In 1795, Mr. Samuel Mackay was appointed Professor of the French Language. He terminated his connection with the College in 1799, and from that time the professorship was discontinued. Mr. Mackay was born in the town of Chamberly, Canada, in 1764, and died in Sullivan, Maine, in 1831. The French language was his vernacular tongue, and, though said to have been somewhat wanting in dignity of deportment, he was a successful teacher of that language, and acquired some reputation as a historian.

From 1796 to 1798, Jeremiah Day, since President of Yale College, and Henry Davis, since President of Middlebury and Hamilton Colleges, were tutors in this institution.

The Academy continued for several years in connection with the College. It was found to be a convenient place for preparatory studies, and students more advanced had the privilege of reciting with the College classes.

The President's house was built in 1795, and he began to occupy it in November of that year. The thanks of the Corporation were presented "to David Noble, Esq., for his generous present of one acre of land for the house-lot for the use of the President."

The first Commencement was held on Wednesday, September 2, 1795; and Samuel Bishop, John Collins, Chauncy Lusk, and Dan Stone, three from Stockbridge and one from Lenox, were the first who received academic honors at this institution. Lusk pronounced the Valedictory. The second class, graduating in 1796, consisted of six members. The third class consisted of ten, and the fourth of thirty. So rapid was the early growth of the College.

A society called the Adelphic Union was formed in College some time previous to 1795, but precisely when is not known. It consisted of all the members of College, and a few of the more advanced students of the Academy. This society had a library, which was kept in the southwest corner room of the fourth story, — West College. The number of books in 1795 did not vary much from one hundred.

In the fall of the year just named all the members of the Freshman class, and those who had newly entered the upper classes, were admitted into the Adelphic Union Society. This society held its meetings in the fourth story of the West College, in the northeast corner room. Its members had now become so numerous that they could not all be conveniently accommodated in the place of meeting, and a committee was appointed to report a plan of division. Such a plan was presented. It was discussed for several evenings, and the result was the formation of the Philologian and Philotechnian Societies; the two to be known by the old name of The Adelphic Union, and the library to be in common. The individuals most active in bringing about these changes are said to have been Knapp and Mason of the Senior class, and Towner of the Junior. After the East College was built, the weekly meetings of the societies were held alternately in the Senior and Junior recitation-rooms; and the library was kept in the third story of the West College, in the room over the east entry-way. These societies have continued until the present time, and hold their meetings every Wednesday evening in their respective halls, which occupy the third story of South College, and are handsomely furnished. Each society owns a valuable library, comprising in the aggregate ten thousand volumes. There is a pleasant and healthful rivalry between them, manifesting itself as much in connection with their past history as with their present condition.

In 1795 a College Catalogue was published. It contained the names of seventy-seven students. The following note was appended: "Besides the above members of College, there are about fifty students in the Academy connected with the College." This catalogue, according to Dr. Robbins, the antiquarian, was the first catalogue of the members of a college published in this country. The same thing was done at Yale in the year following, and the plan was subsequently adopted by the colleges generally. It was at first printed on a single sheet, but since 1821 it has been printed in a pamphlet form, and has contained the names of the Trustees, which before were omitted, together with a list of the studies required for admission, and an outline of the College course. The Triennial Catalogue was first issued in 1779, and has since been regularly continued.

The first three Commencements were held in the small meeting-house, the first one built in the town. This was found to be so inconvenient that the Trustees voted to hold their succeeding Commencements in Pittsfield or Lanesborough, unless the town would provide a more suitable place. But before the next Commencement measures were adopted to erect a new and more commodious edifice. Towards the expense of this building the Corporation contributed one hundred pounds, on condition that seats should be reserved for the students, and that they should have the use of the house on all public days. The fourth Commencement was held in the present house, then in an unfinished state. The early Commencements were attended by a numerous collection of people from the vicinity, as well as by many from a distance, and by various distinguished and literary characters. At the first Commencement, President Fitch delivered an address to the graduating class; but this practice was afterwards discontinued, and a Baccalaureate discourse has been delivered on the Sabbath afternoon preceding Commencement, by all the Presidents, with only an occasional exception.

In January, 1796, the Legislature granted two townships of land, which were sold in May following for about $ 10,000, and the avails, with a considerable sum besides, amounting in all to

$12,400, were applied to the erection of the old East College, in 1797. It was a brick building, four stories high, one hundred and four feet by forty-eight. It was convenient for students; contained thirty-two rooms and two recitation-rooms, and was regularly occupied until the fall of 1841, when it was destroyed by fire. With a portion of the grant from the Commonwealth at the time of the incorporation of the College, a small but well-selected library was procured, and some philosophical apparatus.

According to a general estimate made by Dr. Fitch, the expenses of the Free School and College, from 1789 to 1800, were as follows: — For West College, $11,700; President's house and land, $2,400; for East College, $12,400; for the meeting-house, $333; for library, $567; total, $28,000. The funds received for the same time were: — The Williams fund, $11,000; from the lottery, $3,500; subscriptions, $2,000; legislative grant, $4,000; two townships of land, $10,000; total, $30,500; leaving a balance in the College treasury at the close of the year 1799 of $2,500.

For a series of years after its incorporation, the College continued to advance in reputation and prosperity. Such was the rapidity of its growth, that in 1804 it enrolled on its catalogue one hundred and forty-four students. In 1802, the number of volumes in the library amounted to over two thousand, and in the Adelphic Union library to three hundred and seventy-five. Some of the causes that contributed to the early prosperity of the College were, that the necessary expenditures of the students were less here than elsewhere; its sequestered location, and the high moral character of the surrounding community, presenting few inducements to extravagance and dissipation. The President and Tutors were men of high attainments and reputation. The institution was always popular among the clergy in this part of the country. It was early distinguished by a decidedly religious character. Through the influence of Dr. West, of Stockbridge, Dr. Hopkins's System of Divinity was, for a time, one of the text-books of the Senior Class. In March, 1797, the President writes: "In future we shall read Doddridge's Lectures, in lieu of Hopkins's System."

We can give our readers no better idea of the condition and prospects of the College in these early days, than they will derive from extracts from some of President Fitch's letters, written about this time. They are selected from the Memoir of Dr. Fitch, published in the American Quarterly Register,* and will be read with interest in this connection.

January, 1796. "The number of students is increasing rapidly, so that we already want another college edifice. We hope to obtain from the State a grant of two townships of land in Maine,† which,

* Vol. XV. pp. 363, 364.

† It will be recollected that Maine at this time belonged to Massachusetts.

if obtained, will enable us to erect another building. At present we have a very likely collection of young men. They are very studious and orderly, and scarcely give us any trouble."

January, 1799. "Things go on well in our infant seminary. Our number is hardly so large as last year. The scarcity of money is one cause of the decline; some leaving through mere poverty. But our ambition is to make good scholars, rather than add to our numbers; and in this we mean not to be outdone by any college in New England. Perseverance in the system we have adopted will eventually give reputation to this institution in the view of all who prefer the useful to the showy."

June, 1801. "Our College is prospering. We have admitted forty-five Freshmen and nine Sophomores, and expect to make the number up to sixty before Commencement."

January, 1802. "Our Freshman class this year is not so large as usual, but we expect it will increase to twenty-five or more. A large number, however, are professors of religion, and will, I hope, make pious and useful ministers."

April, 1802. "We have lately had trouble in College. The judgments we drew up and published to the classes respecting their examinations in March gave offence. Three classes in succession were in a state of insurrection against the government of the College. For ten days we had a good deal of difficulty; but the Faculty stood firm, and determined to give up no right. At last, without the loss of a single member, we reduced all to due obedience and subordination. Never had I occasion for so much firmness and prudence, — not even in the great rebellion of 1782 at Yale. Most of the students are now much ashamed of their conduct. The present generation, I trust, will never burn their fingers again. They have found that we will support our authority."

March, 1803. "We have both our College buildings full of students. This is truly encouraging."

In the year 1798, when our country resolved to resist the aggressions of France, and pledged itself to the support of government by various addresses, one was sent by the students of Williams College, with the approbation of the Faculty. President Adams returned a polite answer, commending the patriotism of the students, and spoke in flattering terms of the flourishing state of so young an institution.

In 1804, a strip of land of no great value was granted to Williams and Bowdoin Colleges, and in 1805 another township of land was granted, which sold for $4,500, and also one in 1809, which brought nearly $5,000.

Among the friends and patrons of the College who were called to their rest at a comparatively early period was the Hon. David Noble, who was one of the principal inhabitants of Williamstown. He was born at New Milford, Conn., December 9, 1744, was graduated at Yale College, 1764, and came to this town from Fairfield, in 1770. He read law, and followed that profession a number of years. He afterwards engaged in mercantile pursuits, and acquired a very handsome estate. He was an extensive land-owner. He was a man of activity and enterprise, of probity and intelligence, and a considerable benefactor and one of the original Trustees of the College. He gave the College a bell, and the land on which the President's house stands. In 1797 he was made a Judge of the Court of Common Pleas, and died March 4, 1803, in his fifty-ninth year.

In 1804, Hon. John Bacon resigned his connection with the College as a Trustee. He was born in Canterbury, Conn. in 1737, and died in Stockbridge in 1820, aged eighty-three years. He was graduated at Princeton College in 1765, under Dr. Samuel Finley. He was settled as a minister of the Presbyterian order on the Eastern Shore of Maryland in 1768, where he remained until 1772, when he went to Boston and became the pastor of the Old South Church, which he left in 1775, and settled as an agriculturist at Stockbridge. After this he preached occasionally, but was almost constantly employed, until within four years of his death, in the various public offices and as a member of both branches of the Legislature of Massachusetts. He was President of the Senate in the year 1803-4; member of Congress from 1801 to 1803; and first judge of the County Courts for about twenty years. He was a man of strong powers of mind, much given to argumentative discussion, and was firm and tenacious in his opinions and purposes. He entered largely and zealously into the ecclesiastical, educational, and political controversies of the day in which he lived. He was the classmate, and afterwards the correspondent, of the younger Jonathan Edwards, and of David Ramsey, the American historian.

The Commencement of 1807 was a mournful occasion. President Fitch's eldest son, having been admitted to College, died the evening before the Commencement. The President presided at the exercises with great propriety, and the next morning attended the funeral of his son, at which most of the students were present. When the corpse was deposited in the grave, the deeply afflicted father in a calm and collected tone remarked, "I do not deposit in this grave silver or gold, but my first-born, the beginning of my strength." He was a professor of religion, and a youth of great promise.

"At a meeting of the Board of Trustees, September, 1805, it was voted to break and discontinue the former seal of the corporation, and to adopt a new one with the following device, viz. a globe, telescope, inkstand, and pens, below a wreath of laurel, above a morning glory, with this motto, 'E liberalitate E. Williams, Armigeri.'"

In the year 1806, a Professorship of Mathematics and Natural Philosophy was established, and Mr. Gamaliel S. Olds, formerly a tutor, was elected to this professorship. At his inauguration, October

14, 1806, he delivered an oration, "On the Importance of Mathematical and Philosophical Science," which was published. It was also voted at this time to discontinue the grammar school, on account of the paucity of students.

The Rev. Seth Swift, a Trustee of the Free School, and afterwards of the College, died suddenly February 15, 1807. He was a native of Kent, Conn., was graduated at Yale College in 1774, and was ordained at Williamstown, May 26, 1779. At the time of his settlement, the church consisted of sixty-one members. His ministry continued nearly twenty-eight years, and the average of admissions to the church varied but a fraction from ten a year. Two of his sons were graduated at Williams College, and entered the ministry. The church records contain the following entry: "At about 9 o'clock, A. M., the Rev. Seth Swift, our much esteemed, dearly beloved, and very faithful and laborious pastor, died, in the midst of great usefulness, while God was pouring out his spirit here, and giving him many seals of his ministry." Mr. Swift was rather above the middling stature, with a strong frame and large features. He was not studious of the graces of dress, manners, or conversation. He was warm and open in his temper, evangelical in his religious views, and serious in the general tone of his intercourse with his people. He was zealous in his ministerial labors, prudent and energetic in his measures.

In 1808, the Rev. Daniel Collins resigned his

place on the Board of Trustees. He was born at Guilford, Conn., 1738, and was graduated at Yale College, 1760, where he sustained the reputation of a good scholar. He studied theology with the Rev. Dr. Bellamy, and was ordained in Lanesborough, April 17, 1764. Here he sustained the character and discharged the duties of a pastor for nearly half a century, exerting an extensive and salutary influence in forming the manners and habits of his people. Some seasons of special refreshing from the Divine presence occurred under his ministry. He possessed good sense, dignified manners, and exemplary piety; and was greatly beloved and esteemed in all the relations of life. He was a gentleman of the old school; tall, erect, and quick in his movements, and polite to everybody. He wore a wig and three-cornered hat all his days. He was a trustee of the Free School, and afterwards of the College at Williamstown. He was deeply interested in the College, and devoted much time to its early establishment, on the ground that he fully expected it would become a seminary where many young men would receive their training for the service of the Church. He died August 26, 1822, in the eighty-fourth year of his age.

In the spring of 1808, another early and efficient Trustee of the College was called to his rest, the Hon. William Williams, who was the second son of Hon. Israel Williams of Hatfield; he was born June 10, 1734, and was a cousin of the founder of the College. He was graduated at Yale College in 1754. Returning to his native town, he was shortly after appointed Clerk of the Court of Common Pleas in Hampshire County. This office he held for about twenty years. At the commencement of the war with Great Britain, not coinciding with the majority of the people respecting the propriety of the Revolution, he was left out of office. Yet such was the general estimation in which he was held, that he met with but few trials or little opposition on this account. But deprived of the employment which had afforded a comfortable support, he left his native place and removed to the west part of Dalton, where he spent the remainder of his days. He married Miss Dorothy Ashley, of Deerfield, and when he died left nine surviving children. He held many civil offices of trust, was a deacon of the church in Hatfield, and also in Dalton, and was one of the original Trustees of Williams College. He died greatly lamented, March 1, 1808, and was interred in the cemetery in Pittsfield. Dr. Shepard preached a sermon at his funeral; and Dr. West of Stockbridge preached a sermon in commemoration of his life and character in Dalton, on the 15th of May following, which was published. In this discourse he gives Mr. Williams a very high character as a citizen and Christian. "He was leader and guide to the people for many years; an ornament and glory of the town as a citizen and Christian."

Thus far, with the exception of the disturbance

alluded to in President Fitch's letters, nothing had occurred to check the prosperity of the College, or to cause any difficulty. In the summer of 1808, however, some disturbance took place among the students, of which Professor Dewey of Rochester furnished the following account: —

"In the spring and summer of 1808, there was an attempt of the Sophomore class to prevent the continuance of some of the officers of the College after the Commencement. The students supposed the Tutors to be elected annually, and that, by a petition to the Trustees against a re-election, the desired end would be secured. To effect this object they enlisted the interest of two members of the Senior class, then about to graduate. So much was said and done by these two Seniors, that the Faculty obliged them to make some acknowledgment of the impropriety of any such interference on their part, before they could be admitted to perform their parts at the Commencement, and receive their degrees. Though the Seniors believed a change of Tutors to be important, they were sensible that it was not their part to meddle with such a matter, and the affair was settled with them. The Commencement passed off pleasantly, and, as the Tutors remained in their office, it was supposed the whole matter was settled; and the students returned after vacation, with the intention, as they said, of going on in peace and good-will.

"Professor Olds had felt that the students were too much disposed to present petitions on subjects over which they had no control, and in which their interference was entirely improper. This practice he wished to have broken up, and this he designed to effect. He felt that the Tutors had been injured by the course of the students, and that the Faculty were abused by it. He had led the Seniors, by direction of the Faculty, to make their acknowledgment in the case, and he expected to bring the class more particularly concerned in the petition to do the same. The Faculty agreed on the course to be pursued, and the President and Professor Olds presented the subject to members of the offending class, which was now under the care of the Professor. When the acknowledgment of the wrong and the renunciation of the practice were proposed, *each individual refused* to put his name to the paper. The Junior class was now, therefore, in direct opposition to a measure resolved on by the Faculty. Recitations were suspended in that class, and the whole College was in a state of high excitement. The expulsion of some of those most deeply implicated was feared.

"When the state of things was reported to the Faculty, the President, with the advice of one of the Trustees, refused to sustain the officers in the attempt, and disclosed that he had been mistaken in the facts, or he should not have consented to require the Juniors to make the proposed acknowledgment. He took a stand in favor of the students, and against the Professor and Tutors." We have been told that a committee of the students waited on the President, in the midst of the excitement, and informed him of the ground on which the objectionable petition had been presented; that their motive in presenting it was to sustain the reputation and usefulness of the College; that if they had erred, they had done so in discharging what they deemed to be a duty. These representations produced a change in the President's course, which was unexpected to the other officers. "He said the matter had been managed by Professor Olds, in whom great confidence was placed, and who had great influence with the Faculty and students; and that Professor Olds had come to conclusions, and had led them to adopt measures, which the true state of the facts, and the feelings and intentions of the students, did not authorize. He therefore told the Professor that the proposed measure was not proper or called for, and must be given up. Professor Olds felt that his honor was compromitted, that he could not hold a respectable standing in the eyes of the students, and that he must be sustained, or leave the College. In a few hours the resignation of the Tutors was sent to the President, and soon after that of Professor Olds.

"The College was then without any officer except the President; and as the vacancies could not be supplied immediately, a recess of four weeks was given to the students, and they returned to their homes.

"A few were disgusted by the procedure, and took dismissions from the College. At the end of the recess most returned, and, Chester Dewey, John Nelson, and James W. Robbins having been called to the tutorships, the remainder of the year was employed in quiet and profitable study. For two years the students pursued an unexceptionable course in all things. Order, peace, study, and good feelings ruled.

"Professor Olds felt that he was greatly injured by the decision of the President, and his failing to sustain him when the trial came. The President, whom the Trustees judged to have decided correctly, felt that he had been led into a mistake by the representations of Professor Olds, not as intending any error, but carried beyond the facts of the case by the influence and strong feelings of the Professor. He regretted that he had not earlier scrutinized the case, but believed he had now taken the only wise, because the only right course.

"Professor Olds doubtless misjudged on the dishonor of his situation. So high was the estimation of his talents by the students, and so great his influence with them, and so strong their attachment to him, that they uniformly declared many times in the year or two following, that they should have entertained all respect and regard for the Professor, as they believed he had erred honestly, and with the best intentions. By resigning, and leaving the College, he lost much of their respect, as it seemed to charge them with a criminal intention, which they disowned. There is another apology for Professor Olds, to be found in the fact that he had labored to support the Tutors; and as they could not consistently remain, he was bound to share with them the results."

When the students reassembled, the instruction of the refractory Junior class was assigned to Mr. Dewey; thus placing him in a most trying and responsible position. His opinion, early formed, was that it was not best for a teacher to say much about government, but so to influence students that they shall govern themselves. Accordingly, when he met the class for the first time, he frankly confessed to them his inexperience, reminded them of the unfavorable reports which had gone abroad respecting them, and assured them that the only way to counteract these reports, and do away their injurious influence, was by a faithful and manly performance of duty in future. The appeal produced the desired effect. They felt that they were thrown upon their individual responsibility. Subordination and order were at once restored; study was cheerfully and heartily pursued. Years afterwards, the Hon. Daniel Kellogg, one of the judges of the Supreme Court of Vermont, a member of the class, remarked: "I remember as if it were but yesterday, that first recitation of Mr. Dewey's, and his address to the class. He put us on our honor, and after that we would not for all the world have done a rebellious deed."

But who were among the leading members of the class which Professor Olds considered so refractory, and so suddenly and unceremoniously abandoned? The late Dr. Justin Edwards, the Rev. S. M. Emerson, Hon. Judge J. H. Hallock, Hon. Judge Daniel Kellogg already mentioned, Hon. Darius Lyman, Hon. William H. Maynard (the founder of the Law School in Hamilton, N. Y.), the Rev. Luther Rice, one of the early missionaries to the East, the Rev. John Seward, and others who might be named.

Still, "from this shock," says Dr. Griffin, "increased by exaggerated reports respecting the extent of the disorders which prevailed, the College did not recover during the administration of Dr. Fitch. The institution was then at its height. The rooms in both buildings were nearly full, and the four classes then on the ground produced more graduates than any other four successive classes have done [up to this time, 1828], to wit, 115. The next largest number was 113, and consisted of the classes that were in College in the summer of 1808, when the difficulty began. The class which entered the fall after the rupture produced but 20; and the four classes which entered next after that event produced but 89. Other colleges had sprung up to increase the effect." It is manifest, that from this time forward, for a series of years, we shall witness the gradual decline of the College. It was not to be expected that officers who left under such circumstances would exert an influence in favor of the institution.

Professor Olds was born in that part of Granville, Mass., which is now Tolland, February 11, 1777. His parents in his early life moved to Marlborough, Vt.; he was graduated at Williams College in 1801, with a high reputation as a scholar; he was a Tutor in his Alma Mater, from 1803 to 1805; in 1806, he was elected Professor of Mathematics and Natural Philosophy, and resigned his office in 1808. He studied theology with Dr. West, and at Andover; he was ordained pastor of the Congregational Church in Greenfield, November 19, 1813, where he remained about three years. He was then solicited to accept of a professorship in Middlebury College, but owing to some misunderstanding or disagreement, which occasioned some public discussion, he never entered upon the duties of that professorship. From 1819 to 1821 he was a Professor in the University of Vermont, and from 1821 to 1825 was one of the Professors in Amherst College. For some few years he held the same office in a college in Georgia. Returning to the North, he resided some years at Saratoga Springs, and in 1841 removed to Circleville, Ohio, where he passed the remainder of his days. He died June 2, 1848, by a distressing casualty. Returning on Monday from the place where he had passed the Sabbath, when about twelve miles from home his horse took fright, and threw him from his carriage some twelve feet down a steep bank. He lingered a few days, and died in peace.

His mind was of a high order. He was a fine linguist; and the whole system of mathematics taught in our colleges he had perfectly at his command. But his keen sensitiveness led him to terminate his connection with institutions in such a sudden manner, that many years of his life were sadly embittered. But his last years were spent in the service of the Church; and when he died, honorable testimony was borne to his character, fidelity, and usefulness.

Hon. Thompson J. Skinner died at Boston, January 20, 1809. He was a son of the Rev. Thomas Skinner, and was born in Colchester, Conn. Having served out his time as an apprentice, he came to Williamstown, and acquired extensive influence. He was one of the original Trustees, and an efficient friend of the College. He became Chief Justice of the Common Pleas Court, State Treasurer, and Treasurer of the College.

In 1808, the Faculty were authorized by the Trustees to give the students leave of absence from their rooms from 9 to 10 o'clock, P. M.

In 1809, public worship was attended on the Sabbath in the chapel. And the Trustees voted to pay "the Faculty a hundred and eighty dollars for supplying the pulpit thirty-six Sabbaths." And a hundred and fourteen dollars were paid for preaching in the chapel the next year.

In 1810, Mr. Chester Dewey was elected Professor of Mathematics and Natural Philosophy, in place of Professor Olds, resigned.

In May, 1811, Woodbridge Little, Esq., of Pittsfield, made a donation to the College, for the purpose of aiding pious and indigent young men in their preparation for the Christian ministry. Mr. Little was a native of Colchester, Conn., and was born in 1741; was graduated at Yale College, in 1760; studied theology with the Rev. Dr. Bellamy; was licensed to preach the Gospel; and soon after came to Lanesborough, where he was employed as a candidate one or two years. For some reason he then commenced the study of the law, and was admitted to the bar, and settled as the first lawyer in Pittsfield in 1770. He was one of the original Trustees of the College, and ever manifested a deep interest in its prosperity, and in the civil, educational, and ecclesiastical affairs of the county. In 1811, a pious student* came to Dr. Fitch, the President, to request a dismission from College, solely on the ground of his pecuniary embarrassments. Dr. Fitch informed him that he had that very morning received a letter from Mr. Little, of Pittsfield, pledging the College twenty-five hundred dollars for the purpose of aiding pious, indigent, and promising young men in their preparations for the Christian ministry. The young man did not leave till he had completed his college course. At his death, which occurred in June, 1813, Mr. Little left twenty-seven hundred more to the College for the same purpose.

In February, 1811, the Legislature granted $3,000 per year, for ten years, from a tax on

* John Woods, the Valedictorian of his class.

banks, the interest of one fourth of which constitutes a fund for the payment of the bills of such students as may require assistance. This was a most providential benefaction, and served to sustain the College through the troubles which followed the resignation of Dr. Fitch.

In September, 1812, the Rev. Stephen West, D.D., of Stockbridge, in view of his age and infirmities, resigned his connection with the College. He was one of the original Trustees, and was chosen Vice-President at the first meeting of the Board; and had contributed, in no small degree, to give the institution its deep religious character. Dr. West was born at Tolland, Conn., November 13, 1735, and was graduated at Yale College in 1755. He studied theology in Hatfield with the Rev. Mr. Woodbridge, and commenced his ministerial labors as chaplain at Hoosac Fort, where he remained one year, perhaps a little longer. He then went to Stockbridge to succeed the distinguished Edwards in 1758, and was ordained there June 15, 1759. The church at that time numbered twenty-one English members. He married, for his first wife, Miss Elizabeth Williams, daughter of Colonel Ephraim Williams; they had no children. In person he was below the middle stature, but of uncommonly dignified bearing and aspect. He exerted a controlling agency in the organization of most of the early churches of Berkshire. It was through his agency mainly that most of the churches in this county were early blessed with such thoroughly orthodox confessions of faith. Many of the early pastors of these churches had been his pupils, — Dr. Catlin, the Rev. Seth Swift, and some others. Among the distinguished divines of his day he was *primus inter pares*, — "little in stature, but mighty in spirit," — a man of such extraordinary intellectual powers, that he was at home in the depths of metaphysical discussions, or when analyzing and unfolding the most difficult passages in the writings of Isaiah or Paul. During his ministry he passed three times through the New Testament, "expounding the sacred oracles verse by verse with a propriety, acuteness, and vigor of which this country has seen no parallel." He was greatly blessed in his labors. He died May 15, 1819, aged eighty-three years, having ministered to that people over sixty years.*

At the meeting of the Trustees in September, 1814, Hon. Daniel Dewey resigned the office of Treasurer of the College, which he had held since the year 1798. Judge Dewey was connected with the College from its earliest days, holding for a time the office of Secretary, and subsequently that of Treasurer, and also that of Professor of Law. He had been one of its devoted friends, and an active agent in procuring the earlier grants by the State, and was much resorted to by President Fitch for his counsel and advice in relation to the affairs

* The College has a portrait of Dr. West, painted by Keeley, and presented by Dr. Duncan.

of the institution. He was a distinguished lawyer, and held various offices of public trust. He was a member of the Executive Council of Massachusetts in the years 1809 and 1812, a member of the Congress of the United States in 1813, and was appointed to a seat upon the Bench of the Supreme Judicial Court by Governor Strong in 1814.

Judge Dewey was born in Sheffield, January 29, 1766. He was two years a member of Yale College. He came to Williamstown and settled in the practice of law in May, 1787. His death occurred May 26, 1815. In an obituary address delivered by his associate on the Bench, Chief Justice Parker, we find the following: "Judge Dewey is now no more. The seat destined for him on this circuit is vacant, and all that remains to us of him is the remembrance of his past life, his amiable temper, his modest and retired manners, his diligence and activity in business, his wise and impartial administration of justice, his true love of his country, and his exemplary piety and devout obedience to the will of God."

It is certainly a ground of gratitude that so many of the early friends and patrons of Williams College were men of liberal education and of broad and generous views. And every reader of its history must be struck with the absence of self-interest on the part of most, if not all, its friends and founders. Among these the Hon. Theodore Sedgwick, LL. D., of Stockbridge, holds a conspicuous rank. He was one of the original Trustees, and continued in that position till his death. He was a native of Hartford, Conn., and was born in 1747, was graduated at Yale College in 1765, and studied law with Col. Mark Hopkins, in Great Barrington. After residing a few years in Sheffield, he removed to Stockbridge. He was a leading individual in procuring the abolition of slavery in Massachusetts; was an earnest advocate for the adoption of the Constitution of the United States in the State Convention; and also a member of the State Legislature, and Speaker of the House of Representatives. He was afterwards a Representative and Senator in Congress, and a Judge of the Supreme Court of this State. He guided the studies of many law students. He was appointed to deliver a course of lectures on Law and Civil Polity to the students in College. Thus active, honored, esteemed, and useful, he died at Boston, January 24, 1813, aged sixty-six.

In May, 1815, a Professorship of Languages was established, and Mr. Ebenezer Kellogg, then a student at Andover, was appointed Professor. At the same meeting of the Trustees, the Prize Rhetorical Exhibition, on the evening preceding Commencement, was instituted. Those who receive the appointment to speak for the prize have always — we know not the origin of the term — been called "Moonlights."

We have now glanced at the history of the College, as far as to the year 1815. For twenty-two years Dr. Fitch had presided over it with ability, and with a good degree of success. But now, by the concurrence of circumstances, it had been for a time on the decline. Since 1808, the institution had not enjoyed the reputation and prosperity of former years, notwithstanding the exertions of the President and other officers, aided by the counsel and co-operation of a judicious prudential committee. A secret influence was at work against the College, in its present location, and it began to be whispered that it was desirable and expedient to have a younger and more popular man at the head of the institution. The funds of the College were small; and the salary which Dr. Fitch received was inadequate to the support of his large family. And in addition, he could not bear to see this object of his affection and early and earnest labors droop under his care. Especially he could not endure the thought of having this decline attributed to himself. Under all these circumstances, Dr. Fitch thought it his duty, and judged it expedient, to resign. He accordingly tendered his resignation to the Trustees, May 2, 1815. By permission, he immediately left College for the summer, his salary continuing until the fall. During his absence, Professor Dewey discharged the duties of President. Before leaving, Dr. Fitch delivered an affectionate parting address to the students, which made a deep impression on their minds, and in the end was productive of much good. He returned to College in August, presided at Commencement, inducted Professor Kellogg into office as Professor of

Languages, and then carried into effect his resignation. He remained in town a short time to receive his successor, and left early in October.

At a meeting of the President and Trustees of Williams College, held May 2, 1815, the following vote was unanimously passed: — "Whereas, The Rev. President Fitch has signified his intention of resigning, at the next Commencement; and whereas, in consequence of the state of the funds, the Corporation has not been able to give him such a salary as his station and expenditures have required, — *Voted*, That there be granted to the Rev. Dr. Fitch the sum of $ 2,200, to be paid in one year from the time of his resignation." This sum was paid him as a remuneration for his long and faithful services, and was esteemed by him as an act of generosity; by the Board, as an act of justice. It was both.

The following letter is from the Hon. William C. Bryant.

"ROSLYN, LONG ISLAND, July 19, 1859.

"MY DEAR SIR: —

"I regret that I can contribute so little from my own recollection in aid of your undertaking. I will endeavor, however, to answer your inquiries.

"I entered Williams College in the autumn of the year 1810, — almost half a century since, — having prepared myself in such a manner that I was admitted into the Sophomore Class.

"At that time Dr. Fitch was President of the College, and instructor of the Senior Class. I have a vivid recollection of his personal appearance, — a square-built man, of a dark complexion, and black, arched eyebrows. To me his manner was kind and courteous, and I remember it with pleasure. He often preached to us on Sundays, but his style of sermonizing was not such as to compel our attention. We listened with more interest to Professor Chester Dewey, then in his early manhood, the teacher of the Junior Class, who was the most popular of those who were called the Faculty of the College. Two young men, recent graduates of the College, acted as tutors, superintended the recitations of the two lower classes, and made their periodical visits to the College rooms, to see that everything was in order. These four were at that time the only instructors in Williams College.

"Before my admission, it had been the practice for the members of the Sophomore Class, in the first term of their year, to seize upon the persons of some of the Freshmen, bring them before an assembly of the Sophomores, and compel them to go through a series of burlesque ceremonies, and receive certain mock injunctions with regard to their future behavior. This was called *gamutizing* the Freshmen. It was a brutal and rather riotous proceeding, which I can, at this time, hardly suppose that those who had the government of the College could have tolerated; yet the tradition ran, that, if it was not connived at, at least no pains were taken to suppress it. There were strong manifestations of a disposition to enforce the custom after I became a member of the Sophomore Class, but the Freshmen showed so resolute a determination to resist it, that the design was dropped; and this, if I am rightly informed, was the last of the practice.

"The College buildings consisted of two large, plain brick structures, called the East and the West College, and the College grounds consisted of an open green, between the two, and surrounding them both. From one College to the other you passed by a straight avenue of Lombardy poplars, which formed the sole embellishment of the grounds. There was a smaller building or two of wood, forming the only dependencies of the main edifices, and every two or three years the students made a bonfire of one of these. I remember being startled one night by the alarm of fire, and going out, found one of these buildings in a blaze, and the students dancing and shouting round it.

"Concerning my fellow-students I have little of importance to communicate. My stay in College was hardly long enough to form those close and life-long intimacies of which college life is generally the parent. Orton and Jenkins — I am not sure of their Christian names, and have not the catalogue of graduates at hand — were among our best scholars, and Northrop and C. F. Sedgwick among our best elocutionists. When either of these two spoke, every ear was open. I recollect, too, the eloquent Larned, and the amiable Morris.

"The library of the College was then small, but I recollect was pretty well supplied with the classics. The library of the two literary societies into which the students were divided was a little collection, scarcely, I think, exceeding a thousand in number. I availed myself of it, however, to read several books which I had not seen elsewhere.

"Where the number of teachers was so small, it could hardly be expected that the course of studies should be very extensive or complete. The standard of scholarship in Williams College, at that time, was so far below what it now is, that I think many graduates of those days would be no more than prepared for admission as Freshmen now. There were some, however, who found too much exacted from their diligence, and left my class on that account. I heard that one or two of them had been afterwards admitted at Union College. There were others who were not satisfied with the degree of scholarship attained at Williams College, and desired to belong to some institution where the sphere of instruction was more extended. One of these was my room-mate, John Avery, of Conway, in Massachusetts, a most worthy man and a good scholar, who afterwards became a minister of the Episcopal Church, and settled in Maryland. At the end of his Sophomore year he obtained a dismission, and was matriculated at Yale College, New Haven. I also, perhaps somewhat influenced by his example, sought and obtained, near the end of my Sophomore year, an honorable dismission from Williams College, with the same intention. I passed some time afterwards in preparing myself for admission at Yale, but the pecuniary circumstances of my father prevented me from carrying my design into effect.

"Such is the sum of my recollections of Williams College, so far as they can have any interest for one who is writing its history, which I am very glad to learn that you have undertaken, and which I hope you will find ample encouragement to complete and put to press.

"I am, sir, yours with great regard,

"WM. C. BRYANT.

"TO REV. CALVIN DURFEE."

CHAPTER V.

RELIGIOUS HISTORY OF THE COLLEGE FROM 1793-1815.

Williams College was evidently intended, in the economy of God, to subserve a religious end. The moral and religious state of the institution in its earliest days will be best understood from the testimony of those who were then connected with it. The Rev. Jedediah Bushnell, a member of the first Freshman class, and for many years a venerable clergyman in Cornwall, Vermont, near the close of his life furnished the following: —

"Respecting the religious state of things in College during my residence in it, I have no very favorable account to give. It was the time of the French Revolution, which was, at that time, very popular with almost all the inmates of College, and with almost all people in that part of the country. French liberty and French philosophy poured in upon us like a flood; and seemed to sweep almost everything serious before it. Not that I believe, or ever did believe, that the greatest part of the students were in theory settled infidels; but I did fear at that time, and now as much fear, that a number of talented young men of the several classes did fix down on those infidel principles, from which they never afterwards were recovered. Some, however, who thus made Volney their oracle, and openly professed it, have renounced it since, and become pious and useful men. But French principles at College had a commanding influence, and bore the multitude onward in its course. The influence was so great, that it was very unpopular for a sinner to be convicted of sin, or be converted or say or do anything on the subject of experimental piety. There were two or three old professors of religion whom the wicked very rarely treated with indignity; but the moment a sinner began to have serious thoughts, the wicked would load him with ridicule and shocking abuse. This spirit ran so high, that none dared manifest seriousness except those whom God had truly made serious. Respecting the morals of the College, some infidels were moral men according to the common acceptation of that term; but, as a general rule, the College suffered about as much in morals as it did in the theory of religion. Comparatively with colleges now in New England I think we were quite immoral.

"Notwithstanding this state of things, there was a redeeming spirit in the College as long as I was a member of the institution. There was some solid active piety in a few which remained unmoved. The number of professors of religion was very few; but one in my class at that time who belonged to any church, — none in the higher classes.

The classes which entered afterwards were larger, and contained several professors of religion, one or two instances of decided piety. This spirit of piety, though limited to a small number, had an enlightening and restraining influence on many, at times, beyond what is easily imagined, so that it gave comfort and hope. About three or four were deeply convicted or hopefully converted while I was a member of College. Others have informed me since, that they received impressions then which were never effaced from their minds, until they found the salvation of the Lord."

After speaking of a weekly conference, generally though not uniformly sustained, the writer proceeds to make the following interesting statement: "But that which in my judgment had the most influence of all things, under God, was a prayer-meeting every evening in the week at the ringing of the nine o'clock bell. One of the students opened his room for that prayer-meeting. The meeting was much in the form of our usual family prayer. We read the Scriptures, commented on the truth, exhorted one another, and closed by prayer. Our number hardly ever exceeded twelve, sometimes nine or ten, commonly six, seven, or eight. We usually spent twelve or fourteen minutes in those meetings at a time. All were invited to come who wished. Some non-professors came; some of them would come for a while, and then retire for a season, and then others would come. This meeting was sustained uniformly for four years during my whole College life, and I believe will be remembered with joy by some in another world. Those evening meetings were solemn, and sometimes soul-refreshing, and they constituted a rendezvous for any serious mind in College. As wicked as we were at that time, I do not recollect of a single insult on the room during the time of our devotions, or where we held those prayer-meetings during the space of four years. The ground, during the time of our worship, seemed in the view of all to be sacred ground, which was a wonder to all thus associated, and to me is a wonder now." Notwithstanding the darkness of the period, the writer adds, "I have always been glad that I was there at the time I was, and still hold the scenes which there passed in sweet remembrance."

The above extract needs no comment. In a time of prevailing and even persecuting opposition to religion, to maintain a meeting every evening during four years of such power and interest as to call in, not only Christians, but professedly impenitent persons (the latter class, it would seem, sometimes constituting a majority), indicates not only great practical wisdom in relation to the most efficient mode of combating infidelity, but an integrity of purpose and maturity of Christian character of which we find few examples among young men placed in such circumstances. Need we wonder that God showed his favorable regard towards such a spirit by granting convictions and conversions in connection with the exercise of it?

The greatest darkness, it is sometimes said, precedes the dawn; such was the case now. A brighter day was approaching, which changed, to a considerable extent, the moral aspect of things in College. Allusion has been made already to the fact that religious revivals had begun to make their appearance in various parts of the land. Commencing first in the south part of this county, and in the borders of Connecticut under the ministration of Dr. Hyde, Dr. Griffin, and others, they came soon to attract the attention of the churches generally. Rev. Mr. Swift, the clergyman of Williamstown at that time, "was strongly impressed with the belief that he should live to see a revival under his ministrations." In the year 1805, this blessing began to be realized. "It commenced in the spring of that year, and was great through the summer." Professors of religion in College were aroused. Upon the impenitent, however, little impression was made, except in the way of exciting opposition to the work. So far from having gained an influence over them by mingling in their vain and sinful practices, those with whom they had thus mingled were found ready "to turn and rend them," when any direct effort was made to bring about a change in the existing state of things. A few, however, whose light it would seem had shone in the darkest period, were unable to refrain from exertion. Among these, repeated mention has been made to me, by those who were conversant with the times, of a young man by the name of

Bailey (Algernon Sidney). He appears to have been a terror to the wicked, both in town and in College, insomuch that attempts were set on foot to mob him. He was mighty in prayer. On one occasion, we are told that, when the wicked were lying in wait for him with a view to offer indignity and violence to his person, "several of them were brought suddenly under convictions of sin." This young man, with a few others, set up a meeting in the summer of 1805, at a distance from College, it not being deemed prudent to meet for such a purpose in the College buildings, "as at that period we could hardly have held a prayer-meeting in College without ridicule and interruption." This meeting was somewhat secret. Numbers, however, rallied around the standard, and the meeting filled up, though the house was a considerable way off (near the bridge over the Hoosac on the road which leads to Bennington). "This was a blessed meeting," says one who was a member of it, "and there I have always thought the revival began." About the same time, another meeting was set up, also private, and out of College, probably for the same reason.

In the spring of 1805, the accession to College was favorable to religious influence. Samuel J. Mills,* of whom something will be said hereafter, and James Richards, were members of this class. The standard of religion was elevated. Christians

---

* Mills joined College in April, 1805.

walked more consistently, and of course were more respected. Opposition became less virulent, and meetings began to be held in College at a tutor's room. The revival, meanwhile, continued in town, interrupted partially by the inclement weather of the winter; but in the spring it broke out again afresh, "and was great through the summer of that year." In College God seemed to hold his people off. The struggle had now been protracted "amidst much contention" for nearly a year and a half, and yet, at most, but here and there a mercy drop had fallen. In those days, however, revivals were regarded as great events, of infinite moment. Years of toil were not thought a great sacrifice to secure the enjoyment of them. We are to remember, too, that, during all this period, Christians were becoming matured in their religious experience. "The trial of their faith worked patience," and a sense of their dependence on the Divine sovereignty. Hence the revival which followed was marked by some traits of a peculiar character, as we shall see in the sequel.

It was not until the summer term of 1806 that the work became deep and general in College. It was now that conversions began to be multiplied, it would seem somewhat early in the term. Says Mills, in his diary, under date of June 26: "Attended conference this evening, composed principally of the Freshman class. A very good meeting, — many very solemn. It was very evident God was striving with some of his disobedient creatures." We may remark here, that revivals of religion in college often spend their strength mainly on particular classes, whilst others remain comparatively or not at all affected. In the present instance, the Freshman class shared most extensively in the work. The higher classes, however, owned its power. Under date of August 1, we hear Gordon Hall, of the Sophomore class, mourning over his dark prospects and lost estate, acknowledging himself to be "in the gall of bitterness, and under the bonds of iniquity," and yet rejoicing in the glorious work which was then going on. The conversion of this single individual, we may safely say, was worth shaking the College to its centre. It pleased a sovereign God, also, just on the eve of Commencement, to arrest the attention of a member of the graduating class, who, for a series of years afterwards, was made extensively instrumental in promoting a spirit of revivals in the College, and to whose recollections the writer is indebted for several important particulars, both in reference to this and subsequent periods.

One conversant with the scenes just described, and a member of the prayer-meeting above alluded to, speaks of the effects of this revival as decided and happy upon the state of things in College generally. "Some in all the classes shared in it. It brought religion into the ascendant. The institution of the Theological Society was one of the fruits of it, and I have no doubt it was directly concerned in bringing out and maturing the foreign mission spirit." The truth couched in the last clause of this extract is one of deep interest. Weighing the importance of events by their consequences, we shall be led to regard the revival of 1806 as of interest, more from the development of the spirit there alluded to than from the worth of individual souls, brought to a saving acquaintance with the Redeemer, through the agency of it. The long protracted struggle which gave this revival birth, seemed to indicate that God intended to bring out of it something more than temporary results. Painful travail in the Church, as a general thing, precedes her brightest deliverances. Great throes go before great movements which rock the foundations of public sentiment and practice, and go to settle things on a new basis. Aged Christians have told me, that they never knew before nor since such a wrestling spirit as that which prevailed at this time. The prayers of Bailey and some others seem to have struck, with a kind of wonder, those who had been conversant only with the ordinary state of things which prevailed in the churches. This spirit of prayer was expansive; it embraced a wider sphere than that circumscribed by the walls of College. The world, with its dark and dying population, presented its claims. A deep-toned sympathy for millions of the human race, deprived by sinful sloth and griping penury of Gospel offers and Gospel hopes, was kindled and fostered in these little bethels. Here indeed this spirit was fanned into a flame, which so soon after enlightened the American Church into a knowledge, not only of the wants and woes of heathenism, but of her duty in reference to it.

That quick and tender conscience in reference to Gospel precepts, as absolutely, imperatively, and at the present time binding, which is wont to be excited where the Spirit of God moves with power, fixed now with peculiar strength on the dying command of Christ, "Go ye into all the world and preach the Gospel to every creature." Where there is obedient will, the eye will naturally be arrested by those commands which apply most appropriately to the circumstances of the individual. From this fact, in part, we may account for it, that young men, setting before themselves as the object of life the furtherance of Christianity, should have had their attention arrested by such precepts as that above quoted. Other young men, however, had been similarly situated, outwardly, and had had the same precepts before them. It is reasonable to conclude, therefore, that there was a simultaneous movement upon several minds, by one and the same Spirit. I would not say a special movement, — not special, at least, in any other sense than this, that things were now viewed as they were, lucidly and clearly, being seen in the concentrated light of that spiritual atmosphere which gathered around the praying part of College during the long protracted struggle which preceded the awakening. Samuel J. Mills was at this time a somewhat mature Christian, having been the subject of an awakening in 1801. Characterized in his early religious experience by convictions of uncommon pungency and strength, he became a radically serious person, and brought on with him a more than common weight of religious feeling and influence. In the spirit which was falling upon the institution he participated largely, and seems to have been among the first whose mind was deeply wrought upon in reference to his duty personally to the heathen. "He reflected long, and prayed much," says his biographer, "before he disclosed his views, and when he determined to unburden his mind, by conversing with two or three of his fellow-students, it was in a manner which deserves to be related. He led them out into a meadow, at a distance from the College, to a retirement, probably familiar to himself, though little exposed to observation, or liable to be approached, where, by the side of a large stack of hay, he devoted the day to prayer and fasting, and familiar conversation on this new and interesting theme; when, much to his surprise and gratification, he found that the Spirit of God had been enkindling in their bosoms the flame which had been so long burning in his own. The reader will not be surprised to learn, that this endeared retreat was often made solemn by the presence and hallowed by the piety of those dear young men. It was to this consecrated spot they repaired to cherish the high-born influence, and dedicate themselves renewedly to Christ in this blessed cause; to spend many a precious day in humiliation, fasting, and prayer, and there to offer to a present God those early and fervent supplications to which may be traced the institution of foreign missions in the New World."

So high and exalting an object, commending itself to youthful enthusiasm as well as Christian philanthropy, might well have been expected to elicit strong feeling; and it would seem that measures were immediately set on foot, which proved that the idea of evangelizing the world was not a speculative chimera, a beautiful fancy of young poets, made to exercise the invention or furnish food for philosophical reverie. It did not rank among the day-dreams and frenzied theories of the ancients, in reference to a golden age about to dawn; but was evidently something which the youthful originators intended, with all possible despatch, to put to the rigid and solemn test of practice. It was proposed that the students of Williams College should constitute a Missionary Board, and although the declaration of Christ and the law of Christian charity equally recognized the world as the field, yet it was deemed that the heathen of our own continent had a local and paramount claim. It was proposed, therefore, that the pioneers should furnish themselves with knapsacks and guns sufficient to kill game for their subsistence, and march westward into the wilderness. Does the reader think this enthusiasm? What could be done? The Foreign Missionary Society was not yet formed; the Church was slumbering

11

over the woes of the heathen, and there must be some outlet for their benevolence. "Remember," says Hall, "that there is a dead love, a dead sympathy, a dead compassion, as well as a dead faith, — being without works." Such a sympathy had been common in the Church, and needed no outlet. But an active sympathy could not be restrained. The Foreign Missionary Society, to be sure, sprung into being shortly after; but had that institution not been originated, this feeling would have found vent. "I tell you," says Christ, "if these should hold their peace, the stones would cry out." In a letter to Hall, Mills says, "I wish we could break out upon the heathen like the Irish rebellion, forty thousand strong."

From the scenes which transpired here in the years 1805 and 1806, an influence spread, not only to the remotest East, where the bones of Hall and Richards were laid, but also to the remotest West. It deserves to be mentioned, that it was one of the converts in this revival who afterwards picked up and fostered Henry Obookiah. God seems to have directed this heathen youth to a point where he knew that his path would be crossed by a ray of the missionary light. From this beginning emanated the Sandwich Islands Mission, which has been the theatre within a few years past of such miracles of grace.

In speaking of the origin of the revival, I have already adverted to the labors of the Rev. Mr. Swift. "God blessed his labors as the means of incalculable good," and early in the succeeding year called him to rest from them. And here it will be doing no more than justice to mention the name of another individual, "who for a long time exerted a great influence in College." This was Deacon Stratton. He used to hold conference meetings in College, which the students were fond of attending. Those who were here in the dark days of French infidelity have told me, that, when the ungodly saw good Deacon Stratton coming, they would take their hats and go into the conference to hear him pray and exhort. With humble talents and a limited education, he was willing to work, and would work, wherever he could find an opportunity to do good. He did not fear the ridicule of the students, hoping, "by any means, to save some." His name deserves to be mentioned among the bright lights of the times, whom God employed to direct many a dark mind homeward, — heavenward.

I cannot conclude this brief sketch, without pausing to observe, that several of the most busy actors in the scenes just described died early. This was the case with Robert C. Robbins, who is spoken of by a correspondent "as one of the master-spirits of the period." It was the case with Bailey and Hall and Mills, though, in the significant language of the latter, they lived to exert an "influence on the other side of the globe," and died in the prime of life. This should be a warning to youth, and especially those engaged in the preparatory stages of education, not to defer the hour of activity to an uncertain hereafter.

After the death of Mr. Swift, the town did not enjoy, for several years, the labors of any settled pastor. College and town worshipped together, and of course sympathized, to a greater or less extent, in matters of religion. Men and times changed rapidly, as in a shifting community like a College they must do. A lax morality and want of religious principle crept in. "I do not think, however," says one familiar with this period, "that the departures from right were ever so great as before the revival." Still, there was "much want of principle," and the times grew turbulent. The social condition of a community constituted like a college becomes necessarily unpleasant, and is liable to become quite intolerable, where there are no effectual religious restraints, no Christian benevolence, and no high aims. In such a state of things, the ingenuity of the young, their scheming and planning powers, instead of being exercised on such expansive and ennobling objects as those to which the attention of the reader has been above directed, are employed in conceiving various kinds of mischief, and in practising low and malicious annoyances, either upon themselves or their teachers. This state we have already described as having grown into a habit, previous to the revival of 1805 and 1806. In 1811, we find the same system, though not perhaps to the same extent; still so much so, that, with serious men, it became a trial to live in College, especially in the building occupied by the two lower classes. The number of professors of religion in College had become reduced to twenty; of these, several were inefficient as Christians. The Senior class appears to have embodied most of the active piety which remained; and as this class entered upon its last year, distressing apprehensions began to be entertained lest religion should altogether go out in the institution. In this gloomy and distressing state of things appearances of awakening began to be manifest in the town, and during the winter the work increased, and was "great in town," but College remained unmoved. It seemed to be like the parched heath around which heavenly showers were falling. In the spring term a member of the Senior class returned, visited all the professors of religion in College, proposed a Sabbath morning meeting, which was then established, and has since been continued; being now observed generally in the colleges and theological seminaries as a concert for colleges. Meetings became thronged. Few or no cases of conviction among the students, however, occurred, till about the time of the State Fast. At that time a special meeting was held, and under the "preaching of the word," some of the most ungodly in College had their attention powerfully arrested. The institution became almost immediately solemn. It became again evident that "God was striving with his disobedient creatures." The unquiet and disorderly spirit, which, a little before, had been so painfully annoying, was hushed, and the solemnity of death reigned in both College buildings.

During the revival of 1812, as is the case generally in powerful awakenings such as this was, many incidents occurred of deep interest. The following, as it relates to one whose character is somewhat extensively known, and who now rests from his labors, may be admitted as a specimen of others not less interesting.

"After the revival had been apparent a few days," says Professor Dewey, "and affected the three lower classes much, Jenkins, who had been a deist, a strong-minded man, and twenty-two years old perhaps, now a Junior and under my teaching, came one forenoon to my room, and said, 'We (the class) wish not to have a recitation at eleven, but to meet in the recitation-room at that hour, and hear you on the subject of religion.' I was startled, and said, 'Why, what is the matter?' He replied, 'Many of us are too deeply affected by the conviction of our sinfulness to study to any purpose. Besides, we wish to be taught what to do.' His voice faltered, and the big tear stood in his eye. Knowing his past views, I said, 'Are your own feelings interested, and do you wish this for yourself?' He replied in the affirmative, with a tone that convinced me, knowing the strong mind of the man, that the *strong-hold* was shaken. He said, 'The truth was now all before him, and he could not find a refuge in error.' Some of the other classes, getting knowledge of what was going on, obtained leave to go in. The feeling was so deep that some minutes elapsed before anything could be said. The place was truly a Bochim. 'In a few days,' the account adds, 'Mr. Jenkins was a new man: the deep solemnity of the grave was gone; a happy smile was on his face, and he told me of the change of his feelings, and of his frame of mind. He became a decided Christian from that hour.'" This was the late Rev. Charles Jenkins, of Portland, whose sermons are before the public.

I here insert extracts from another communication. They are as follows: — "The dealings of God with Williams College are worthy to be recorded. They will be had in everlasting remembrance; and when the scenes of Bennington, Saratoga, and Bunker Hill shall be forgotten, there will, I doubt not, be before the throne of God and the Lamb a precious company of redeemed spirits, who, with ever-growing ardor and joy, will celebrate the grace which reached and subdued their hearts, while connected with that institution. It was an account of a revival of religion, in and about the College, I should think as early as about 1805 or 1806, that determined me to go to that place.

"The revival of 1812, of which you request an account, was an interesting work. Its fruits remain to this day. As I entered one year in advance, the class of 1810 were Seniors during my first year. That class contained a good proportion of pious students, and the interests of religion, until they left, were pretty well sustained. In the next class there was a less amount of active, ardent piety. Religion was in a low and languishing state. It was a period of much political excitement. Wickedness abounded, and the love of many waxed cold. 'College scrapes' were frequent, and some of a very daring character. The chapel Bible was several times removed, or nailed to the seat. Once, at least, it was supposed to be burnt. There was some intemperance; I had not the means of knowing how much. In one carousal, I was credibly informed, there was a mock celebration of the Lord's Supper. In my class, nearly one third were professors of religion; but the state of religious feeling with some stood very low. Almost everything around me seemed hostile to a state of living piety. Some of the forms of godliness remained, but its life and power had fled. In the class after me, previous to the revival, there were but two or three professors of religion. The low and declining state of religion was truly alarming. In the fall of 1811, Mr. Nott, one of the first missionaries to India, was employed to preach in Williamstown. His labors were blessed. An interesting revival of religion commenced among the inhabitants. Good old Deacon Stratton's meetings became very full and interesting. But the College, at this time, was like the mountains of Gilboa, on which fell neither dew nor rain. It was a scene of so much noise and confusion, that I seriously contemplated hiring a room in some private house, where I might prosecute my studies with less interruption. At the commencement of the spring term in 1812, one of the pious students in the Senior class, who had been absent most of the winter teaching school, visited and conversed with every professor of religion in College. As the result of his interviews, a prayer-meeting was appointed, privately, for professors of religion only, at his room, at the ringing of the first bell, Sabbath morning, to pray especially for a revival of religion in the College. At the first meeting, nearly or quite all attended. Inquiry was made at the close, whether we should meet again. Some proposed meeting again the next Sabbath morning. He at whose instance the meeting was held inquired if we could not spare time to spend one hour in united prayer on a week-day; and it was concluded to meet again at nine o'clock, Thursday evening. The meetings were continued at different rooms regularly, Sabbath morning and Thursday evening, about three weeks, when (the spring examination being near) the meeting on Thursday evening was so neglected or forgotten that but two attended; and he by whose exertions the meetings had been established went to his room entirely discouraged. Another meeting, however, was appointed for the next Sabbath morning, with an engagement to notify, personally, every professor of religion of the time and place. Again, nearly or quite every one was present, and one in the Senior class, who had been much more engaged in politics than in religion, arose and made a most melting confession of his backslidings. It was a new and unlooked-for event. He was older than any other member in College, and stood high as a scholar. Every one present was deeply affected. Just as all were in a flood of tears, a very thoughtless student from the opposite room, who knew nothing of the meeting, opened the door, and stood for a moment amazed at what he saw; then silently drew back and shut the door. Immediately it was noised abroad through College, and many were saying, 'Why did you not let us know that you had such meetings? We should be glad to attend.' The meetings, after that, were so thronged, that a private room would not contain them. Very soon it was ascertained that one in the Sophomore class was deeply awakened, said to be by a letter from a pious sister. Within a day or two, others became serious. Meetings began to be not only crowded, but very solemn. The week for the annual Fast arrived. Professor Dewey suggested, in a written note to the pious members of the Senior class, the propriety of dispensing with the usual meetings of the literary societies on Wednesday evening, and holding a religious meeting. It was done; and some of the Faculty invited to conduct the meeting. The portion of Scripture read and remarked upon was the parable of the unfruitful fig-tree, Luke xiii. One young man, who had been very thoughtless and profane, attended from curiosity. On hearing the passage read, he thought the audience were to be entertained with a lecture on agriculture, and so concluded to give attention. He found that he was the unfruitful tree, spared only because Christ had made intercession for him, and yet he had never once thanked him for it. A sense of ingratitude stung him to the heart. He became exceedingly distressed. Sleep and rest were impossible. In a few days he found peace in believing; and it was 'great peace.' His bosom overflowed, and he expressed strong desires that his friends might share the happiness he felt. 'His tongue broke out in unknown strains.' Instead of profaneness, was the language of humble prayer. The change was great. It seemed to electrify the whole College. There was no room left for unbelief. All cavilling was silenced. A Junior with whom he had been intimate, and who had been taught and accustomed to ridicule revivals and experimental religion, said he could no more doubt it was the work of God, than he could doubt his own existence; yet, he added, 'I know my heart is opposed to it.' From this time his conviction became deep and pungent. He could not study, and requested his teacher to meet his class and pray with them, and tell them what they must do to be saved. It was done. The meeting was one of deep solemnity. After a day or two it was held at one o'clock instead of eleven, and nearly every student in College attended. Instead of the noise and disturbance which had prevailed a few weeks before, the College was now a scene of great stillness and quiet. The suppressed groanings of some wounded soul might sometimes be heard, or the low voice of prayer, amid the silence and darkness of the night. Recitations now went on as usual, but many for a time had to ask to be excused. They could not study classics. The long-neglected Bible claimed their attention. Professor Dewey was very active and faithful. The work was deep, noiseless, and powerful. It changed exceedingly the aspect of College. The whole number who cherished a hope was between thirty and forty, nearly all of whom were in the three lower classes. The Junior and Sophomore classes shared most largely. Had I a graphic pen, I could describe scenes of deep and thrilling interest. One of the converts, after relating to me how he was awakened and brought, at last, to submit himself into the hands of the Saviour, said, 'O, how this will rejoice my mother!' 'You have a pious mother then?' said I. 'Yes,' said he; 'and many a time, at midnight, have I heard her praying for me.' Another, laying his hand upon his Bible, said: 'This blessed book that my mother gave me and charged me to read every day, — it has lain at the bottom of my chest, and has not been opened until a few days since. It is God's book. O how I have despised and treated God!' Another said, 'O how I should rejoice now to preach the Gospel to my father's slaves!' And he was seen that day, several times, conversing with colored persons in the street, on the salvation of their souls. One very manifest fruit of the revival was peace, quietness, and good order. Government was easy. There was also a great increase of brotherly love. Christians met each other with warm expressions of affection, that could not be counterfeited. One scene which resulted from this state of feeling I shall never forget. It was at the last social religious meeting which my class attended. The exciting scenes of the revival had then passed away. The strong ties of brotherly affection which bound the pious students to one another were about to be sundered. The meeting was tender, and interesting throughout. It devolved on me to preside. In selecting a hymn to close, my eye chanced to fall on the one beginning, 'Blest be the tie that binds.' I had never seen or heard it before. I succeeded in reading it without much, if any, faltering. A tune was named, and singing commenced. About the third verse, Brother Burt [Rev. Federal Burt, of Durham, N. H.], now in heaven, who then stood by my side, turned away and wept aloud. The next verse was attempted. But voices failed. The place became a Bochim. We hung upon each other and wept and wept, and so closed the meeting, and went to our rooms to weep alone.

"At the close of the spring term it was customary for the Junior class to have a public exhibition. By request of the class it was that year dispensed with, and a religious meeting held in its place, and Professor Dewey preached on the occasion."

This revival "was a great and good work;" a

more decided and happy change, perhaps, was never wrought in the moral tone of an institution, than that which accompanied and succeeded. The results were permanent. Those various petty mis chiefs and tricks which had been so common before entirely disappeared, and during the three years which followed, the students pursued their appropriate pursuits in an atmosphere quiet and tranquil, congenial to mental improvement as well as growth in divine things.

I shall close this chapter with a brief account of the revival of 1815. This first made its appearance in the summer term, near the commencement of it. Professor Dewey thinks that the first indications of seriousness were in connection with the preaching of President Fitch, which was, at this time, more than commonly pungent. It is less difficult to trace the instrumental than the real causes of religious awakenings. The following anecdote has been stated to me, and, though not committed to writing at the time, may be substantially relied upon. A member of College had been West, during the spring vacation, and fallen into a place where the Lord was pouring out his spirit. His feelings, which had previously been in a low state, became aroused. As he approached the College buildings on his return, a few days after the term opened, he said within himself, Why might not the Lord do a similar work here? Before getting out of the wagon, a pious student came up. Said he, "Do you wish to see a work of grace here?"

Being answered in the affirmative, "Then," said he, "let us have a prayer-meeting *to-night.*" "Where shall we have it?" "At my room." The room-mate of this individual was a professor of religion, but tinctured with Arminianism. He became immediately downcast and unhappy, and for a few days could scarcely engage actively in religious services. At length, he met his room-mate one morning at the door, exclaiming, "O glorious sovereignty! glorious sovereignty!" From that time his piety became active, ardent; and he now ranks among the most learned and devoted of modern missionaries. This private meeting became so crowded, that, in less than a week, it was found necessary to adjourn to a recitation-room. This also filled up immediately, and the work went on with power. "It came," says one of the subjects of it, "in the majestic stillness of God, and scarce a heart but felt its near and intimate relations to the great things of the future. The aspect of College was suddenly changed. Our rooms were places for prayer, and for religious conversation. We resorted to those Christians, in whom we had seen the Christian character exemplified, for instruction and counsel. The exercises of the classes were not suspended, except in a few cases, though classical improvement became a secondary matter."

The proximate causes of religious awakenings, as has been already hinted, may be often minutely traced. The intimate and true causes, however, are more difficult to be detected. They lie veiled in the bosom experience of the pious, and are among those secrets of which we gain only occasional, and, as it were, accidental glimpses. These glimpses are deeply refreshing, when we are so fortunate as to be favored with them, and deserve to be recorded as samples of what will be found, no doubt, among the most affecting disclosures of the day of judgment. A convert in this revival said to me, with tears, that he could never think of it without being affected. His attention was arrested, he became deeply serious; at length, in anguish and self-despair, he was led to cast himself upon the sovereignty and mercy of God. The mother of this youth, residing at a distance, and knowing nothing of what was here taking place, just at this time had her feelings drawn out, with remarkable fervor, toward her son. On the night of his submission, sleep departed from her, and she wrestled with the angel of the covenant "till the breaking of the day." So calm was her assurance in the morning, that she informed her family of the event, either as something which had taken or would immediately take place. The disclosures of eternity will, no doubt, reveal agonizing throes in the secret chamber, as the springs of those movements which have suddenly revolutionized the moral aspect of communities, to the astonishment of by-standers, and the wonder even of Christians themselves.

CHAPTER VI.

BIOGRAPHICAL SKETCH OF PRESIDENT MOORE.

THE Rev. Zephaniah Swift Moore, D.D., the second President of Williams College, was the son of Judah and Mary Moore, and was born at Palmer, Mass., November 20, 1770. When he was seven or eight years old he removed with his father's family to Wilmington, Vt., where he worked upon a farm till he was about eighteen. From early childhood he evinced great inquisitiveness of mind, and a thirst for knowledge; in consequence of which his parents, who were in humble circumstances, consented to aid him in acquiring an education. Having prosecuted his preparatory studies at the Academy in Bennington, Vt., he entered Dartmouth College, in his nineteenth year; and was graduated in 1793, when he delivered the philosophical oration, "On the Causes and General Phenomena of Earthquakes."

On leaving College, he took charge for one year of an Academy at Londonderry, N. H. He studied theology under the direction of the Rev. Dr. Charles Backus, of Somers, Conn., and was licensed to preach the Gospel by the Association of Tolland

County, February 3, 1796. After preaching to acceptance in different places, especially in Tolland, Conn. and Peterborough, N. H., he finally accepted a call from the church and congregation in Leicester, Mass., and was ordained there January 10, 1798. Here his labors were acceptable and useful. During a portion of the time that he resided here, he joined to his duties as a minister those of Principal of Leicester Academy.

In October, 1811, he accepted the chair of Languages in Dartmouth College. Here he was respected as a man, as a teacher and preacher; and if his attainments were not of the highest order in his department, they were at least such as to secure his respectability and usefulness.

In 1815, he was elected President of Williams College, then vacant by the resignation of Dr. Fitch. He accepted the appointment, and was regularly inducted into office at the Commencement in September of that year. Shortly after his removal to Williamstown he received the degree of Doctor of Divinity from his Alma Mater. His connection with Williams College was attended with circumstances of peculiar embarrassment, in consequence of the efforts which were made about this time to remove the College to Northampton, or some other town in Hampshire County; and in these efforts Dr. Moore took a prominent part. The measure failed in consequence of the refusal of the Legislature to sanction it.

In the spring of 1821, the Collegiate Institution

at Amherst having been founded, he was invited to become its first President. He accepted the invitation, taking a large number of students with him, and was inaugurated in September following. The institution, then in its infancy, and contending with a powerful public opinion for its existence, put in requisition all his energies; and the ultimate success of the enterprise was no doubt to be referred in no small degree to his earnest and untiring efforts. In addition to his appropriate duties as President, and Chairman of the Board of Trustees, he heard the recitations of the Senior class, and a part of the recitations of the Sophomore class; besides all his personal efforts to increase the funds of the institution. His constitution, naturally strong, was overtaxed by these unremitting efforts, and had begun perceptibly to yield, before the last violent attack of disease, which terminated his life.

On Wednesday, June 25, 1823, he was seized with a bilious colic, which reached a fatal termination on the Monday following, — not two years after he left Williamstown. During the brief period of his illness, the greatest anxiety prevailed in College, and unceasing prayers were offered on his behalf. His own mind appeared to be tranquil, and he anticipated the closing scene, and passed through it, with apparent Christian composure. He was fifty-two years seven months and five days old. His funeral solemnities were attended on the Wednesday following, when an appropriate discourse was delivered by the Rev. Dr. Snell, of North Brookfield.

Shortly after his settlement at Leicester he was married to Miss Phebe Drury, of Ward, Mass. They had no children. Mrs. Moore died November 10, 1857.

In personal appearance, Dr. Moore was above the middling stature; was corpulent, was rather prepossessing, modest, and retiring in his appearance. "The turn of his mind was metaphysical, and the duties of his vocation led him to cultivate this branch of study."

"As a College officer," says one who knew him well, "he had few superiors. He knew men and students almost instinctively, and had great skill in moulding and managing them. Mild and persuasive in his manners, never flurried, and rarely severe, he was as firm and immovable in what he thought was right and duty as Greylock itself, and every student understood it, and rarely ventured to set up his own will against his." As a director of the studies of the Senior class, Dr. Moore always appeared to good advantage. "As a preacher he had many high and excellent qualities. He was a clear thinker, and his style was remarkably neat and pure. His elocution was good, though not what might be called eloquent. He was earnest, sincere, and winning, rather than rousing and hortatory in his sermons."

In the spring of 1819, Dr. Moore preached a sermon in the Court-House at Lenox, before the

Berkshire County Education Society, for aiding pious young men in their preparation for the ministry. It was the only time I ever heard him preach. His text was the glowing vision of the prophet Isaiah xl. 6 – 9: "*The lion and the Lamb shall lie down together*," &c. In that discourse he adduced "some Scriptural evidence that the kingdom of righteousness and peace will, at some future period, be extended through the whole world; and then showed by what means it would be thus extended; and particularly the place which the preaching of the Gospel holds among those means." In preaching, he had but very little action. His voice was not loud, but clear and pleasant. His manner was dignified and impressive; adapted to arrest and fix the attention of the hearers. He used but little figurative language, and there was no aim at rhetorical effect. He left a deep impression of his sincerity on the minds of his hearers, and his manner indicated that he felt the importance of the truths he uttered.

Dr. Moore published a Thanksgiving sermon, delivered at Peterborough, N. H., November 17, 1796; two sermons preached at Leicester, January 23, 1798, — the second Sabbath after his ordination; an oration delivered at Worcester, July 5, 1802; a sermon at the funeral of Ensign Winthrop Earle, October 20, 1807; a sermon at the ordination of the Rev. Simeon Colton, at Palmer, June 19, 1811; a sermon at the ordination of the Rev. Jacob Allen, at Tunbridge, Vt., October 6, 1813;

Massachusetts Election Sermon, May, 1818; a sermon at the ordination of the Rev. Dorus Clark, at Blanford, Mass., February 5, 1823; and an address to the public in respect to Amherst College, in 1823.

There is at Williams College a bound volume, containing fifteen of Dr. Moore's manuscript sermons, — a present from Mrs. Moore. They are written in a full and fair hand.

The following letter from Rev. Dr. J. C. Brigham may fitly close this biographical sketch of Dr. Moore.

"BIBLE-HOUSE, New York, February 22, 1859.

"DEAR SIR: —

"You ask for my impressions as to the character and course of Williams College, under the Presidency of Dr. Moore. I will give you some of them briefly. When he came to the institution in 1815, it was, as you are aware, in a reduced condition as to Faculty. Rev. Dr. Chester Dewey was there as Professor, exerting a decided and happy influence on learning and religion, as he has done in other positions to this day. Rev. E. Kellogg, who proved to be a ripe scholar and thorough teacher, came at the same time with the President as Professor of Languages. My class also entered at this juncture.

"As to the President, his whole figure and manners are still distinctly before me. He was then in middle life, of more than ordinary height, rather fleshy, a little stooping, hair smoothly combed down in front, small clothes and knee-buckles, after the old Puritan style. In manners he was gentle, affectionate, yet decided where there was any infraction of College rules. As an instructor in mental and moral philosophy he was thorough, adhering perhaps a little too much to the *letter* of the text-book.

"As a preacher he was clear, earnest, and evangelical, though with no great compass of voice, and little of action. At evening prayers in the chapel, he was always present and conducted the exercises. Occasionally the students were convened, as on fast days, when he took decided pains to impress religious truth on their minds. And though there was no special revival of religion in College during his presidency, there was at times much seriousness among the professing students, which he warmly encouraged, as did the other members of the Faculty. During my Sophomore year he was seriously ill for several weeks with fever. Individuals were called to spend the night in watching with him, in which service I twice participated. From the tone of his conversation, he impressed me with a belief that he was truly a man of God, — submissive to His will, yet desirous, if so ordered, to live and labor for the welfare of his new charge. He recovered, and everything in relation to the College seemed for nearly three years to be prosperous. Near the close of this period a topic came up which afterwards produced great and wide-spread agitation. I refer to the removal of the College to Hampshire County. In my Senior year this was the absorbing theme. The President and the students who resided east of the mountains were for removal. I, as a Berkshire man, was of course averse to the measure. But while many censured the President for the leading part which he took, I was never inclined to question the goodness of his intentions. He evidently felt that the College would not long live where it was, but would flourish on the banks of the Connecticut. Other great and good men, ministers, and laymen, thought it would flourish where it now stood. That question was never decided. Divine Providence, infinitely wiser than both parties together, interposed, and has proved that at each place a college of high rank can be sustained and made widely useful.

"You have thus some of my impressions of the College and its Faculty while I was a member. You will infer that in my judgment the President commenced his career auspiciously, and might have succeeded well had his *heart* been with his body west of the mountains.

"I will add, that if all the Faculty, students, and their friends had been with the President in favoring removal, it might probably have done well in Hampshire County. Let us then praise the Lord for ordering two colleges in place of one, neither of which could be spared without great detriment to the cause of education and of the Gospel.

"Yours most truly, &c.,

"J. C. Brigham.

"To Rev. C. Durfee."

CHAPTER VII.

ADMINISTRATION OF PRESIDENT MOORE. 1815-1821.

On the 2d day of May, 1815, the Board of Trustees accepted the resignation of President Fitch; and on the same day elected the Rev. Leonard Woods, D. D., of Andover, President and Professor of Divinity. The Rev. Dr. Hyde was appointed a committee to notify Dr. Woods of his appointment. At the same meeting, the Rev. Zephaniah Swift Moore, Professor of Languages in Dartmouth College, was chosen to the same office; and Dr. Packard was authorized to inform him of it, in case Dr. Woods did not accept. It was likewise voted to raise the President's salary from $ 1,000 to $ 1,400 per annum. Dr. Woods declined the appointment; and Dr. Packard then notified Professor Moore of his election, who accepted the appointment.

At the same meeting of the Board at which Professor Moore was elected President, Dr. Packard of Shelburne introduced the following motion, which was adopted: "That a committee of six persons be appointed to take into consideration the removal of the College to some other part of the Commonwealth; to make all necessary inquiries which have a bearing on the subject, and report at the next meeting." The committee consisted of the Hon. Joseph Lyman, the Rev. Samuel Shepard, the Rev. Theophilus Packard, Joseph Woodbridge, Esq., Theodore Pomeroy, Esq., and the Hon. Daniel Noble; and they reported at the next meeting of the Board, in September, that "a removal of Williams College from Williamstown is inexpedient at the present time, and under existing circumstances."

At the time of this decision it was understood by the Board "that a full and fair experiment should be made to revive and build up the College in its present location;" and as any further agitation of the question of removal would directly tend to blast all efforts which might be made for its success, and frustrate the experiment about to be made, it was very properly agreed that the question of removal should be considered as at rest during this experiment.

Dr. Moore (for he had just received that degree from Dartmouth) was inaugurated President of the College, with appropriate ceremonies, September 3, 1815. His inaugural discourse has been described as an able and finished production. It was not published, but it is said to have contained an expression of his views in favor of the removal of the College.

Still, though such an expression of personal opinion had been intimated, it was reasonably expected that the President and Faculty of the College would heartily unite their influence and efforts to give success to the experiment now to be made. Indeed, there seemed to be an implied understanding among the friends of literature and religion in this section of the State, that an experiment should be fairly made for the College in its present location.

When this experiment (if so short a period can be called one) had been in operation three years, it became very apparent that nothing was wanting but the united and hearty co-operation of the Trustees, Faculty, and friends of the College to crown the experiment with all reasonable success. If any entertained doubts respecting the future growth and prosperity of the College when the Presidency of Dr. Moore commenced, those doubts were soon seen to be groundless. The pleasing assurance soon began to be cherished, that the College would flourish again in its present location.

Such were the animating hopes and prospects of the College, at the Commencement in 1818, when a sad scene was suddenly opened in the history of this institution. Amidst the most cheering prospects, for the College, and while its early and long-tried friends were congratulating each other on the bright prospects which were dawning on the College,— while they were speaking its praise and predicting its success,— just as the Board were about to adjourn, a petition was presented by one of their own members, the Rev. Dr. Packard, as an agent for Amherst Academy, "requesting the Board to unite this College with a proposed literary institution, which they contemplated locating in the town of Amherst." And Dr. Moore now declared himself to be favorable to such a project. This proposition met with a decided negative from the Trustees of Williams College, their only action upon it being a vote, "That the said Trustees of Amherst Academy have leave to withdraw the communication which they have submitted to this Board." Dr. Packard now predicted that the Board would be summoned to attend an extra meeting in less than three months; and his prediction was verified.

When the Trustees were assembled, November 10, 1818, the President immediately submitted to them a proposition for the removal of the College, connected with an expression of his purpose to resign the office of President, unless the proposition should be sustained. He now stated, that, at the time he accepted the Presidency of the institution, he had no idea that the College was to remain at Williamstown, but had all the while supposed it was to be removed to Hampshire County. The following action, says a competent witness, "was principally owing to the influence exerted on that occasion by Dr. Moore." In view of all the circumstances which presented themselves, the Trustees finally concluded, on certain conditions, to submit a petition to the Legislature for a removal of the College, in order that the question might, by the highest authority in the Commonwealth, be put to rest. And that the Legislature might act in this matter with all proper information as to the *place* of removal, provided it should be judged expedient to change the location, a most respectable committee was appointed by them, to determine, upon actual view, in what town in Hampshire County the College should be located.

At this meeting of the Board the following conditional resoulutions were adopted, nine out of twelve voting for them: —

"*Resolved*, That it is expedient to remove Williams College to some more central part of the State, whenever sufficient funds can be obtained to defray the necessary expenses incurred, and the losses sustained by removal, and to secure the prosperity of the College, and when a fair prospect shall be presented of obtaining for the institution the united support and patronage of the friends of literature and religion in the western part of the Commonwealth, and when the General Court shall give their assent to the measure.*

"*Resolved*, That, in order to guide the Trustees in determining to which place the College shall be removed, and to produce harmony and union, the following gentlemen, viz. Hon. James Kent, Chancellor of the State of New York, Hon. Nathaniel Smith, Judge of the Supreme Court of Connecticut, and the Rev. Seth Payson, D. D., of Rindge, N. H., be a committee to visit the towns

* The three individuals who voted against the removal were Israel Jones, Daniel Noble, and Levi Glezen.

in Hampshire County, and determine the place to which the College shall be removed; the Trustees pledging themselves to abide by their decision, provided the requisite sum be raised."

The Board then adjourned to meet at Pittsfield in May next, at which time and place the committee reported that the proper place to remove to was Northampton. An address to the public was also prepared and printed, setting forth the reasons for the intended removal of the College, and requesting donations to increase its funds, and to promote its prosperity at its new location, viz. at Northampton.

The following reasons were set forth in the address, which was extensively circulated: "That, since its establishment in 1793, other colleges have sprung up about it, and had almost wholly withdrawn the patronage it had formerly received from the North and West. That, owing to the want of support, its funds have become so reduced that the income falls short of the expenditures, and the Trustees, for this reason, are unable to maintain the institution in its present state, and enable it to compete with other colleges. These circumstances have induced the Trustees, after mature reflection and deliberation, to think a removal of the College to a situation more central and more convenient of access necessary to its support and continuance in usefulness."

We pause here to record the death of one of the Trustees, and the resignation of another.

In 1815, Elijah Williams, Esq. died at Stockbridge, aged eighty-three. He was born at Newton, November 15, 1732, and was a half-brother of the founder of the College. When a young man he settled in what is now West Stockbridge village, and was an enterprising farmer. The latter part of his life he passed in Stockbridge, in order to enjoy the ministry of his brother-in-law, the Rev. Dr. West. For many years he was Sheriff of the county, was one of the original Trustees of the College, and was a Christian gentleman of the old school. His only child, William Henry Williams, was graduated of Williams College in 1798.

In 1819, the Hon. Stephen Van Rensselaer, another original Trustee, resigned his connection with the College. He was born at Albany, N. Y., November 1, 1764, passed most of his days in his native city, was an elder in the Dutch Reformed Church, was distinguished for his wealth, activity, and beneficence, and died January 26, 1839, aged seventy-four years.

The public agitation and discussion of the question of removing the College to Hampshire County was now commenced in earnest. President Moore, from this time, was untiring in his efforts to effect it, and many were induced to believe that the College would never prosper in its present location. Others, too, were earnestly in favor of a removal, and published many anonymous articles on this subject.

These earnest pleas in favor of removal were ably and triumphantly answered by the friends of the College. The leading arguments in favor of a change of location were: "That the state of the funds and the number of students were such as to threaten the destruction of the College, and fully to authorize the assertion that it could not continue to go on in its present location with any hopeful prospect." "It was asserted that it was not enough to say that Williamstown is a place where a good education may be obtained. Our country is not so filled with people that it is necessary to go so far to find a place lonely and sequestered enough for purposes of education." "Williamstown may be a good place for retirement from dissipation; but does this advantage compensate for all the disadvantages of its situation? It is not a single difficulty which the College has to encounter. It might, perhaps, overcome any *one*. It is their number and concurrence that produces discouragement." "Besides a bad location, it has great wants, which cannot be supplied, even by the funds which have been raised in consequence of the measures towards a removal." "A chapel is needed." "More permanent officers are requisite." "The library contains only fourteen hundred volumes, and many of these not very valuable." "The College has extensive wants in other departments to be supplied." It was urged, "that students could never be induced to resort to so retired a place as Williamstown to obtain an education." "Nothing can show more decisively than the present low state of the College that the public are not, and will not be, satisfied with the present location. It can never regain the ground it has lost."

On the other hand, it was urged, "that the funds of the institution are so considerable, and the number of students is so great, that the income from both exceeds, at this time, the annual expenses of the College." It was claimed, "that it was unnecessary and inexpedient to remove the institution on the ground that it was more likely to prosper elsewhere than here; additions to its number of students may soon be confidently expected, sufficient to insure the respectability and usefulness of the institution. The present diminished number of students may more justly and philosophically be attributed to accidental and transient causes, than to anything connected with its location." The prospect of its removal, it was shown, prevented many from entering the institution. In 1818, the College, its friends claimed, would have contained more than a hundred, instead of eighty-seven, but for the agitation of the question of removal. "And there is good reason to expect that in years to come the number will be much and permanently increased, if this agitating question is put to rest." It was strenuously maintained that Williams College had been greatly useful to those for whom it was principally intended; that it had been a College of the character which the Legislature of 1793 designed it should be; and had thus far, in its present location, answered, and, if suffered quietly to do its work, would continue to answer, the views and intentions of its founders."

The community generally became interested in the subject, and conflicting opinions were entertained, and freely and frequently expressed. Pamphlet succeeded pamphlet, and newspaper article followed newspaper article, on this unwelcome and exciting subject, for more than two years. There was a large convention held at Northampton, August 3, 1819, composed mostly of gentlemen from that vicinity, to take measures to effect the removal of Williams College to Hampshire County. At this meeting Dr. Moore presided. Resolutions were adopted in favor of the removal of the College, and committees were appointed to solicit subscriptions for that purpose.

A large convention was held in Pittsfield, October 6, 1819, for the purpose of expressing the views and feelings of the county in relation to the removal of the College. The Hon. William Walker of Lenox presided. Resolutions against the removal of the College, and an address to the public, were reported and adopted. It was "the deliberate opinion of this meeting that nothing was necessary to preserve for Williams College, in its present location, the character of a highly respectable and useful institution, but the cordial co-operation of the friends of literature, science, and religion, in the western section of the State." In this address to the public they say: "If the removal of the College should result in some pecuniary losses, — if some widows and men of wealth were to suffer by it, — these losses might be endured; but we know not what would restore to the community that confidence which sweetens life and binds society together; nor where would be found that balm which would heal the wounds which this measure would inflict."

On the 2d day of November, 1819, at a meeting of the Trustees in Williamstown, it was voted that it is expedient to petition the Legislature for permission to remove Williams College to Northampton. Fifty thousand dollars had been subscribed in a short time, by the inhabitants of Hampshire and adjoining counties, to defray the expenses which would be incurred, and the losses which would be sustained by the removal. And a committee was chosen to present the petition to the Legislature.

A proposition was also made to the Trustees of Amherst Academy, requesting them to unite their charitable funds with the College, in case it was removed to Northampton; but it was rejected, unless they would change the location to Amherst. The petition of the President and Trustees to the Legislature, on the subject of the removal of Williams College, met with a spirited opposition on the part of the inhabitants of the town and county, and, upon their own responsibility, they raised a subscription of $17,500, which was laid before the Legislature, and which was to be paid to the College, in case it should not be removed.

This subscription, raised against the wishes of a majority of the Trustees, and which they could not refuse without a fraud upon the Legislature, was made payable in ten years. At the expiration of this time, the subscribers were called on, and in some cases payment was refused. So much dependence had been placed on this fund by the College, that it was found impossible to do without it, and legal measures were reluctantly resorted to. One case was carried to the Supreme Court, and the decision being in favor of the Corporation, the remainder was collected without difficulty. It was, however, unjustly made the ground of much ill-feeling, and much odium was thrown on the College on account of the measures pursued. This subscription, it must be remembered, was procured by those not connected with the College, and was one of the reasons that influenced the Legislature to refuse permission for removal; and under these circumstances, the collection of this sum, guaranteed to the College by the subscribers, could not have been otherwise than honorable and just.

The site for the College in Northampton had been mentioned, and the subject of its removal was the principal topic of discussion in the western part of the State.

The prospects of the College in Williamstown were indeed gloomy. It seemed to be on the verge of ruin. Even its warmest friends were in doubt whether it could much longer be retained in its present location.

The number of students began a second time to decline.* The College hardly supported itself, but in some instances drew upon its friends for maintenance. Only a few of the students were in favor of retaining it in Williamstown.

The petition to the Legislature was finally laid before that body in February, 1820, and after a long and anxious discussion and consideration, — in consequence of the subscription of $17,500, and of the representations and remonstrances from the inhabitants of Berkshire County, and also from a deep conviction that it would be a plain violation of the will of the founder of the institution, and others who had given funds to maintain an institution in Williamstown, — the Legislature refused to grant the Trustees permission to remove the College.

In their report (which was adopted by a large majority in both branches of the Legislature †), the committee say (after reviewing all the proceedings of the Legislature from 1785 up to that time, in relation to the College): "They have supposed it their duty to notice that Woodbridge Little, Esq., of Pittsfield, some persons in Williamstown, some in Vermont, and some in New York, have made donations to Williams College; and the

* The College year commenced in 1815 with fifty-eight students. This number increased in the second term to sixty-four. In three years the number had increased to ninety-one; and then began again to decline, amid the excitement about the removal.

† In the Senate, 31 to 5; in the House, 120 to 25.

committee suppose they ought not to disregard the presumption that the *location* of this seminary constituted some parts of the motive to the bounty. And they cannot, therefore, but doubt the *justice* of removing this seminary to any place not contemplated by such donors, to be the site of the future use of their charities."

The committee further state, that, in their opinion, so important a measure as the removal of Williams College "ought not to take place without *a reasonable and unembarrassed conviction that some great benefit will result therefrom, not attainable in its present location.* The committee are by no means satisfied that mere location determines the degree of estimation and respect in which any literary institution may be held. It is reputation which constitutes attraction; and this is founded on the modes and means of instruction. And although it might be a very interesting question whether fifty or a hundred thousand dollars should be originally expended at Northampton or at Williamstown; yet considering the length of time since the establishment of Williams College in the place where it is; that a considerable part of its funds were given in contemplation of its continuance there; and considering that no change of a very imposing cast is likely to be effected immediately, or before the lapse of some years, in the future usefulness of the institution, if at all, by removal, — the committee have come to the result, that it is *inexpedient* to remove Williams College to Northampton."

In conclusion, the committee state that "they do most highly appreciate, and most profoundly respect, the motives of the petitioners; these are unquestionably founded in a truly honorable and elevated desire to extend the usefulness of this respectable College, in promoting learning, virtue, piety, and religion; and under these impressions, the committee feel the most sincere regret that their perception of duty compels them to submit to the two Houses that it is neither *lawful nor expedient* to grant the prayer of the petition."

And thus Williams College was permitted to remain in its present beautiful, rightful, heaven-blest location. It was a hard-fought battle on both sides, each party taking the ground distinctly that but one College was needed or could be sustained in Western Massachusetts. The question of removal went to the Legislature with this distinct avowal; and hence the general expectation was that the decision of the Legislature would be final. So the friends of Williams thought; so thought the people of Northampton, who have ever since shown a commendable disposition and desire to patronize and sustain Williams College.

But there were those who were not in this way to be defeated in what they had undertaken. Strong expectations had been excited that there would be a college in Hampshire County; and the people of Amherst, taking advantage of this state of things, raised a large subscription, and commenced August 9, 1820, to erect buildings for the accommodation of students, with the expectation of obtaining a charter, or of establishing a collegiate institution there. They organized a Board of Trustees, and Dr. Moore, instead of following the example of Drs. Hyde, Shepard, and some others, by acquiescing in the decision of the Legislature, and exerting himself to build up Williams College, accepted an invitation, extended to him in May, 1821, to place himself at the head of that institution, and unite himself with the destinies of that enterprise.

Early in the summer term, Dr. Moore announced in the College chapel that he had received an invitation to go to Amherst, and had accepted it, with the understanding that he should perform the duties of his office at Williamstown until Commencement; or he should leave before that time, if the Trustees desired it. From the general respect which the students entertained for the President, and the gloomy prospects which at that time surrounded this institution, it would not have been surprising if they had resolved to follow him in a body. But, instead of this, there soon sprang up a division of feeling among them. There were nearly eighty students in College at this time. Full one half were determined to remain, while most of the rest concluded to go to Amherst. During the summer term there was probably as much debating as studying in College. At the close of the Senior examination, the venerable Dr. Hyde called the students together in the College chapel, and remarked that the President whom they valued was about to retire; but the guardians of the College would remain, and stand by it; and, by Divine assistance, it would be sustained. That so cautious a man as Dr. Hyde should venture to make such an announcement, at such a time, was truly cheering to that portion of the students who were steadfast in their adherence to the College. Those who were resolved to leave, however, now called a meeting, and, after a protracted discussion, passed a resolution to carry the library belonging to the Philologian and Philotechnian Societies with them to Amherst, and chose a committee to carry this resolution into effect. This undertaking, however, was defeated. The same kind Providence which had watched over Williams College in times past, for good, and prospered the early efforts of its friends, again signally interposed for its deliverance and prosperity. The resignation of Dr. Moore, though much regretted at the time, opened the way for the introduction of a man to the Presidency who was eminently qualified for the office, and who was ardently attached to the College, and to the College *as then located.*

At the meeting of the Board at which Dr. Moore's resignation of the Presidency of the College was received and accepted, the Trustees unanimously elected the Rev. Thomas McAulay, LL.D., Professor of Natural Philosophy in Union College, to the office of President, and Dr. Shepard was appointed to notify him of his election. The Trustees at this time published a circular, announcing the election of Dr. McAulay, and their determination to stand by the College (now that the question of its location was settled), and restore it to its former respectability and usefulness. Dr. McAulay visited Williamstown, and several other towns in the county, but finally declined the appointment. The Rev. Professor C. A. Goodrich, of New Haven, was then elected, and declined. The condition and prospects of the College were now discouraging. Commencement was at hand. The two men who had been elected did not feel disposed to leave permanent and useful positions elsewhere, and place themselves at the head of an institution whose future existence was so precarious. The students who had nobly stood by the College hitherto, began to be discouraged. The prospects of a Commencement were dark. Some had already asked for dismissions, in order to take their degrees at other colleges; others were now wavering. In these discouraging circumstances, the Senior class called a meeting, to determine what to do, when two individuals, with a noble determination to sustain the reputation and honor of their Alma Mater, addressed the class. They declared their intention to remain, and to have a Commencement; that if left alone they would still graduate in the usual manner, and, if necessary, would perform the several parts which had been allotted to their classmates. The names of these individuals ought to be recorded on these pages, — the Rev. Emerson

Davis, D. D., of Westfield, and the Hon. Erastus C. Benedict, of New York, both of them afterwards Tutors, and now (1859) associate and efficient Trustees of the College. Another member of that class, Hon. Henry L. Sabin, M. D., has for some years been an efficient member of the Board of Trustees.

Influenced by such examples, the remainder concluded to stand by the College. The Commencement was a memorable one. Thirteen took degrees. Dr. Moore presided at the exercises for the last time. They were well attended. At twelve o'clock Dr. Griffin, "a man of most commanding figure and presence," arrived in town, and took his seat on the stage in the afternoon, to the unspeakable joy of the friends of the College. Now it was known, for the first time, that he had been elected to the Presidency, and had come on to settle the question of acceptance. The hopes which his majestic presence inspired caused the exercises of the day, which were commenced in gloom, to pass off with cheerfulness, and even with raised expectations of the future. The Valedictory oration, by Emerson Davis, entitled, "To be Useful, the Duty and Happiness of Man," and the Master's oration, "On Home," by Mr. William A. Porter, were of a high order, and gave great satisfaction to the audience. In a few days Dr. Hyde received a letter from Dr. Griffin, announcing his acceptance of the Presidency; and the cheering intelligence was shortly circulated through the length and breadth of the land.

From the commencement of his Presidency, Dr. Moore had been understood to be in favor of the removal of the College to Hampshire County. During all the latter part of his connection with it, he labored to accomplish this object with distinguished ability and untiring perseverance. In all his efforts, however, to effect its removal, he was undoubtedly influenced by honorable and Christian motives.

It is undeniably true that there was an understanding between Dr. Moore and a portion of the Trustees, when he came to Williamstown, that the College would be removed to the valley of the Connecticut, — to Northampton or Amherst. Some of the Trustees were warmly enlisted in favor of this measure, at the time of Dr. Moore's election. They believed the College could never flourish in its present location. And when their views and purposes on this subject were fully disclosed, an unusual excitement was created in Williamstown, and, indeed, throughout the entire county. Dr. Moore now assigned, as the reason in justification of the part he had taken in the movement, that he came to Williamstown with the confident and honest expectation that the College would be removed. The disaffection towards him, however, was not so great as it was towards a portion of the Trustees. Still he had been free and frequent in the expression of his opinion that the College could never flourish in the valley of the Hoosac, one of the handsomest valleys in the world.

He fully believed that the interests of learning, and especially the cause of Evangelical religion, required the removal of the College to a more central position in the State. Entertaining such views, he never made a vigorous attempt to fasten it in its present location, nor threw the whole of his influence in favor of building it up on this ground. Had he entered with the same energy and zeal into the interests of this College, which he afterwards displayed in behalf of Amherst, there is reason to believe it would have enjoyed a greater degree of prosperity than it did during the latter part of his connection with it. If the *location* of the College was the cause of its previous decline, on what ground shall we account for that uncommon degree of reputation and prosperity, which, notwithstanding all its subsequent embarrassments, it has enjoyed since 1821?

CHAPTER VIII.

RELIGIOUS HISTORY OF THE COLLEGE FROM 1815 - 1821.

THE question of the removal of the College to Hampshire County did not begin to be publicly agitated at the commencement of Dr. Moore's administration. True, the subject was first introduced to the notice of the Trustees at the time of his election to the Presidency; still, it was about three years before it was generally understood that he was earnestly in favor of such a measure. As students are a consequential class of the community, when this was known, they began to hold meetings on the subject. They were much divided in opinion. The influence of all this was evidently unfavorable to religious impressions or improvement.

There was another subject which produced much excitement during the administration of Dr. Moore, namely, the rivalry and animosity between the two literary societies. It was finally allayed by an agreement that each Freshman class should be equally divided between the two societies. During all these agitations Christianity was losing ground, from two causes, — a diminished number of professors of religion, and a general want of spirituality. Says a correspondent: "Professors were hardly distinguishable, as a body, from the impenitent members of College. There were some exceptions."

As a natural result of worldly conformity in the Church, various species of immorality became prevalent; — the general habit of drinking wine and brandy on all special occasions, especially on the election of officers of the two societies. At the close and commencement of each term, wine and spirits were freely used. It was customary for some to keep them in their rooms. It was no uncommon thing for professors of religion to mingle in these scenes of hilarity, giving them their countenance and encouragement. Card-playing (a most dissipating amusement) was not uncommon, "and there was an almost constant succession of low tricks."

In the midst of this state of things, a powerful and extensive revival of religion was enjoyed in the town, in the winter and spring of 1819; and, for a time, there was much feeling manifested on the subject of religion in College. Some of the most wild and thoughtless were brought under serious impressions, and, for a short season, the realities of the future seemed to hold the predominance over the pursuits of time and sense. As a matter of course, the Bible came into demand. Professors of religion now came and made confessions to each other, and to the awakened. But the cloud which, for a time, portended a plentiful shower, finally passed over with only here and there a single drop.

The following letters will be read with interest, in this connection. The first is from the Rev. B. F. Clark, of the class of 1820: —

"No deep and long-continued religious interest was witnessed in College, so far as I recollect, while I was a member. I think in the spring term of 1819 Christians were more active than usual. Some who, though professors, had not been much known as such, were revived; and about this time Johnson Baldwin and Simon C. Ewers obtained hopes. The Rev. Joshua N. Danforth, D. D., was a brand plucked from the burning, as we hoped, some time before this. His case excited much interest for a time; but I do not know that any other student began to hope near that time.

"I have no distinct recollection of efforts made by the Faculty to elevate the standard of piety, or to awaken the careless. But I have never thought that any of them were unusually deficient in their official duties as the temporary guardians of the spiritual interests of the students. I was always interested, instructed, and gratified by Dr. Moore's preaching and prayers, and always feel an emotion of gratitude when I think of him. And if it was not invidious, I would say the same of Professor Dewey. I loved both as teachers and Christians.

"I think the rivalry between the two literary societies had an unhappy influence on the religious state of College. Christians were alienated from each other, and I have reason to suppose from members of the society to which they did not belong.

"In the latter part of my College course, the removal of the College from Williamstown began to excite interest, and the students suffered their feelings to be enlisted; some very strongly, leaving not much room for Christ and his cause. Such like causes I have no doubt had influence to prevent works of grace in College, and to discourage any who would have rejoiced in the work of the Spirit."

The Rev. Dr. William A. Hallock, of the class of 1819, writes: —

"To your inquiries as to the religious state of Williams College from September, 1815, to September, 1819, I cannot record any special or extensive outpouring of the Spirit; but I felt from first to last that our religious privileges were great. The whole influence of our worthy President seemed to me most salutary, without any abatement or drawback whatsoever. He seemed in all respects to aim at the best interests of the College, and of all its members, and pre-eminently to seek the highest spiritual interest of all under his care. The thought never occurred to me that the diminished number of students when he came to the College, or any question as to its future history or prosperity, abated his fidelity; he rather appeared to me to labor the more earnestly for the highest and best good of the institution and all its members. In my last year the labors of the Rev. Mr. Gridley, the pastor in Williamstown, were much blessed, and the College to a considerable extent felt the happy influence. There was a fine foreign missionary spirit in some of the students. There was one very marked case of conversion, that of a prominent student * who was far from God, and whose labors have since been greatly blessed in revivals of religion, and who has been long in a prominent pastoral charge. My recollections are all pleasant of the piety and excellence of the officers of the College, the pastor and leading members of the church with which we worshipped, and of the members of the church within the College. If I had any complaint to make, it was of myself, for not more wisely improving the rich privileges I then enjoyed. May God preserve and bless the institution down to the day when our glorious Redeemer "shall see of the travail of his soul, and shall be satisfied."

In the early part of this chapter, we may have over-estimated the influence of the unsettled state of

* Rev. Joshua N. Danforth, D. D.

things, and the dark prospects of the College on the tone of religious feeling and morals. Certainly, in these respects, there does not appear to have been any marked or radical change or improvement, until the question respecting the location of the College was permanently put to rest.

> "The Spirit, like a peaceful dove,
> Flies from the realms of noise and strife."

CHAPTER IX.

BIOGRAPHICAL SKETCH OF PRESIDENT GRIFFIN.

THE Rev. Edward Dorr Griffin, D. D., third President of Williams College, was born at East Haddam, Conn., January 6, 1770. He was the son of an enterprising farmer. He fitted for college with the Rev. Joseph Vaill, of Hadlyme, entered Yale College in 1786, and was graduated in 1790. He excelled in every department of study, and attained the highest station in his class.

On leaving College, he became principal of an academy at Derby, Conn., and at the same time entered on the study of law. In the summer of 1791 he was attacked by a severe illness, which confined him to his room for some weeks. This was a most important era in the history of his life. Now it was that his mind was brought under a solemn conviction of sin, and he resolved to devote himself to the service of God. He arose from his bed of sickness an altered man. It was about two months before he ventured to hope that he was a Christian. Shortly after this, his mind was suddenly and powerfully impressed, one Sabbath afternoon, with the conviction that it was his duty to enter the ministry. The struggle was short. His private journal contains this record: "From the time the thought first rushed upon my mind, till my purpose was as fixed as it ever was afterwards, was not more than half or three quarters of an hour. From that memorable afternoon, I felt that I should be willing to spend my days among the pagans of the wilderness, if such should be the will of God."

The study of law was now relinquished. His aspirations were directed to something higher. He entered at once upon the study of theology, under the direction of the Rev. Dr. Jonathan Edwards of New Haven, and was licensed to preach the Gospel, October 31, 1792. Early in November he returned to his father's house, — "the only professor of religion in a family of ten," — where his labors were almost immediately attended with manifest tokens of the presence and power of the Holy Spirit. Several in his father's family were brought in a short time to hope in the saving mercy of God. In January, 1793, he began to preach in New Salem, — a neighboring society, — where a revival of religion of great power commenced, which extended into other congregations, and resulted in the hopeful conversion of about one hundred souls. Wherever he preached, the Divine blessing seemed to attend his ministrations.

He was ordained and installed pastor of the Congregational Church in New Hartford, June 4, 1795. A revival succeeded, which resulted in the addition of about fifty persons to the church.

On the 17th of May, 1796, he was married to Miss Frances Huntington, daughter of the Rev. Dr. Joseph Huntington, of Coventry, Conn., with whom he lived in happy companionship until within three or four months of his own death. Their children were two daughters.

In the fall of 1800, he left this field of his early and successful labors, on account of Mrs. Griffin's failing health, and passed the winter in Orange, N. J. In the spring of 1801, he received a call from the First Presbyterian Church in Newark, where he was installed in October following. He remained at Newark about seven years and a half; "and they include the period of his most signal triumphs in the ministry." While here, he admitted to the communion of the church four hundred and thirty-four persons. In six months he received a hundred and seventy-four.

He received the degree of Doctor of Divinity from Union College in 1808.

In the spring of 1809, he resigned the pastoral care of the church in Newark, and accepted the Professorship of Pulpit Eloquence at Andover, and was inaugurated there in June of that year. Soon after he went to Andover he was invited to the pastoral care of the Evangelical Church in Park Street, Boston, then recently organized. He preached the sermon at the dedication of the church, and for a time occupied the pulpit, and the chair of Professor of Sacred Rhetoric. He however resigned the professorship, and was installed pastor of Park Street Church, July 31, 1811. In the winter of 1812 and 1813, he delivered his celebrated Park Street Lectures. In February, 1812, he assisted at Salem in the ordination of the first five missionaries who were sent into the foreign field by the American Board.

Dr. Griffin resigned the pastoral care of the church in Park Street, and returned to Newark in the spring of 1815, and was installed pastor of the Second Presbyterian Church there in June following. In 1816 and 1817, there was a general revival of religion in Newark, which extended into some neighboring towns. In 1817, he published his work on the Atonement. In the spring of 1821, he was elected President of the College at Danville, Kentucky; and also to the same office in a college in Cincinnati, Ohio. Both of these appointments he declined. In August of that year, he was chosen President of Williams College; and the indications of the Divine will were so clear that he said he dared not refuse. "He had precisely the kind of reputation," says Dr. Hopkins, "which was needed for the College at such a crisis." He accepted the appointment, and was inaugurated in November following. And from this time forward the record of his life and the history of the College (during his Presidency) are so nearly identical, that we shall not attempt to give them a separate consideration.

We are unwilling, however, to close this brief sketch of Dr. Griffin's successful and brilliant career without some general statements and remarks respecting him.

1. As to personal appearance and manners, he was tall, six feet and three inches in height; well built, large, and portly. He was prepossessing in his appearance, and was uncommonly suited to excite attention. His towering height, expressive countenance, small, keen eye, and neat costume, altogether gave him such a peculiar aspect, that no one could see him once without a distinct recollection of him afterwards. Dignity, gravity, impressiveness, were borne on his form and features. He was a perfect gentleman of the old school; punctilious in his manners; never passing a student without raising his hat and making his accustomed bow; nor suffering one to pass him without reciprocating that token of respect. He never said *Mister* to a student; and uniformly when he heard that title applied to one, he would say, "Never *Mister* an undergraduate."

2. As a Christian, with earnest endeavor he aimed at completeness, painfully sensible that he had much to struggle against. Like Edwards, he evidently entertained a deep sense of his sinful imperfection all his days. He was a man of prayer. He aimed to be spiritually-minded, to live near to God, and to avoid everything offensive to him. He set apart occasional days for fasting and self-examination. He had a form of self-examination prepared for his pupils and children just after the great revival in 1826, which appears to have aided

him essentially in reaching that full assurance of hope with which he so calmly and triumphantly met the king of terrors in the last conflict.

3. As a man of talents, he must be ranked in the first class which our country has produced. He exhibited a combination of qualities not often united in the same individual, — a discursive and brilliant imagination, and extent and acuteness of research. If some men have excelled him in quickness of apprehension and rapidity of execution, few have been capable of attending to a subject with closer application, or a more profound and patient research. "He had rare powers of abstraction and analysis, and might be called an eminent metaphysician." His vivid imagination and cultivated intellect enabled him to say what was uncommonly bold, striking, and impressive.

4. As a teacher, he particularly excelled in the department of rhetoric. Few have equalled him in teaching young men to write and speak. An associate member of the College Faculty once said of him, "I should not suppose it possible for any one to take young men of the talents and attainments of those composing our Senior class, and prepare them to write and speak with so much power." His powers of criticism, as displayed in the Senior recitation-room every Friday forenoon, his pupils will never forget. On these occasions, while one student read an essay, the rest took notes. Then each in turn was called upon for his criticisms. Then he would criticise both the essayist

and the critic. And woe be to the student that offered trifling criticisms on these occasions. Everything must be graceful and dignified. "By such an exercise he would impress on the minds of the students the leading principles of rhetoric, so that they could be easily apprehended, and not easily forgotten." Besides this exercise, every member of the Senior class was required to bring to his study an original oration for criticism. On reading it, Dr. Griffin would detect and expose error after error, and strike out words and sentences, and make changes until the authorship was sometimes nearly lost. Occasionally, after reading a few high-sounding sentences, he would say, "You mean so, do you not?" "Yes, sir." "Why not say so, then?" His powers of criticism were well-nigh unrivalled. It was on this account, mainly, that so much regret was felt and expressed when he resigned the Professorship of Pulpit Eloquence at Andover.

5. From the commencement to the close of his ministry, Dr. Griffin felt and manifested an absorbing interest in revivals of religion; and in connection with these seasons of spiritual refreshing rendered some of his most important services to the Church. The means of promoting them, he believed, were two, — a clear and earnest presentation of Divine truth, and believing and persevering prayer. His ministry was remarkably characterized with revivals. He was permitted to witness "a continued succession of heavenly sprink-

lings at New Salem, Farmington, Middlebury, and New Hartford (all in Connecticut), until, in 1799, he could stand at his own door, in New Hartford, and number fifty or sixty contiguous congregations laid down in one field of Divine wonders, and as many more in different parts of New England." In the fall of 1800, Dr. Griffin went to Orange, N. J., and passed the winter; a revival followed. From Orange he went to Newark, where he was permitted, for years in succession, to pour forth his enrapturing eloquence amid the wonderful effusions of the Holy Ghost. During his residence in Andover and Boston there was "a continual sprinkling, but things were not ripe for a heavenly shower." Dr. Griffin passed the afternoon of his life in connection with Williams College; and how often and earnestly, and with what animating success, he there besought sinners to lay hold on eternal life, will all be disclosed and declared in that day "when God makes up his jewels." How will his crown sparkle with gems in that day! "Though he spent more time in several other places than in Boston, I have always been impressed with the belief," says Dr. Humphrey, "that his pre-eminent usefulness was on that ground."

6. His interest in the benevolent enterprises of the day was earnest and effective. Next to the lamented Mills, he probably did more than any other man towards originating and bringing forward those great national societies which modern benevolence has planned. "His eloquent voice

was never withheld when the cause of these societies was to be advocated." But for no institution or enterprise did he labor so ardently or successfully as for Williams College. "His fervid imagination," says Dr. Sprague, "never kindled into a brighter glow, his eloquent tongue never gave forth sublimer thoughts, than when dwelling on the past and future of this College."

7. As a preacher, Dr. Griffin rose far above ordinary men. It is not enough to say of him, that "he was the prince of preachers." He was not merely a great preacher. He was pre-eminently a good and effective preacher. He aimed at practical results; never displaying his learning, his knowledge of science, or of polite literature, — never preaching a sermon for the sake of the rhetoric of the sermon. He was successful and useful to an uncommon degree. The seals of his ministry were numerous. Dr. Hopkins has pronounced his eulogy in the following sentence: "Probably the labors of no preacher in his day were blessed to the conversion of more souls than were his." To what was this owing? To refer it to the power of Divine grace solves the inquiry but in part. What was there peculiar in his preaching? The leading characteristics were four. First, *simplicity;* all was on a level with the capacity of a child. Second, *deep emotion;* an element indispensable to effective oratory. Third, he preached in such a manner as to arrest the attention. And fourth, he preached directly to the hearts and consciences of

his hearers. His elocution and manner in the pulpit were peculiar. As a preacher, he was unequal. He was accustomed to say to his pupils, "There can be no mountains without valleys between them, and it is not best to attempt to give every sermon the elevation of a mountain." Sometimes his preaching sounded like declamation. Then he would appear to whisper in melting accents. Then, again, he was majestic in his manner, and "with an eye full of fire, and a countenance beaming with light, and a voice breathing forth the softest and gentlest emotion, or swelling into the majesty of thunder-like tones, he held the complete command of his auditors, — now coming down upon them to break and crush with the fury of the tempest, — and now bearing them on sweet and transporting accents to the very gate of heaven." Sometimes he preached the terrors of the law, but always with tenderness, and often with tears. His chosen theme, however, was the love of God, "and the cross of Christ was with him the glory of every sermon."

His published discourses give no adequate idea of what he was in the pulpit. His sermon, "The Kingdom of Christ," preached in Philadelphia in May, 1805, (and which was shortly after republished by the students of Williams College,) is not found in any collection of his discourses; and yet it may be pronounced the best sermon he ever wrote. Some passages towards the close, says a judicious critic, "are among the finest specimens of human genius." We should be glad to insert some passages from his sermons which might be regarded as specimens of his pulpit eloquence. But we forbear, because no one ever *will*, or *can* hear those passages again as they proceeded from his lips.

Dr. Griffin was not only original and striking in his manner in the pulpit, *but out of it*. He was always attentive to the manners and habits of the students. A single anecdote must serve as a specimen of many that might be related. A few days after two young men had entered College, Dr. Griffin sent for them. As soon as they were pleasantly met, and seated in his study, he said, "I understand you are members of the Church, and have the ministry in view. We shall therefore expect that you will be examples to others in all your studies and duties as members of College. We shall expect you to choose pious students for your associates. There is now some special religious interest in College, and I hope you will enter heartily into the work." By this, one of the students was sitting with his chair tipped a little back, so that it stood on two legs. This posture was offensive to the Doctor's keen sense of propriety. With a pleasant smile, he turned to the young man and said: "Young gentleman, you have come here to learn; you will not be displeased to have your faults corrected; if you were in some places, you would be told that your chair had four legs." He then proceeded: "I have seldom ever known the instance

16

in which a professor of religion occupied the same room in College with one who was not a Christian without an apparent change in one or the other before the year closed. Either the one professing religion became a backslider, or the other was converted, or at least would become more seriously inclined." He next designated the room once occupied by Mills and Hall, and related some of the circumstances connected with Hall's conversion, through the instrumentality of Mills. He closed the interview with expressing the hope that they would be greatly useful while in College.

Dr. Griffin's manner in the pulpit was so peculiar that it is extremely difficult to convey anything like a correct representation of him. There was something in his very *presence* that arrested attention and awakened expectation. He had a voice of remarkable compass and flexibility. He spoke with great deliberation and solemnity. His prayers were always short, and peculiarly appropriate and impressive. Once, at the funeral of a clergyman, he commenced his prayer with these words: "We thank thee, O Lord, that good men may die." In reading the Scriptures, it seemed as though he felt that "correct emphasis is exposition." In reading the psalms and hymns, he threw his whole soul into the exercise, and was much aided by his passionate love of sacred poetry. Watts and Cowper were his favorites. In reading the lines,

"Our love so faint, so cold, to thee,
And thine to us so great,"

he would throw the whole emphasis on the word "*so*." At a meeting of the General Association of Massachusetts, he once commenced the public services with reading the hymn,

"Mighty God, while angels bless thee,
May an infant lisp thy praise?"

and it is said that he produced as deep an impression on the audience as is ordinarily produced by the delivery of an eloquent discourse.

Dr. Griffin insisted that as good an impression might be produced by good reading as by good singing. It was his custom during his last days to devote his Sabbath evenings to songs of praise with his grandchildren. He often spoke of these seasons as among his most precious means of grace. His love of sacred music, connected with sacred song, never forsook him before he went to join the anthems of heaven.

A few paragraphs from his sermon, preached at the dedication of the chapel, September 2, 1828, will throw light on his personal history, and the history of the College.

"In turning to the religious history of the College, and its prospective connection with the Redeemer's kingdom, a subject opens upon us of unbounded interest.

"The year 1792, it has often been said, ushered a new era into the world. In that year the first blood was drawn in that mighty struggle which for more than twenty years convulsed Europe, and began the predicted destruction of the apocalyptic beast. In that year the first of those institutions which modern charity has planned, and which cover the whole face of the Protestant world, arose in England.* And in that year commenced that series of revivals in America which has never been interrupted, night or day, and which never will be until the earth is full of the glory of the Lord as the waters cover the sea.

"For many years I supposed I had been permitted to see, in my native neighborhood and in my father's house, the first revival in the series. But it was with deeply affecting associations that I learned, the other day, that the Vice-President of the College [Dr. Hyde] was allowed to take part in two revivals that same year, one of which was certainly earlier than that which I witnessed.

"It was my happiness to be early carried by the Providence of God to Litchfield County, and to be fixed in that scene where the heavenly influence was to send out its stronger radiations to the different parts of the country; where thrice twenty congregations, in contiguous counties, were laid down in one field of Divine wonders. There it was my privilege to be most intimately associated with such men as Mills and Gillet and Hallock,— names which will ever be dear to the Church on earth, and some of which are now familiar in heaven. Their voices, which I often heard in the silent groves, and in the sacred assemblies which followed, and in the many, many meetings from town to town, have identified them in my mind with all those precious revivals which opened the dawn of a new day upon our country.

"During the first seven years of the existence of the College (in which ninety-three graduated in six classes), there were but five professors of religion in the institution, exclusive of two, who, seven months before the close of that period, were brought into the Church by the revivals in Litchfield County. The seven were, Jedediah Bushnell, who graduated in 1797, Gideon Bent and Nathaniel Turner, who graduated in 1798, a member of one of these classes, who never graduated here, Caleb Knight and Isaac Knapp, who graduated in 1800, and James W. Robbins.

* The Baptist Missionary Society formed at Kittering, by Andrew Fuller and others.

The last two were those who made a profession in Litchfield County. They were both from Norfolk, both obtained their hope at home, in the fall vacation of 1799, and both joined the Church in the winter vacation. In three of the six classes just named there was not a single professor of religion. From the Commencement in 1798 till February, 1800, there was but one professor of religion in College. From the fall of that year, in the four classes, which afterwards sent out eighty graduates, there were but two professors, and both of these had obtained their hopes in the revivals in Litchfield County and its vicinity. These were, Robbins, of Norfolk, who was awakened at home in March, 1799, at the beginning of a great revival, — which I had the happiness to see commence there, — obtained his hope in the fall vacation, and joined his father's church in the following winter. The other was Canning, who, while fitting for College at New Marlborough, obtained a hope, in 1799, in a revival which had extended from Litchfield County, and who joined the Sophomore class in September, 1800. These two young men labored hard, and with many discouragements through the winter, to establish prayer-meetings. But the next spring the religious character of the College received an important change, from the accession to the Freshman class of four young men from Litchfield County, — two from Torrington, and two from Norfolk. Of those from Torrington, one was Gillet, son of my early friend, the Rev. Alexander Gillet; the other was Beach, who fitted for college with him. In this way the influence of the new era gradually crept upon the College, which, from this time, began to rise up to the sacred distinction of being the birthplace of American missions.

"When I received this account from one of the early actors in that scene, it filled me with gratitude and wonder to discover that the religious destinies of the College, which are now opening with such unspeakable interest upon my age, received such an impression from the revivals in which I spent the labors of my youth!

"The spring of 1806 was made memorable to the College by the admission to its bosom of those two distinguished youths,

Gordon Hall and Samuel J. Mills, — the former to the Sophomore class, the latter to the Freshman. Mills was the son of my early friend, the Rev. Samuel J. Mills, of Torringford, Litchfield County, was known to me from a child, and received his permanent impressions in one of the most glorious revivals I have ever seen, — in 1798, — though he did not obtain relief till the month of November, 1801. He at once devoted himself to the cause of missions, and, with a heart glowing with this desire, entered on his course of education. When he arrived in this town he found himself in a revival of religion. He had joined a class in which, to say nothing of the living, there were such men as James Richards and Robert Chauncy Robbins. The spirit of God fell upon the class. In the Life of Mills, it is asserted, on the authority of 'one of his most valued classmates,' that he was much engaged before the event, and during its continuance was more resorted to than any other by the awakened, and was reputed the principal instrument. And yet his modesty and the peculiar structure of his mind prevented him from taking a conspicuous part in public meetings.

"'This revival,' says the author of Mills's Life, 'was among the most signal expressions of favor to the Church.' He alludes to the well-known fact, that, by means of this influence, Mills prevailed to diffuse through a circle of choice spirits that zeal for missions which actuated his own breast. On Wednesday afternoons, they used to retire for prayer to the bottom of the valley south of the West College; and on Saturday afternoons, when they had more leisure, to the more remote meadow on the bank of the Hoosac; and there, under the haystacks, these young Elijahs prayed into existence the embryo of American missions. They formed a society, unknown to any one but themselves, to make inquiries, and to organize plans for future missions. They carried this society with them to Andover, where it has roused into missionaries most that have gone to the heathen, and where it is still exerting a powerful influence on the interests of the world. I have been in situations to *know* that from the counsels formed in that sacred conclave, or from the mind of Mills himself, arose the American Board of Commissioners for Foreign

Missions, the American Bible Society, the United Foreign Missionary Society, and the African School under the care of the Synod of New York and New Jersey, besides all the impetus given to domestic missions, to the Colonization Society, and to the general cause of benevolence in both hemispheres. If I had any instrumentality in originating any of those measures, I here publicly declare, that in every instance I received the first impulse from Samuel John Mills."

When Dr. Griffin retired from public life, he returned to Newark, for the third time, — a place endeared to him by a thousand tender and hallowed associations. Here he lived a little more than a year. On the 15th day of September, 1837, at a most interesting meeting of the American Board, he was present and closed the services, offering, in a sitting posture, his last public prayer, while the audience were affected to tears; many of them at the thought that "they should see his face no more." In the house of his son-in-law, Dr. Lyndon A. Smith, he found his last earthly home. Here he was soothed with the kindest attentions of his two daughters, "who witnessed the triumphs of his faith, and watched his progress up to the gate of heaven." He died November 8, 1837, having lived sixty-seven years, ten months, and two days; and had preached the Gospel forty-five years.

"Servant of God! well done;
Praise be thy new employ;
And while eternal ages run,
Rest in thy Saviour's joy."

The following is a list of Dr. Griffin's publications: —

A Sermon, — The Kingdom of Christ, — 1805.
Sermon at Dr. McWhorter's Funeral, 1807.
Farewell Sermon at Newark, 1809.
Inaugural Oration at Andover, 1809.
Sermon at the Dedication of Park Street Church, 1810.
Sermon at Portsmouth, N. H., — Orphan Asylum, — 1811.
Dedication Sermon at Sandwich, 1813.
Park Street Lectures, 1813.
Sermon, — What wilt thou have me to do? — 1814.
Sermon, — Living to God, — New York, 1816.
Address in behalf of African School, 1816.
Plea for Africa, — a Sermon, — 1817.
Address of Managers of the United For. Miss. Society, 1817.
Extent of the Atonement, 1819.
Sermon, — Foreign Missions, — 1819.
Sermon, — Claims of Seamen, — 1819.
An Appeal on the New Test in the Pres. Church, 1820.
Address before the American Bible Society, 1820.
Baccalaureate Address (Commencement Day), 1822.
Address before the Jews' Society, New York, 1824.
Address before the Pres. Education Society, New York, 1824.
Sermon, — The Art of Preaching, — Boston, 1825.
Address before the Am. Ed. Society, Boston, 1825.
Sermon before the A. B. C. F. M., Middletown, Conn., 1826.
Baccalaureate Sermon, Williamstown, 1827.
Sermon at the Dedication of the College Chapel, 1828.
Convention Sermon, Boston, 1828.
Letter on Open Communion, 1829.
Address before the Am. S. S. Union, Philadelphia, 1829.
The Prayer of Faith, — a Sermon, — National Preacher, 1830.
The Heavenly Mind, — a Sermon, — National Preacher, 1830.

Murray Street Discourse, New York, 1830.
Address before the Bible Class, Williamstown, 1830.
Regeneration not wrought by Light, — National Preacher, 1832.
Letter to Dr Sprague, on Revivals, 1832.
New Doctrines, and New Measures, 1833.
Letter to Rev. A. D. Eddy, 1833.
A Work on Divine Efficiency, 1833.
Sermon, — The Causal Power in Regeneration, — National Preacher, 1834.

Dr. Griffin was a contributor to the Connecticut Evangelical Magazine; and he also wrote a series of articles for the Panoplist, on the history of missions. After his death, two volumes of his sermons, with a memoir, were published, in 1839, by the Rev. Dr. Sprague of Albany; and in 1844, another volume of his sermons was published, by M. W. Dodd, New York.

CHAPTER X.

ADMINISTRATION OF PRESIDENT GRIFFIN. 1821 - 1836.

Dr. Griffin had been for some time much interested in Williams College, from its connection with the early foreign missionary operations, and from his intimate acquaintance with some of the pioneers in that enterprise, Hall, Mills, Richards, and others, prominent graduates of the institution. As soon, therefore, as he was invited to take the Presidency, he came directly on to meet the Trustees at Williamstown, and settle the question of his acceptance. A feeling of despondency had taken possession of the minds of those who were interested in the continuance and prosperity of the College; but his unexpected arrival at that time revived their hopes, and thenceforward things began to assume a brighter aspect.

Having accepted the appointment, Dr. Griffin was inaugurated President and Professor of Divinity, November 14, 1821. A large number of people were drawn together, from the neighboring towns, by the interest of the occasion. The Rev. Dr. Hyde, the Vice-President, after making a short Latin address to the President elect, and receiving his answer, and after the blessing of Heaven had been invoked on the President in his new station, by the Rev. Dr. Shepard, proceeded to invest him with the office in the usual form, and committed to him the instruction and government of the institution in a serious and interesting manner.

An inaugural address was then delivered by the President, in which he traced the influence of the higher institutions of learning upon all the inferior schools, their connection with the happiness of society, the interests of civil and religious liberty, and the cause of vital piety, in our own and other lands. He alluded, with great eloquence, to the exertions of Mills and Hall, which led to the establishment of the American Board of Commissioners for Foreign Missions, and waked the churches to a great and long-neglected duty. In the course of this able and elegant discourse, he showed how all the principal branches of study conduce to such valuable results. This was followed by a congratulatory address from Professor Kellogg, in Latin. A sermon was also preached by Rev. Dr. Humphrey, in the evening, from the encouraging words (1 Samuel vii. 12), "Hitherto hath the Lord helped us." The College choir performed two or three pieces, selected and executed with good taste.

Confidence was now revived. A comparatively large class had entered, and from this time onward the College began to increase in numbers and prosperity.

The Commencement of 1821 will ever be a

memorable one in the annals of the College. It was on this occasion that the Alumni, being desirous of doing something to aid and sustain the College in its depressed situation, formed themselves into a society, to be called "The Society of Alumni." The object of this society is perhaps best explained by the following notice, calling the meeting together, which we extract from one of the newspapers of that day: —

"A meeting of the Alumni of Williams College will be held, at the College Chapel, September 5, at 9 A. M., to consider the expediency of forming a Society of Alumni. The meeting is notified at the request of a number of gentlemen, educated at the institution, who are desirous that the true state of the College may be known to the Alumni, and that the influence and patronage of those it has educated may be united for its support, protection, and improvement. A general meeting is requested."

To Governor Washburn belongs the honor of having first suggested the above-named project. In the summer of 1821, that dark day in the history of the College, he wrote a letter to the Hon. Daniel Noble, urging a general meeting of the Alumni at the next Commencement, for the purposes named in the above notice. And Mr. Noble issued the call for the meeting.

The meeting having assembled, pursuant to notice, in the chapel, in the West College, the following Preamble and Constitution were adopted: —

"For the promotion of literature and good fellowship among ourselves, and the better to advance the reputation and interests of our Alma Mater, we, the subscribers, graduates of Williams College, do form ourselves into a society, and adopt the following Constitution: —

"Art. I. This Society shall be called the Society of Alumni of Williams College.

"Art. II. This Society shall meet annually, at the College, at the time of the Annual Commencement.

"Art. III. An address shall also be delivered at each meeting, by one of its members, chosen for that purpose.

"Art. IV. The officers of this Society shall consist of a President, Vice-President, Secretary, and an Executive Committee of three members, to be chosen by ballot at the Annual Meeting."

The remaining articles specify the duties of the officers, &c., and are of no special interest. The first President was Dr. Asa Burbank. The Hon. Elijah H. Mills, a distinguished United States Senator, was elected the first orator. This appointment was not fulfilled. The first oration was delivered in 1823, by the Rev. John Woodbridge, D. D., of Hadley, which was well worthy of the occasion. "The Obligations of Literary Men to embrace with Ardor, and maintain with Constancy, the Divine Religion of the Gospel," was the appropriate and animating theme which he illustrated and enforced with great energy and beauty. The address was published and widely circulated. Since that time the annual oration before the Alumni has seldom failed. This was the first association of the kind ever formed in this country, and the example has since been followed by nearly every college in the United States. And who can tell how great the influence of such associations may become in cherishing kind feelings, in fostering literature, in calling out talent, and in leading men to act, not selfishly, but more efficiently, for the general cause, through particular institutions?

The Berkshire Medical Institution, having been established at Pittsfield about this time, was placed under the care and supervision of the College, the degree of M. D. being conferred by the President at the regular Commencements. This connection was dissolved after a few years.

We have now come to a most interesting epoch in the history of the College. Steadily, under the able and efficient management of Dr. Griffin, was it recovering from the embarrassments under which it had been laboring, when misfortunes again began to gather around it; and for a time it was doubtful whether it would long maintain its corporate existence. The question now came before the Legislature whether a third college should be chartered in this Commonwealth. For three successive years the subject had been presented and contested before the Legislature. While it had been a mere question of *location*, the excitement had been principally confined to the western part of the State;

but when it was proposed to establish another college, it touched the friends of Harvard, and they became interested in the discussion. When the subject was brought before a committee of the Legislature, the meeting was held in the Representatives' Hall, and it was crowded even to the galleries. It was an hour of conflict and trial. There was the Hon. Daniel Davis, an eminent advocate, and the Rev. Dr. Humphrey, to plead for Amherst. There was Homer Bartlett, a mere youth, who had nobly exerted himself to prevent the removal of the College, to plead for Williams, — firmly and manfully resolved, that, while many were forsaking, and some were opposing her, his Alma Mater should never be able to turn to him and say, "Et tu quoque, mi fili?" His speech occupied over two hours in the delivery, and was one of great power. Among his auditors were such men as Chief Justice Parker and Amos Lawrence. Mr. Lawrence, at that time a member of the Legislature, has been heard to say that he then made up his mind that if ever he aided either of these colleges, it should be Williams.

After a long discussion in the Legislature, a charter was finally granted to Amherst College, in February, 1825, by a small majority. Great efforts had been made to prevent this by the friends of Williams College. It had been often and earnestly urged, as an argument in opposition to that institution, that two colleges could not be sustained in Western Massachusetts, and "the inference now was that Williams College must die. A panic seized the public mind, and extended to the College. A number of the students immediately took dismissions, while a very small class entered at the ensuing Commencement. The whole number sank from one hundred and twenty to eighty, and little prospect appeared of there being any increase. It was now seen that, in order to extract the seeds of consumption which had lurked in the College for eleven years, something must be done to convince the public that it would live and flourish on this ground. It was believed that nothing was needed to give stability to the institution but to fasten this conviction in the public mind. It was evident, notwithstanding interested reports to the contrary, that it was well situated for a healthful, moderate-sized college, — in one of the most beautiful valleys in America, in a region perfectly healthy, far removed from the temptations of cities and large towns, in the midst of a population distinguished for morality and religion, where living was as cheap as in any town in the United States, and where sufficient range was still left for a college."

As a last resort, therefore, the Trustees determined to raise twenty-five thousand dollars, to found a new professorship and build a chapel. This resolution was adopted at the earnest request of Dr. Griffin. Such an addition to the funds, he believed, would certainly restore confidence in the public mind. But this fund *was to be* raised.

"Unless it could be done, and the institution be placed on a stable and prosperous footing, two of the Professors had determined to leave, and a third was apparently sinking into the grave, while the Trustees, disheartened and discouraged by eleven years' conflict and troubles, would have given up in despair of doing anything further." It must be evident to every one who reflects on the condition of the College at that time, that the crisis had come, and that its fate was staked on raising the twenty-five thousand dollars; the subscription being void unless completed before the last day of November, 1826. The attempt to raise this sum seemed hopeless. The most practical men pronounced, with emphasis and concern, that, in the embarrassed state of the country, it never could be done. Notwithstanding, Dr. Griffin, encouraged by a powerful revival of religion, undertook the work, opening the subscription himself with one thousand dollars, and accomplished what, seemingly, no other man could have accomplished.

A few days after the resolution to attempt to raise twenty-five thousand dollars had been adopted by the Trustees, Dr. Griffin went to Northampton to attend the annual meeting of the American Board. This was in the fall of 1825. While there he met, one evening, a number of the friends of the College, and stated to them the effort that was about to be made, and the necessity of that effort in order to place the College on a permanent basis. He closed by stating that it was his intention to open the subscription with one hundred dollars. The late Dr. Porter, of Catskill, a man of a large heart, and a warm friend of the College, at once remarked that if the subscription was commenced with that sum, the undertaking would inevitably fail. He said that Dr. Griffin must commence the subscription with one thousand dollars, and then the work would be accomplished. Dr. Griffin said he could not, and assigned the reasons for it. After a long interview they parted for the night. The next morning, when these friends met, Dr. Griffin stated that he had passed a sleepless night, — that he had looked over the whole subject, and had concluded to put down the one thousand dollars. "Now," said Dr. Porter, "the work is done. The twenty-five thousand dollars are secure."

And the work *was* accomplished. At a time of considerable financial embarrassment in the country, twelve thousand dollars were raised in four weeks. A Professorship of Rhetoric and Moral Philosophy was endowed, and the building of the College chapel was immediately commenced. With the utmost propriety, therefore, might the President afterwards, in his sermon at the dedication of the chapel, exclaim: "Heaven has decreed that this College shall live." He was convinced that it was "an institution dear to Christ;" and he devoted his powerful energies to its upbuilding, with an enthusiasm which such a conviction alone could have inspired. He could not but exclaim: "This

College has been saved by the Holy Ghost, and to the Holy Ghost let it be forever devoted, as a scene of revivals of religion, to raise up ministers and missionaries for Christ and his Church." "I will go and preach this doctrine to the Trustees, and Faculty, and students, and the people of the town, and to all the friends of Williams College. I would it were written on the broadside of heaven, where all the friends of the College might read it till the final conflagration."

Such is a brief history of the darkest period in the annals of the College. From that time it has been felt that the institution is permanent. Its course has since been steadily onward and upward, uniformly doing the work for which it was organized and endowed.

In 1827, Professor Dewey resigned the chair of Mathematics and Natural Philosophy, which he had acceptably filled for seventeen years; and Mr. Sylvester Hovey, a graduate of Yale College, was elected in his place. Mr. William A. Porter was at the same time chosen Professor of Rhetoric and Moral Philosophy.

Professor Dewey was born in Sheffield, October 25, 1784, fitted for college with the Rev. Mr. Robbins of Norfolk, Ct., entered Williams College in 1802, and was graduated in 1806, ranking among the first in his class. During his Senior year there was a revival of religion in College, when he was led to consecrate himself to Christ, and to the work of persuading his fellow-men to lay hold on eternal life. He studied theology with the Rev. Dr. West, of Stockbridge, and in October, 1807, was licensed to preach the Gospel by the Berkshire Association. During a part of 1807 and 1808 he preached in West Stockbridge, and a part of the year in Tyringham, where he was favored with an extensive and powerful revival. In November, 1808, he was invited to a tutorship in his Alma Mater, which was endowed with all the responsibilities of a professorship. In 1810 he was transferred to the Professorship of Mathematics and Natural Philosophy. He continued to occupy this post until 1827. During these seventeen years several extensive revivals were enjoyed. He now became Principal of the Gymnasium at Pittsfield, and in 1836 Principal of the Rochester Collegiate Institute, and in 1850 was elected Professor of Chemistry and Natural Philosophy in Rochester University, N. Y.

A brief notice is here due to Israel Jones, Esq., who was born at Weston, September 21, 1738. He descended from a pious and worthy ancestry. When a young man, he settled in the central part of Pittsfield, but in 1766 he removed to Adams, and purchased the farm on which Fort Massachusetts stood. The next year he married a daughter of the Rev. Mr. Todd, with whom he lived fifty-nine years. They had nine children. He was a member of the church in Williamstown, and regular in his attendance on public worship. He manifested a uniform Christian spirit. He ever cherished a deep sense of his unworthiness, and looked for salvation through a Redeemer. His assurance of a glorious immortality rendered his expected departure from this world an agreeable subject of contemplation. He was often appointed to posts of civil trust and honor. He was repeatedly a member of the State Legislature. He was a Trustee of the Free School, and then of the College, at Williamstown. On the 11th day of September, 1828, in the forenoon, he rode some ten or twelve miles on horseback, in his usual health. After dinner he retired, as his custom was, to rest awhile, and expired suddenly, without a struggle or a groan, about two o'clock.

In 1828 the chapel was completed, at a cost of ten thousand dollars, and on September 2d, of the same year, Dr. Griffin preached the dedication sermon, from Deut. viii. 2: "And thou shalt remember all the way which the Lord thy God led thee." In this discourse he gave a concise history of the College. The sermon was published, and was well worthy of the occasion. Dr. Hyde offered the dedicatory prayer.

During this year, the Hon. Joseph Burr, of Manchester, Vt., left to the College a legacy of one thousand dollars.

This year, too, Dr. Ebenezer Emmons was elected Professor of Chemistry and Natural History.

At the same time, the Trustees voted that any member of the Corporation who shall hereafter neglect to attend the meetings of the Board for three years in succession, without giving satisfactory reasons for such absence, shall be considered as having so far neglected to perform his duties as to vacate his seat.

In 1829 Mr. Albert Hopkins was elected Professor of Mathematics and Natural Philosophy, in place of Professor Hovey, resigned.

In April, 1830, the Rev. William A. Porter, Professor of Rhetoric and Moral Philosophy, died, in the thirty-second year of his age. He was born in Spencertown, N. Y., October 3, 1798, but was brought up in Catskill; fitted for college with his father, was graduated at Williams College in 1818, when he pronounced the valedictory oration. In 1819 he was appointed a Tutor in College, and officiated in that capacity two years. In 1821 he delivered the Master's oration, which was much admired. In the summer of 1825, having spent two years in the study of theology, mostly at Princeton, he was invited to preach at Burlington, Vt., as a candidate for settlement; and while there he received the appointment of Professor of Languages in the University of Vermont. He was soon after appointed to the same office in Williams College, it being intended at that time to transfer Professor Kellogg to the department of Natural Philosophy. But Mr. Porter had accepted the invitation from the University, before receiving information of his appointment in his own College. He remained in Vermont two years. In the fall of 1826 he was married to Miss Mary A. Noble, daughter of the Hon. Daniel Noble, of Williamstown. In the fall of 1827 he was called to the new Professorship of Rhetoric and Moral Philosophy in his Alma Mater. He was much respected for his talents and accomplishments. He was a warm friend, a diligent student, and a devout Christian. And, with his acknowledged talents and attainments, it is impossible to say what he might have accomplished in the cause of learning and religion, had he lived to the ordinary age of man. After his death, a small volume, prepared by Professor Kellogg, containing a sketch of his life, a lecture on the domestic relations, four of his sermons, and his valedictory oration, was *printed*, but not published.

> "Thou soul of God's best earthly mould,
> Thou happy soul! and can it be
> That these . . . .
> Are all that must remain of thee!"

In August, 1830, Dr. Mark Hopkins was elected Professor of Rhetoric and Moral Philosophy, as successor to Professor Porter, deceased.

In the fall of 1830 it became necessary for the Hon. Daniel Noble to visit Portland, Maine, on business connected with the College. On his way there he took a severe cold, and died November 22, in the fifty-fourth year of his age, in the chamber which he first entered on reaching that city.

Mr. Noble was a native of Williamstown, was born July 7, 1776; was graduated at Williams College 1796; and studied law with the Hon.

Judge Dewey. He commenced the practice of law in the village of South Adams, where he remained till 1811, when he removed to Williamstown.

Mr. Noble was a devoted friend and liberal patron of the College. He was the first Alumnus who was a member of the Board of Trustees. For sixteen years he had been the College Treasurer. When a powerful effort was made to move the College to Hampshire County, he threw the whole weight of his powerful influence against the measure; and though the number who co-operated with him was small, yet their efforts were finally crowned with success.* Mr. Noble was repeatedly

---

* The following letter from Mr. Noble to Mr. Glezen will be read with interest: —

"WILLIAMSTOWN, January 7, 1820.

"MY DEAR SIR:

"I find the public are expecting a Memorial from the minority of the Corporation, in the case of the petition to remove Williams College. I should have been much gratified to have had this written by yourself; but not being able to see you, I have availed myself of a few hours' leisure, amidst my almost unceasing calls, to place on paper a few of my thoughts in the shape of a Memorial to the Legislature. I have been less particular than I should have been had we not a very full memorial from this Town, in which the subjects are discussed in detail; and this Town Memorial is to be printed. I wish you to examine the memorial which I send you, and put your own name to it. You will please leave room for Esquire Jones's name first, yours second, and mine third and last.

"We feel in tolerably good spirits as to the College question. We mean fairly and honorably to discharge our duty, and be prepared for any result. There has, on the whole, been a noble spirit of liberality manifested on the occasion. Whatever shall be the issue, I trust we shall retain a high sense of gratitude to our friends, in various directions, for the part they have taken upon this interesting occasion.

"I am very respectfully yours,

"DANIEL NOBLE."

a member of both branches of the State Legislature, was two years a member of the Governor's Council, and was once a candidate for the office of Lieutenant-Governor. He was a professor of religion, a liberal contributor to the benevolent enterprises, and an earnest advocate of the moral reforms of that day.

In this connection, we are induced to pay a passing tribute of respect to two other members of the Board of Trustees, Mr. Glezen and Dr. Pomeroy.

Levi Glezen was born at Stockbridge, near the line which separates it from Lenox, December 15, 1775; fitted for college mostly by himself in his father's house; and was graduated at Williams College in 1798, ranking among the first in his class. Soon after his graduation he became the first Preceptor of Lenox Academy, which was incorporated by an act of the Legislature in 1803, and received a small grant of land, one half of a township in the State of Maine. For a number of years this land was wholly unproductive; but was finally sold, and produced a small income, the avails of which were appropriated to the support of the Institution. The Academy acquired under Mr. Glezen's tuition a very respectable standing. The institution was generally judicious and thorough. Mr. Glezen was a fine linguist, sustained a fair Christian character, and was successful in fitting young men for College. He was very near-sighted, and his eyes must have been peculiar. We recollect handing him a letter one evening in the street, and he read it with ease by starlight. Sometimes a student would take advantage of this short-sightedness, and the result was no little merriment was created in school. Still many students here laid the foundation of their future eminence and usefulness. The first individual who was prepared for college at this Academy, under Mr. Glezen's tuition, was the Hon. Samuel R. Betts, a Judge of the District Court of the United States for the Southern District of New York. The Academy was extensively patronized. The average number of students from the beginning was not far from seventy. Mr. Glezen was a Trustee of Williams College from 1813 to 1826, during which time he fitted many young men for admittance to his Alma Mater. When a powerful effort was made to remove the College, he firmly withstood those efforts to the last. In 1824 Mr. Glezen accepted an invitation to take charge of an academy at Kinderhook, N. Y., where he remained about six years. He then removed to Sheffield, Mass., where he died October 21, 1843, in the sixty-seventh year of his age.

Thaddeus Pomeroy, M. D., was born at Northampton, October 23, 1764; was graduated at Harvard College in 1786. He studied medicine, but afterwards became a partner in a druggist's establishment in Albany. In 1794 he married Eliza Mason Sedgwick, eldest daughter of the Hon. Theodore Sedgwick of Stockbridge, "a woman whose wisdom and loveliness qualified her to perfect every good tendency in his nature." In 1806 he removed to Stockbridge, and devoted his time to the cultivation and improvement of his farm and the best interests of the town. In his religious opinions he adhered to the faith of his orthodox fathers, but honored Christianity under any name. In the peace and confidence of a Christian he died March 2, 1847, aged eighty-two. Dr. Pomeroy went to Newark in August, 1821, to persuade Dr. Griffin to accept of the Presidency of the College, and by his personal influence Dr. Griffin, who had just declined two similar appointments, was induced to come to Williamstown and consult the Trustees before giving his answer.

In 1832 the time of holding Commencement was changed from the first Wednesday in September to the third Wednesday in August.

In the same year a measure of great importance was undertaken by the Society of Alumni. In consideration of the meagre condition of the philosophical and chemical apparatus, it was voted, at a meeting held September 5, to raise the sum of four thousand dollars, to be expended for the benefit of these respective departments. Immediate action was taken upon this subject, and in a comparatively short time the sum (including interest) of $4,511 was subscribed and paid. This sum has since been applied, under the direction of a committee, for the purchase of instruments. In the raising and appropriating of this fund great credit is due to Professor Kellogg, for his unwearied and constant exertions.

In the month of December, 1833, the Rev. Alvan Hyde, D. D., died at Lee, aged sixty-five years. For more than thirty years he had been intimately associated with the friends and patrons of this College. From 1812 until the time of his death he had held the office of Vice-President. He was Chairman of the Prudential Committee of the Board twenty-three years. He had educated four sons at this College. While his funeral services were attended at Lee, there was a service in the College chapel, and Professor Mark Hopkins delivered an address to the students, in which he delineated the character and services of Dr. Hyde. He was born at Norwich, Conn., February 2, 1768; was graduated at Dartmouth College, 1788; studied theology partly with the Rev. Dr. Backus of Somers, Conn., and partly with Dr. West of Stockbridge, and was ordained in Lee, June 6, 1792. He was a sound divine, an earnest and solemn preacher, and a model pastor. Few ever saw his equal. The many virtues which he manifested in the various relations of life which he sustained, especially the untiring and valuable service which he rendered to the College, will cause his name to be held in long and grateful remembrance by its Alumni and friends.*

In July, 1829, the Hon. Ezra Starkweather, of Worthington, tendered his resignation as a Trustee of the College. We make a brief quotation from

* The College has a portrait of Dr. Hyde, a present from his sons.

his letter: "Being acquainted with the origin of the College, and early attached to its interest, and believing in its extensive usefulness to the community, it is matter of consolation that, in reviewing its progress, various measures, and their results, to the present time, nothing has transpired to diminish my confidence in its rising eminence and important benefits to the Church and State. The smiles of Heaven have manifestly attended the institution from the beginning; and though at times it has been under a cloud, and its affairs somewhat perplexed, the result has uniformly been the elevation of the seminary. And I doubt not of its permanence, and its high standing among the literary institutions of our country. In conclusion, permit me to add that I recollect with pleasing emotions the series of social and devotional meetings which I have been permitted to attend with my brethren of the Board, in relation to the concerns of the College. These meetings and services have been among the most agreeable of my public life, and they would be cheerfully continued if age and approaching infirmities did not demand my retirement. Accept the assurance of my prayers that the members of the Board and Faculty may ever be under the Divine protection, and be guided, in all their ways, by that wisdom which is from above."

Dr. Starkweather was born at Stonington, Conn., December 15, 1754. He was the eldest of nine sons, four of whom lost their lives in the Revolutionary struggle. Dr. Starkweather was in the army a short time himself, and left only on account of the failure of his health. Leaving the army, he settled as a physician in Preston, Conn., and remained there till 1785, when he removed to Worthington. There in public and private life he gained that respect which talent, joined with integrity, never fails to win. For many successive years he was a prominent member of the State Senate. And, though filling offices of honor and usefulness in public life for so many years, yet his pacific and controlling character was felt, if possible, more in the church than in civil society. He was a professor of religion, and a man of acknowledged piety. He was facetious and affable in his conversation and manners. In connection with his resignation, he sent to the College a present of one thousand dollars, the interest of which goes to aid indigent students. He died on the 27th of July, 1834, aged eighty years.

June 15, 1834, a church was formed in the College for the sake of giving the students the advantages of its watch and care. The members of the Faculty, and the students who were professors of religion, presented their certificates, and being called on by the President, as Professor of Divinity and Pastor, they arose in the chapel (it being *the Sabbath) and publicly* assented to the articles of faith drawn up for the new church, and renewed their covenant with God, and entered into covenant with each other, and thus formed themselves into a distinct church. The three first named on the church records are Mark Hopkins, Albert Hopkins, and Simeon H. Calhoun. During a portion of the time Dr. Griffin was President, the students attended worship in the chapel; but uniformly, during the Presidency of Dr. Hopkins, they have worshipped in the meeting-house. They are in the habit of having regular church-meetings, and one communion season in each term, in the College chapel.

In 1834 Professor Albert Hopkins went to Europe, to procure the philosophical and chemical apparatus for which funds had been previously procured. He went at his own expense; his salary was, however, continued during his absence.

A Professorship of Chemistry was established at this time, and Mr. Edward Lasell was appointed to the chair.

At this time, for the sake of increasing the funds of the College, or rather to keep it from drawing upon its scanty means of support, the respective officers, with a spirit of generous self-sacrifice, voluntarily agreed to relinquish a portion of their salaries; each professor, from the small salary of $800, giving up $100, while the President, with a salary of $1,400, reduced it to $1,000. Such a spirit is not often met with in our public men, and is worthy of mention and remembrance. It is to this unity of attachment and feeling that the preservation of the College, during so many and successive misfortunes (greater than which have not been encountered by any similar institution), is in a great measure attributable.

In 1835 the Rev. Joseph Alden, Pastor of the Congregational Church in Williamstown, a native of Cairo, N. Y., and a graduate of Union College, of 1828, and of Princeton Theological Seminary, was elected Professor of the Latin Language, and was afterwards transferred to the department of History, Political Economy, and Rhetoric.

The Society of Natural History proposed an expedition to Nova Scotia during the fall vacation of 1835. A company of about twenty members of College, with three of the officers, Professor E. Emmons, Professor A. Hopkins, and Tutor S. H. Calhoun, sailed from Boston, August 25, in the sloop Flight, Captain Hallett. They sailed up the Bay of Fundy, and visited many places of interest. The expedition brought to the College a large accession to the Cabinet of Minerals, and gave to the members the nucleus of a cabinet, and did much to awaken an interest in the study of mineralogy and geology.

Dr. Griffin continued to preside over the institution with distinguished ability and success till the spring of 1833, when it became evident that his services were drawing to a close, and that the infirmities of age and disease were gathering upon him. From this time, however, notwithstanding occasional attacks of paralysis, he continued to exert himself for the College, until 1836, when he found it necessary to resign, which he accordingly did at the meeting of the Board of Trustees in August.

His resignation was accepted with the deepest regret that circumstances rendered this step necessary, and with strong emotions of gratitude for the services he had rendered.

As soon as arrangements could be made, he left Williamstown, the scene of his useful labors, forever. A few days before he left, the Faculty invited him to a social dinner at the Mansion House. And on the morning of his departure (September 28) the students waited on him in a body, to take their leave of him, and presented him with a respectful and affectionate address. He was much affected, and with overflowing feelings replied to them from his carriage. He now returned to Newark, having been President of the College fifteen years.

Providence appears to have brought him to Williamstown just in season to secure the College from extinction. His reputation, his talents, his personal efforts, were the means of raising it from obscurity and deep depression, and of giving it rank and standing among kindred institutions. He cheerfully assumed the charge of the College when its only chance of life seemed to stand in the reputation, ability, and efficiency of its President. When others had declined this responsibility, he cheerfully and confidingly came, and placed his reputation and learning, his eloquence and influence, at the service of the College, so completely identifying his interests with its interests that he practically said: "If this College lives, I live; if it dies, I die." His reasoning was, that an institution which had been so signally favored in the Providence of God as Williams College had been, would not, must not, be forsaken now; and it was a warranted conclusion. The results have abundantly verified and confirmed the correctness of his reasoning. The broad seal of God's approbation has been placed on his labors. And so, "after he had served his own generation by the will of God, he fell on sleep." "The memory of the just is blessed." *

* The College has a portrait of Dr. Griffin, a present from his son-in-law, Dr. Lyndon A. Smith.

CHAPTER XI.

RELIGIOUS HISTORY OF THE COLLEGE FROM 1821 - 1836.

WHEN Dr. Griffin assumed the charge of the College, its prospects began at once to brighten. Students in greater numbers now resorted to it. He had commenced his ministerial career, as appears from his life, just at the opening of that series of religious revivals which began to be enjoyed shortly after the American Revolution. Some of the earliest of them occurred under his personal ministry. Regarding this ground as in a sense sacred, from its character as the birthplace of American missions, he came on, feeling that in so doing he was identifying himself with the cause of God. Though past the meridian of life, he had lost, at this time, but little of his native vigor. Ardent in his temperament, uncommonly commanding in person, and not inferior, perhaps, to any of the pulpit orators of that day, his preaching was generally admired; and being of a pungent cast, it was calculated also to work upon the consciences of his hearers. No sensible impression of an awakening character, however, appears to have been felt till the spring of 1824. Quite a number, at this time, were impressed. I conclude that the influence was somewhat deep and general, from a remark made by Dr. Griffin: "Is it possible that God has shaken this College to its centre to bring out one conversion?" We might, however, remark, as in the case of Hall, that that conversion was worth this; yes, and infinitely more. It took place in the person of William Hervey, who afterwards died in India, and who, for simplicity and purity of heart and life and devotion to the great interests of the missionary work, has had few superiors. His name is embalmed in the memory of many here, who afterwards witnessed "how holily and unblamably he behaved himself;" and, although he fell an early prey to death, it is believed that his life told sensibly on the great work of evangelizing the world. It was thought by Dr. Griffin that the idea of the annual fast for the conversion of the world originated with him.

The two following years were years of great spiritual drought and declension. Iniquity in various forms abounded, and the love of many waxed cold. There was a good deal of dissipation at this period; treating at elections and at other times was common. Drunkenness was an occurrence not unfrequent, when holidays were given. I should think the gravest men in College, certainly with one or two exceptions, did not scruple to drink (at least drank) on set occasions. The order of College, at this time, was not good. I am not aware that any religious meetings were held during the week. On Saturday evening and Sabbath morning, there were meetings, but very thinly attended. The majority, probably, did not know that such meetings were held.

During the summer term of 1825, some of the more considerate and serious Christians began to consult with each other, and to make the condition of things in College a matter of prayerful consideration. It is understood that, towards the close of that term, a small number met to pray specifically for a revival of religion in the College, with a determination to continue the meeting into the next year. In the fall vacation, a member of the Senior class, who had professed religion during his college life, but had not honored it, was reclaimed, and came back a new man. There was a solemnity on his countenance which was noticed. There seemed to be a small sound, as it were, the moving of a leaf in the topmost bough, indicating, in the ear of those who had been waiting for it, that a breeze was coming. They began, accordingly, to bestir themselves. It deserves to be mentioned, that the movements of the Church were so entirely still that those around were not aware that anything was going forward more than usual, except as they gathered this from the countenance and altered deportment of their fellows. I was not aware, until I commenced this account, that deep feeling pervaded the Church so early in the term. An individual has informed me that, returning a few days after its commencement, he was met in the College yard by his room-mate, with the salutation, "Chum, God is here." An accidental opening of a door, between breakfast and study hours in the morning, disclosed a band of Christians, kneeling and pouring out their hearts in prayer. Other trivial circumstances may have led individuals to suspect something unusual. The impenitent part of the College, however, in the main, had no knowledge whatever of any special movement, during the first two months of the term. I say in the main, for it afterwards appeared that one or two were seriously impressed quite early in the term.

About the time of the annual Thanksgiving, in the latter part of November, some indications of more than usual wakefulness began to be evident. The author of this notice was called, providentially, just at this crisis, to leave the institution for a season. He well remembers, one morning, of hearing a very profane young man say to some of his mates standing before the College, "Come, my friends, let us go up and attend to the concerns of our souls." There will be occasion to refer to this young man again. The remark is introduced to show that at this time, probably the day before Thanksgiving, there began to be some impression on the minds of the hitherto unawakened.

About the middle of the next week there came to Williamstown two delegates from the south of Berkshire, whom the churches, in compliance with the example of primitive times, had sent to look in upon the state of religious affairs in this section, and to pray with and exhort the people. These delegates were the Rev. Dr. Hyde of Lee, and Dr. Field of Stockbridge. As a matter of courtesy to the churches and their messengers, in part, and it is believed not without some strong desires that the anticipated visit might result in the revival of God's work, the church in town agreed to set apart the day of their visitation, and observe it as a fast. Intelligence of this was communicated to the Faculty of College, and it was determined to suspend literary exercises, for the purpose of giving to any who wished, liberty to hear these brethren, and also to furnish to the students an opportunity of prayer and conference among themselves. This was announced, it would seem, at evening prayers the night before, and occasioned no small stir among the students, who had begun to be already somewhat sensitive on the subject. As is usual at such times, Satan took advantage of the natural enmity of the carnal heart, and excited the wicked to throw off the convictions which had began now to hover around, if not to settle upon them. I have been told that there were mock meetings, that night, all over College. There was, also, another meeting at the Junior recitation-room, attended by Dr. Griffin, at which one heart at least was stricken. Next morning, the aspect of things was rather tumultuous. A meeting had been appointed, however, at the Senior recitation-room, under the idea that most of the religious part of the College would be present, and some, at least, of the impenitent. The hour arrived, and immediately there began to be a flocking to the place. Some left their rooms, without the least intention of going to the meeting. Their account of it is, that they found themselves there, they knew not how. Few had manifested any particular seriousness. Many were very bold sinners, and came in whirling their hats across the room, as if in derision. The room became directly crowded. Every student from both College buildings at length found his way in. The meeting began with marked stillness, such as is wont to be noticed when a crisis is at hand, and the spirit of God intimately near. Tutor Hervey, who had been from the first, in his meek and quiet way, exceedingly active, and his associate in office, now the President of the College, were present to take the direction of this meeting. In a short time, however, it became evident that the great Master of assemblies was himself present to take the lead. The exercises of the meeting had not proceeded far, when a student, the hitherto notoriously profane one already alluded to, arose in the assembly. The deep solemnity of his countenance, the altered air and strange attitude of the speaker, conspiring with that deep impression of the Divine presence which previously pervaded the meeting, was sufficient to bring about a sudden and most extraordinary crisis. The minds of some were made up before he uttered a word. In a moment, said he, "Will you trifle with your souls?" Every head was bowed, the most hardened were melted, and the meeting became a scene of indescribable interest. Considering the character of those who composed it, and their position in reference to society and the Church, perhaps few private meetings, in our times, are more worthy of remembrance.

In the afternoon was the public meeting at the church; and as little interest as the mass of College took, the night before, in the delegation, probably Paul and Barnabas were not more welcome at Antioch than were these messengers of the churches now. During two or three days succeeding it was impossible to pursue study; there was a prayer-meeting going on in each College building from morning to night, in some room or other. I do not know that the regular recitations were omitted after the fast. So entirely, however, was the mind absorbed with the great realities of religion, that anything like concentrated attention to any book, except that long-neglected one, the Bible, became impossible. *The term was now drawing to a close, and ended with a religious meeting of deep and affecting interest. The majority of those who were in the religious meeting above described obtained hopes nearly at the same time, and not many days after.*

From the influence which descended on the College, feeling spread immediately into the community around, and a very powerful awakening commenced. College assembled, at the opening of the spring term, to experience a renewal of the same scenes which had characterized the closing weeks of that which had preceded. The work went on, with more or less power, until the warm season opened; and a sermon was preached at the close of the term, as had been done in 1812. A synoptical view of the state of the College, at the close of the fall term, which I find among Dr. Griffin's private papers, states the number of actual members of College, at that time, eighty-five; forty-three hopefully pious before, twenty-seven recently hoping; total, seventy. Without hope, fifteen; of these, four on the ground, and eleven absent. Twenty-three of these professed religion soon afterwards, of whom two have fallen away. Of six others, who fell away, three are since hopefully converted, and three are dead. Of those who were active spirits in this awakening, some of the most prominent "have fallen asleep." Among these, it is no more than a tribute due to Christian worth to mention the name of Daniel Freeman. Uniformly consistent as a Christian, he was among the first to take the alarm, in view of the awful and increasing degeneracy of the times before the revival. And probably to no one member of College is so much due as to him, in the way of bringing forward and promoting the work. He was a member of the Senior class, and died about six weeks after his class had graduated. Mr. Hervey, already referred to, was another of the same stamp. Firm, consistent, mild, yet ardent, his example was one uncommonly pure and dignified, and carried great weight with it at that time. To these must now be added the name of the venerable President, Dr. Griffin. The divisions which have since so unhappily distracted the Church, in relation to doctrines and measures, were then unknown. It was not necessary to spend much time, either in hunting after heresy or guarding against it. Dr. Griffin threw himself into the work, with no trammels or scruples to check the ardor of his feelings. Evening after evening, for several months, through darkness, snow, and mud, he went to a school-house, in the east part of the village, and poured out torrents of truth, with an enthusiasm not inferior to that which characterized his best days. He seemed to be nerved up to a great effort, and probably never afterwards appeared to the same advantage, or preached with equal power.

The subsequent year was memorable in the annals of Berkshire County, as a year of great, and probably unprecedented religious interest. Just at the commencement of the year, or rather toward the close of 1826, what were termed in those days church conferences, originated in the south part of the county.* Radiating from the point of their

* The author of this history has long been of the opinion that, for the origin of the church conferences in Berkshire County, we must go back to the fall of 1821. Near the close of the great revival, which was enjoyed that season, in Pittsfield and Lenox, under the labors of Dr. Nettleton, the Rev. Mr. Bradford of Sheffield, and the Rev. Mr. Wheeler of Great Barrington, wrote a joint letter to the Rev. Dr. Humphrey, requesting that two of the brethren might come down and tell them of the work of the Lord in Pittsfield. And Deacon Bissell and Deacon

origin, they illumined all the surrounding region. Scarce a place where the delegates assembled but enjoyed a refreshing. A conference was held in Williamstown, early in the spring, and attended with happy results. In College, there was little remaining material in the three higher classes likely to be wrought upon. In the Freshman class, there were eleven hopeful conversions, only six of which, however, proved permanent.

From the period of which we are now speaking, the religious history of the College became more dark. Various causes may be assigned for this. 1. A want of permanence among the officers of the College, operating, of course, unfavorably to the exertion of any systematic religious influence. Of two professors, inducted at the same time into office, one soon left, the other, the lamented Professor Porter, just as his religious influence was beginning to be more sensibly felt, was removed by death. 2. The removal, in the natural course of things, of those who had shared in the awakening of 1825. 3. The influx of an uncommon amount of impiety, — men of corrupt principles or no prin-

Goodrich were designated to go on this mission. They were absent about two weeks, and a revival commenced in both of the towns visited before they returned. These excellent men are now gone, and the manner in which they went down the county in their one-horse wagon ought to be recorded. It was agreed that one should drive half of the time, while the other was engaged in audible prayer. So they alternated. These visits were not long after repeated. And some would go back to this time for the origin of church conferences in Berkshire; though they were not adopted as a system of measures for promoting revivals until the time named by Professor Hopkins.

ciples, and dissolute life, spoiled before coming, and fitted, of course, only to taint and corrupt the moral atmosphere. 4. A general suspension of Divine influences in this region of country. Owing to the influence, mainly, of these four causes, College soon became again corrupt, probably quite as much so as before the revival of 1825. Intemperance and card-playing prevailed. Also, at this time there was not a little licentiousness. Enjoying great opportunities of association, wicked men "waxed worse and worse." The College buildings, or at least the West College, was repeatedly set on fire, there is reason to believe wantonly. The Bible was stolen from the desk, and *worse* than burnt. This state of things ran on till the fall of 1829, when some engaged Christians instituted a meeting at nine o'clock in the evening, which Dr. Griffin used to attend. This continued into the spring term, when there was some seriousness in College, and two hopeful conversions. "This little refreshing," says a correspondent, "called forth Dr. Griffin's sermon on the prayer of faith, which was published in the National Preacher, and delivered in the church a little previous. The great difficulty seemed to be, that there was not a general waking up among Christians. An impression seemed to prevail that sinners could not be converted till all the professors were awake. Hence the little refreshing was expended in the church."

No decided change in the religious aspect of College occurred till the ensuing winter. Dr. Griffin had been called that winter to labor at Troy, where was a powerful awakening. This was at the commencement of what were then known as four-days' meetings. The Doctor returned, and it was agreed to hold a meeting of this description in Williamstown, the first which was held in this State. The third day, Saturday, was a day which will long be remembered. The meeting was at the church. It was not full, but there was "a sound of a going." "I can hear it," said an aged father, rising in the assembly, and addressing the church and the impenitent, after the afternoon's discourse. "On the evening of the succeeding day," says Dr. Griffin, in his private journal, "—— came to see me, and so overwhelmed, that, as soon as I saw him, I said to myself, the question is decided, there is to be a revival in Williams College." This was the Sabbath before the opening of the term; so that there was considerable interest in the things of religion when the term commenced. This was increased by the coming on of one or two from Troy, who had obtained hopes in the revival there.

Within three weeks, there was a great breaking down among professors of religion. One of this description came out as a new convert, and, "within three days," says a correspondent, "more than twenty professors of religion had given up their hopes. I well recollect three calling at my room at one time, to be prayed for as impenitent sinners." This breaking up of hopes probably will furnish a clew to the awful and reigning stupidity and dissoluteness of morals before adverted to. I did not mention this among the causes which led on to that state of things, as it exists always in periods of declension, and rivets and seals for a sure work those specific causes of deterioration which are liable at such times to exist. About the time of the monthly concert, in March, the work began to deepen among the impenitent. Several became alarmed, and cried out, in view of their undone condition by nature and practice. Very careless persons became awakened. Moralists, also, of whom, at this period, there were not many, grew convinced that they were standing on unsafe ground. There was a great shaking, particularly in the two upper classes. The doctrine of perfection, as that doctrine has since been held by various persons, scattered throughout the country, started, so far as I have been able to ascertain, here at this time. The original principle appears to have been good, but it has since been adulterated with many things. Of those who were awakened in this revival, several went back, some of whom came in the ensuing spring. Some became infidels, of whom two have died since; one, however, renouncing his infidelity on his dying bed.

The spring of 1832 was one of religious interest in town. Rev. Dr. Beman held a protracted meeting here. A number of conversions occurred in College, in the course of the term. Those who came in at this time were, for the most part, made special objects of prayer and labor. They came in lingeringly, one or two in the course of a week, for a considerable time. Not many were awake, but these labored hard. It was a time of much trial in the church, and it is believed that spiritual religion gained ground. The necessity of toiling on under a heavy burden, and working, as it were, at arms' length, on account of the sluggishness of the mass of professing Christians, inured those who came under this burden to severe toil, contributed to form habits of patient, persevering effort; and the College probably has never turned out a more faithful set of working men than those who passed through this ordeal. Indeed, I regard this as in some sense the commencement of a new era in the religious history of the College, and shall take the liberty to enlarge here on what I conceive to be some pretty important principles, which may, perhaps, have in them something of general application.

In the progress of things towards perfection, light comes by degrees, and new light generally breaks in whilst we are working under the guidance and impression of that already enjoyed. There are many simple truths pregnant with others; these last remain in a germ or embryo state till the first strike their roots, so to speak; that is, become fixed and imbedded in the character by being applied to some use. It is probable that, in matters of religion, no practical judgments have ever been formed in advance of those which have preceded, except in compliance with, or at least tacit recognition of that saying of Christ, "That if any man will do his will, he shall know of the doctrine." The Christian system contains in it many things intended to be revealed, not directly, but only in the development of the system itself. So full of truth is this assertion, that no period, probably, will come, either in this world or in eternity, in which it may not be said of the Gospel, as then developed, what Paul said of it, comparing his own times with preceding periods, "the mystery which in other ages was not made known." Now, at present, seeing only "through a glass," we make but slow advances, and these safely only so far as the spirit of that precept guides. This is a salutary and sufficient corrective against vapid and wild theories in religion. The idea, which I think came out more prominently at the period I am alluding to than it had previously done in the history of the College, was the all-important one of a permanent state of religious feeling, and correspondent course of action. In this respect, the experience of our institutions tallies, probably, pretty nearly with that of the churches. This might be expected, college being, as was observed at the commencement of this sketch, only society in miniature. Alternations between high degrees of fervor and low states, quite as near and probably nearer the other extreme of the scale, have given to religion a kind of mutable character, and gone to invalidate the force of its testimony, in the judgment of prudent men, accustomed to regard stability and con-

20

sistency as the only true criterion for detecting principle, and distinguishing it from its counterfeits. I have said that college experience tallies, probably, nearly with that of the churches. The nature of the case would lead us to look for less stability than in the churches generally, on account, first, of the inexperience of Christians; and secondly, numerous cases of excitement, which inevitably spring up in communities constituted as colleges are, over and above those which exist in society at large, which are of themselves sufficient to inundate, one would think, most of the religion in the country at frequent intervals; and thirdly, the interruption of feeling and efforts arising from the occurrence of vacations. Whether the fact accords with what the nature of the case would lead us to expect, I shall not now inquire. It is sufficient to say, that in respect to a permanent, straightforward course of Christian living, there has been, at least, as much to complain of in colleges as elsewhere. It should be noticed, also, that, thrown more nearly together, and in various respects more intimately associated, dereliction of principle and inconsistencies of character are more easily detected, at least force themselves more naturally, and I may say necessarily, upon the attention. It has been said that, of late years, infidelity is increasing in our colleges. Certainly there was, up to the time to which we have advanced in the narrative, a great deal of practical, some avowed infidelity, and, there is reason to believe, much secret scepticism here. This arose, in part, from accidental causes,—causes, however, which might have been counteracted, no doubt, and crippled very much, had there been a mass of consistent, steady, concentrated Christian action. Let me ask any man, who was on this ground and conversant with the times of which I am writing, what he imagines would have been the effect on college principles and college morals, had every professedly religious student here sustained the character of Jesse Lockwood. I mention him, because death has sealed his testimony, and I am sure no one will dare to dispute it. Could the supposition just made have been verified, I imagine that other lurking-places than this would have been sought for infidelity, intemperance, profanity, and licentiousness to have celebrated their orgies in.

I am now going to explain in what way I think the revival of 1832 contributed to a more permanent religious order. It did so, I think, by exercising the principle of personal exertion and self-sacrifice, till it became habitual, and led on to a system which I shall presently give some account of. The principle of persevering, steady devotedness has been firmly established in individual minds, in all ages. But too little has been done to perpetuate this sentiment. One and another has cut his way through the solid rock, and, as it were, filled up the space behind him, so that others have been little benefited, except as they have seen them safe out, and therefore gathered hope, on the ground that such a thing was possible. Peter says, to be sure, "The God of all grace, after that ye have *suffered* awhile, stablish you." But we are not to infer from this that direct means are of no use toward the confirmation of piety. There is, no doubt, in respect to means, such a thing as a millennial order (using the term millennial generically here), and it was towards this that numbers among us were led at this time to look. Having become inured to a pretty steady course of religious action, anxious to persevere in this without faltering, sensible, at the same time, of the sluggishness of nature, and warned by the experience of the past, the inquiry came up, What corrective can be thrown in, what stimulus to excite us forward in an unwavering onward course of Christian action? It was in the way of righteousness, "doing his will," that light was thrown on this subject, — the doctrine of means. It was resolved by the Christians of that period that they would meet together at noon. This, it was thought, would furnish a strong antidote against a tendency, so prevalent everywhere, but perhaps especially in College, to fall in with the tide of worldliness. By setting up, as it were, a dam at midday, it was thought possible to check the current, and thus prevent our Christianity from being overflown, and everything relapsing again into a stagnant and dead state, as had been the case after most previous revivals. I must be permitted to say, that I think the idea of a perfect Christianity, that is, of living in perfect conformity to the injunctions of Christ, without regard to seasons or circumstances, and without reference to the feelings or practices of others, has to do with the institution of this system of means. A very good opportunity was approaching to test it, or at least to test the strength of the resolution which determined on its adoption, namely, the approach of the summer term, when there is uncommon temptation to laxness, and a letting down of the Christian watch. The result proved that the idea was a very practicable one, and very salutary in the operation of it. A few, from five to seven, from the two College buildings, met in rainy as well as sunshiny weather, during the term, and felt improved by it. This meeting, somewhat modified in its character, has continued to the present time, and has more than answered the anticipations of those who originated it. It has served as a balance-wheel, to check the irregular movements of individual action, to temper well-meaning but injudicious zeal. I am just now in from one of these meetings, consisting of from forty to fifty students. The average sometimes ranges considerably higher than this, in times of awakening, and sometimes falls short of it. I have introduced this subject here, because the religious history of the College cannot be given, from this point, without frequent allusions to this meeting, it having become a pretty certain criterion by which the religious pulse of the College may be judged of.

During the year 1833, no special awakening

occurred. The noon meeting increased, during the summer, to fifteen or more, and several persons being attached to it who were devoted to the cause of missions, a spirit of prayer prevailed with reference to that object, more perhaps than at any time since. Towards the close of this year, Mr. Foot, the evangelist, came into the north of Berkshire. He preached in an adjoining town, and the attention of the community was more or less awakened. A protracted meeting was held in Williamstown somewhat early in the ensuing spring. There was special attention to religion at this time in College. A revival in Northampton affected several students who were spending the winter there. These came on changed men. Others were awakened, some under the preaching of the evangelist, and some under the ordinary means. The work was not very extensive, — it did not silence scoffers, — "divers persons were hardened."

The ensuing year, religion gained ground. A Tutor, the Rev. Simeon H. Calhoun, came in, who was much devoted to the work. The noon meeting had increased so much that it was thought expedient to divide. The West College set up for themselves, and the silent influence of their operations appears to have been considerable. An infidel has told me, lately, — one at least who was either tempted or trying to be so at that time, — that the prayers and singing kept him constantly uneasy, so much so that at length he divulged his feelings to his teacher, renounced his infidel principles, embraced religion, and became one of the most steady supporters of the meeting.

The following general view of the several revivals which occurred in this College, previous to 1832, is extracted from Dr. Griffin's most interesting letter to the Rev. Dr. Sprague: —

"The earliest revival known to this town commenced in the spring of 1805, and continued between two and three years. It soon extended to the College, where five began to hope. In the spring a new impulse was given to the work. Mills and Hall entered College that spring. The work seems to have continued beyond the summer, for one account says, 'Thirteen were added to the Church,' of whom nine became ministers of the Gospel. Ten others were supposed to be subjects of the revival.' Another account says, 'Besides those who became church-members from the classes that were graduated in 1805, -6, -7, -8, -9, about seventeen have since become professors of religion.'

"In January, 1812, another revival commenced in town, under the preaching of the Rev. Samuel Nott, one of the first five missionaries who went out that year to India. In April and May it extended to the College, chiefly to the lower classes. Twenty-four were hopefully converted then, and a number afterwards. Another account says, 'Twenty-one were added to the church, of whom thirteen have become ministers of the Gospel. Several others felt the power of this revival, and their lives have since proved that the effects were not transient.'

"In June, 1815, the first President, Dr. Fitch, left the College. His parting sermon had a great effect on the students. A third revival followed. Fifteen were hopefully renewed in the course of the summer. Another account says, 'Twelve were added to the church, of whom nine became ministers of the Gospel. Several others received very salutary impressions, whose lives have since evinced the value of this revival to them.'

"In March, 1824, a fourth revival appeared to commence in

the person of William Harvey. Twelve or fourteen used to attend the inquiry meetings. Several obtained hopes who endured but for a time. Harvey alone persevered. Of the others that were impressed, one obtained a hope in the summer of 1825, another (President Hopkins) joined the church after he was graduated.

"When College came together in October, 1825, the arrows of the Almighty stuck fast in several hearts. Some old hopes were scattered to the winds. A fifth revival ensued. During the latter part of the term the power was astonishingly great, affecting almost the whole College. Of eighty-five students, full seventy thought themselves Christians. The impression was kept up during the spring term, but then it ended. In this revival thirty-five experienced hopes, some of which were soon renounced. For aught I know, from twenty-five to twenty-seven are hoping still, and another who relapsed has apparently been recovered.

"The sixth revival began about the 1st of March, 1827, and continued till vacation. It spent its chief force on the two lower classes, from which six professed religion.

"In October, 1828, some seriousness appeared, which continued through that and the next term. Nine visited me under some impressions. Inquiry meetings were set up. One obtained a hope, which was soon renounced. Not an individual held out. Three of them, however, have since given evidence of a saving change.

"A seventh revival appeared to commence in November, 1829. That month two gave evidence of piety, who still continue. High hopes were entertained, and a determination was taken to pray till the blessing came. Meetings for prayer, accompanied with considerable excitement, were kept up through the term, and through the long winter vacation, and through the spring term. I attended till broken off by sickness in April, 1830. In the course of the winter two more expressed hopes, one of which proved doubtful.

"On the evening of January 6, 1831, I was sent for to visit Troy, where the first in the series of protracted meetings in this region had lately been held, and where a great revival had begun. I went on the 8th, and returned on the 19th. Something hopeful had begun to appear in town before I left home, and on Friday evening, the 21st, I went to a meeting to tell the people what I had seen. One of the students, hearing that a statement was to be made, went, and was awakened. The next week we had a four-days' meeting, beginning with a fast and ending with the communion Sabbath. This was the second protracted meeting in the series, and was attended with an evident blessing. A revival began in town. During the vacation two of the students obtained hopes here, and two more in Troy. When College came together, the 10th of February, it was a time of great solemnity. The month of March was full of power. By the 2d of April, twenty, including those already mentioned, were apparently rejoicing in the truth. Of these, four soon renounced their hope; the other sixteen, for aught I know, still endure, and the greater part appear like devoted Christians.

"These eight revivals the pity of Heaven has granted to this College in twenty-six years, five of which, including two of less extent, have appeared in seven years.

"April 18, 1832. There is at the present moment the ninth revival going on in College. On the 18th of January we had a fast in town to pray for such a blessing in the College and congregation. After that I recommended it to the students, who stayed in vacation, to hold meetings for prayer. The third which we had was on the 1st of February, and I was invited to attend. I found the meeting uncommonly interesting and encouraging. I was then laboring under the commencement of a disease, which confined me till the middle of March. In the interval, a protracted meeting was held in town, and a revival commenced there; and the spirit of prayer was greatly increased in College, and a spirit of inquiry began among the impenitent. The first hopeful conversion in College took place on the 16th of March, two days before I resumed my public labors in the house of God. There are seven students who now venture to hope that they have 'passed from death unto life.' Everything is conducted with perfect stillness and decorum.

"The means employed in these revivals have been but two,— the clear presentation of Divine truth and prayer. The meetings have been still and orderly, with no other signs of emotion among the hearers than the solemn look and the silent tear. We have been anxiously studious to guard against delusive hopes, and to expose the windings of a deceitful heart, forbearing all encouragement, except what the converts themselves could derive from Christ and the promises, knowing that any reliance on our opinion was drawing comfort from us, and not from the Saviour. We have not accustomed them to the bold and unqualified language that such an one *is* converted, but have used a dialect calculated to keep alive a sense of the danger of deception. For similar reasons we have kept them back from a public profession about three months."

C. Currier's Lith. E. Valois, lith. 33 Spruce St. N.Y.

BIRTH PLACE OF PRESIDENT HOPKINS.

Stockbridge, Mass.

CHAPTER XII.

BIOGRAPHICAL SKETCH OF PRESIDENT HOPKINS.

THE time has not arrived to write the life of Dr. Hopkins, the fourth President of the College. Still, in order to bring our history down to the present time, to render it more complete and useful, it is proper to insert the following sketch. He was a native of Stockbridge, and was born February 4, 1802, and the foundation of his future attainments was laid in his early training. His father, Archibald Hopkins, was a farmer in that town, and died January, 1839, aged seventy-three. His grandfather, Col. Mark Hopkins (graduated at Yale College, 1758), was the first lawyer that settled in Great Barrington, and died at White Plains, N. Y., while engaged in the defence of his country, October 26, 1776, aged thirty-seven. He married Electa Williams, a half-sister of Ephraim Williams, the founder of the College. Col. Hopkins was a younger brother of the Rev. Samuel Hopkins, D. D., the first minister who settled in Great Barrington, and author of the System of Divinity.

Mrs. Hopkins, the mother of the President, was Mary Curtis, a native of Stockbridge, and a woman of uncommon strength and excellence of character. She is still living (1860), and has for a few years past resided in Williamstown, in the family of her son. She was present at the first Commencement in Williams College, 1795.

President Hopkins was the eldest of three brothers (there were no daughters), one an artist of promising talents, who died young. The other is Professor Albert Hopkins of Williams College.

President Hopkins was favored with a good early education, and was fitted for college partly at Clinton, N. Y., partly at Stockbridge, under the tuition of his uncle, the Rev. Jared Curtis, and for a short time was a member of Lenox Academy. He entered Williams College in the fall of 1821, joining the Sophomore class, and was graduated in 1824, when he pronounced the valedictory oration.

Directly after leaving College he became connected with the Medical Institution in Pittsfield, and devoted a portion of the year to teaching in his native town. In the fall of 1825 he was appointed a Tutor in his Alma Mater, and officiated in that capacity two years, at the close of which he delivered the master's oration on "Mystery," which was published in Silliman's Journal. The next two years were spent in pursuing his medical studies and in teaching,—partly in Pittsfield, under the instruction of Dr. H. H. Childs, and partly in New York. He received the degree of Doctor of Medicine at Pittsfield in 1829.

Dr. Hopkins made a public profession of religion in 1826, uniting with the church in Stockbridge.

In August, 1830, just as he had completed his arrangements for a permanent residence in New York, he unexpectedly received an appointment to the Professorship of Rhetoric and Moral Philosophy in Williams College, then vacant in consequence of the death of Professor William A. Porter. This appointment he accepted, and entered at once upon the duties of his office. He was licensed to preach the Gospel, by the Berkshire Association, at a meeting held in Dalton, May, 1833.

He was married to Miss Mary Hubbell, of Williamstown, December 25, 1832.

At the Commencement in 1836, Dr. Griffin, in view of his age and infirmities, resigned the Presidency of the College. This event was not entirely unexpected. And at the same meeting of the Board at which his resignation was accepted, Dr. Hopkins was unanimously elected his successor, and Professor of Moral and Intellectual Philosophy. To show the views and motives with which he accepted the Presidency of the College, and entered upon his new and responsible position, we insert the following extract from the closing paragraph of his Inaugural Address.*

"I enter upon the duties of the office to which I am called with no excitement of novelty, with no accession of influence to the College from abroad, and with no expectation of pleasing everybody. I have no ambition to build up here what would be called a great institution; the wants of the community do not require it. But I do desire, and shall labor, that this may be a *safe*

* Miscellaneous Discourses, pp. 254, 255.

College; that its reputation may be sustained and raised still higher; that the plan of instruction I have indicated may be carried out more fully; that here there may be health, and cheerful study, and kind feelings, and pure morals; and that, in the memory of future students, college life may be made a still more verdant spot.

"But deep as is my anxiety when I look at the connection of this College with the interests of science and literature, it is still deeper when I look at its connection with the immortal destinies of those who shall come here, and with the progress of the cause of Christ and the conversion of the world. The true and permanent interests of man can be promoted only in connection with religion; and a regard to man, as an immortal, accountable, and redeemed being, should give its character to the whole course of our regulations, and the spirit of our instructions. This College has for a long time been regarded, and not without reason, with interest and affection by the churches. Of its whole number of graduates, as many as one third have devoted themselves to the Christian ministry, and recently a larger proportion. It is on this ground that American missions had their origin. It was here that Mills and Hall prayed, and their mantle has so descended on the institution, that now we can hardly turn our eyes to a missionary station where one or more of its sons are not to be found. Others are on their way, and there is remaining behind an association devoted to the same glorious work. This College has also been the scene of revivals of religion, pure and repeated and mighty, which have caused, and are still causing, joy on earth and in heaven. It is upon these, and upon the higher standard of consistent piety that follows in their train, that we mainly rest our hopes for the distinguished usefulness of the College. For these let the churches pray, and let them join with us in the words of my venerable predecessor when this building was dedicated, 'In devoting this College to the Holy Spirit as a scene of revivals of religion, and to the blessed Redeemer as an engine to bring on the millennial glory of His Church.' This would we do, not only as the friends of religion, but as the friends of science, and of a pure literature, and of the freest inquiry.

We would do it that we may disabuse the world of the absurd prejudice that the knowledge of God cramps the mind, and disqualifies it for the study of his works; that we may hasten that day, which must come, when it shall be seen and felt that there is a coincidence and essential unity between reason and religion; when the spirit of literature and the spirit of science shall minister before the spirit of piety, and pour their oil into the lamp that feeds its waxing flame; when study shall be nerved to its highest efforts by Christian benevolence, and young men shall grow up at the same time into the light of science and the beauty of holiness."

Dr. Hopkins received the honorary degree of Doctor of Divinity from Dartmouth College in 1837, and from Harvard University in 1841; and that of Doctor of Laws from the Board of Regents of New York, in 1857. During his Presidency the course of instruction in the College has been much extended and improved, and the number of students greatly increased. He has uniformly given instruction to the Senior class in anatomy, metaphysics, and ethics, and in the department of rhetoric, besides preaching one third of the time on the Sabbath.

In 1858, Mr. Jackson established a Professorship of Christian Theology in the College; and the conditions were such, that "if at any time it should be judged expedient by the Trustees to confer this professorship upon the President of the College, to be exercised by him in connection with his office of President, and his other duties," they are authorized to do so. In accordance with this permission, and the known wishes of the generous donor, Dr. Hopkins was appointed to this professorship.

Dr. Hopkins was elected President of the American Board of Commissioners for Foreign Missions, at Providence, R. I., in the fall of 1857, then vacant in consequence of the resignation of the Hon. Theodore Frelinghuysen. To all the urgent invitations which Dr. Hopkins has received to occupy other posts of usefulness, his uniform reply has been, "*I dwell among mine own people.*" From motives of delicacy, we reluctantly refrain from making mention of the acknowledged excellence and efforts of Dr. Hopkins's Baccalaureate Discourses and other pulpit performances and literary labors, choosing rather to leave these and many, many other interesting and edifying details for the historian of our generation to record.

Dr. Hopkins has become extensively known as an author. Among his publications, the most important are his Lowell Lectures on the Evidences of Christianity, which have already become a textbook in some of our colleges. In 1847 twenty-two of his Discourses and Lectures, which had previously found their way to the press, were republished in one volume. His course of Lectures on Moral Philosophy, which he prepared during his professorship, and which have since been delivered to successive classes, it is hoped will soon be given to the public.

The following is a list of Dr. Hopkins's publications: —

Agricultural Address at Stockbridge, 1826.
Oration, — Mystery, — 1827.

Review of the Argument from Nature for the Divine Existence, 1833.

Human Happiness, 1834.

Oration, — Originality, — 1835.

Inaugural Discourse, 1836.

Address at Andover, 1837.

Lecture, — Taste and Morals, — 1837.

Sermon in Commemoration of Dr. Griffin, 1837.

Address before the American Education Society, 1838.

Election Sermon, May, 1839.

Address before American Bible Society, 1840.

Address at South Hadley (Mount Holyoke Female Seminary), 1840.

Address at Pittsfield (Medical College), 1840.

Address at East Hampton (Williston Seminary), 1841.

Alumni Address at Williamstown, 1843.

Sermon before the Pastoral Association, Boston, 1843.

Sermon at the Berkshire Jubilee, 1844.

Sermon before Massachusetts Convention, 1845.

Sermon before the A. B. C. F. M., Brooklyn, N. Y., 1845.

Lowell Lectures on the Evidences of Christianity (octavo volume), 1846.

Temperance Address (for circulation in Massachusetts), 1846.

Sermon Commemorative of Professor Kellogg, 1846.

Sermon at Plymouth, December 22, 1846.

Sermon before the American Sabbath Union, 1847.

Sermon at Dedication in Pittsfield, 1850.

Baccalaureate Sermon, — Faith, Philosophy, and Reason, — 1850.

Baccalaureate Sermon, — Strength and Beauty, — 1851.

Baccalaureate Sermon, — Receiving and Giving, — 1852.

Address before the Western College Society, Boston, 1852.

Sermon Commemorative of Amos Lawrence, 1853.

Oration, — The Central Principle, — New York, December 22, 1853.

Discourse before the Congregational Library Association, 1855.

Baccalaureate Sermon, — Perfect Love, — 1855.

Baccalaureate Sermon, — Self-Denial, — 1856.
Address at Missionary Jubilee, 1856.
Sermon, — Science and Religion, — Albany, N. Y., 1856.
Baccalaureate Sermon, — Higher and Lower Good, — 1857.
Sermon, — The Promise to Abraham, — Bangor, Me., 1857.
Baccalaureate Sermon, — Eagles' Wings, — 1858.
Address at Havana, N. Y., 1858.
The Atonement as related to Sin, and to a Divine Lawgiver, — American Theological Review, 1859.
Baccalaureate Sermon, — The Manifoldness of Man, — 1859.
Religious Teaching and Worship, — a Sermon at the Dedication of the College Chapel, — 1859.

CHAPTER XIII.

ADMINISTRATION OF PRESIDENT HOPKINS. 1836-1860.

THE appointment of Dr. Hopkins to the Presidency of the College was in perfect coincidence with the wishes and expectations of the students and the public. He had been designated as the proper candidate for the place. With the circumstances and wants of the College he was familiar. He had officiated as tutor two years, as professor six years, and had heard the recitations of the Senior class the preceding year. Having accepted the appointment, on the 15th day of September, 1836, he was inaugurated President of the College, and ordained pastor of the College church. The ceremony was performed in the Chapel in the following order: Prayer was offered by the Rev. Dr. Field of Stockbridge; the Hon. D. N. Dewey read the action of the Board in relation to his election; the Rev. Dr. Shepard of Lenox then performed the act of inauguration, and delivered the charge to the President elect; the President then delivered his inaugural address, after which he was ordained pastor of the College church, the Rev. Dr. Cooley of Granville offering the installing prayer; the right hand of fellowship was given by the Rev. E. W. Dwight of Richmond, and the concluding prayer was offered by Dr. Griffin.

During the Presidency of Dr. Griffin, the College had been slowly recovering from its former depression, and its financial condition had been improved. Still there was a great deficiency in its funds, and the number of students was small. The four classes then on the ground furnished one hundred and eleven graduates.

During the first year nothing of special interest or importance occurred. In the spring of 1837 the building known as the Astronomical Observatory (the first of the kind on this continent designed exclusively for such an object) was commenced, wholly on the responsibility of Professor Hopkins. The original plan extended only to the erection of a small edifice, which might serve as a convenient place for the deposit of a small transit instrument; but it was thought best afterwards to enlarge the design so as to accommodate other instruments which at some future time might be furnished. The exterior of the building was finished in the fall of the same year. The work was resumed the ensuing spring, and, in June, 1838, the instruments having been mounted and arranged, the edifice was dedicated by an address from Professor Hopkins. The cost of the Observatory, exclusive of the fixtures, was not far from two thousand dollars, to aid in defraying which, four hundred dollars were subscribed by four gentlemen in

Worcester, Boston, New York, and Williamstown, the remainder devolving upon Professor Hopkins. This sum has since been partially repaid to him by the Trustees, and, in honor of his efforts and generosity, it was unanimously voted that the building be called the "Hopkins Observatory."

In the summer of 1842, with the money thus repaid by the Corporation, Professor Hopkins also constructed and presented to the College a Magnetic Observatory, together with the ground on which it stands.

In 1838 the Professorship of Mathematics and Natural Philosophy was abolished, — the department of Professor Hopkins being termed the Professorship of Natural Philosophy and Astronomy, — while a new Professorship of Mathematics was at this time established, and Mr. John Tatlock, who had been for two years a Tutor in College, was transferred to the new professorship.

In the spring of 1840 an expedition through Berkshire County was undertaken by the Lyceum of Natural History, with a view, partly, to study the natural history of the county, to explore its interesting deposits of iron, marble, etc.; and also to give its members an opportunity to see the beautiful scenery of the county. The expedition, generally, and always when it was desired, held a public religious meeting at night, in the place where they pitched their tent. In this way many useful impressions were made, and much good accomplished. The expedition was accompanied by

Professor Hopkins, who, like Goldsmith's village pastor, has, for more than thirty years in this College,

> "Allured to brighter worlds,
> And led the way."

Sunday, October 17, 1841, the building long known as the East College was destroyed by fire. The fire took in the afternoon while the students were at church, and was communicated, as is supposed, from a stick of wood falling from the fire-place upon the floor, in a room situated on the north hall, fourth story, and west side. The building being old, the flames spread with great rapidity, and in a short time the edifice, which fond recollections had rendered dear to many, and which, for nearly half a century, unscathed, had withstood so many storms and partial burnings, was soon a smouldering ruin. The students were, however, enabled to save most of their furniture and books, with the exception of those which were in the immediate vicinity of the fire.

While the south end of the College was burning, the Astronomical Observatory was at times in great danger, and was saved only by covering the combustible parts with wet blankets. The theological library was entirely destroyed. But the loss that fell with the greatest weight upon the students was the destruction of the rooms belonging to the literary societies. These apartments had been but recently fitted up in this building, and were situated in the third story. The major part of the society libraries and furniture was removed, though not without great injury, the students exerting themselves to the utmost, and not deserting their posts until compelled by the overpowering heat.

The fire, though severely felt by some, on account of the loss of books and furniture, did not break up the regular course of studies, even of the Junior and Senior classes, for more than one day. The students, by the activity of the Faculty, and the kindness of the people of the town, were without exception furnished with comfortable rooms before the close of the next day. There being no insurance, the loss fell heavily on the College, but a meeting of the Trustees being immediately called, active measures were at once taken, and in a comparatively short time nine thousand dollars were subscribed to aid in rebuilding. A petition was also sent to the Legislature for aid, but it was not successful. During the ensuing spring and summer, two new buildings, called East and South Colleges, were erected, at an expense of eleven thousand dollars.

In 1842, a full suit of the minerals of the State of New York was presented to the College by Professor Ebenezer Emmons.

On Wednesday, August 16, 1843, in accordance with previous arrangements, the Society of Alumni celebrated the semi-centennial anniversary of the founding of the College. This occasion brought together a great number of graduates (probably not far from three hundred), and with them, a large crowd of interested spectators.

On Tuesday evening, near a beautiful sunset, his Excellency Governor Morton and Lieutenant-Governor Childs were escorted into town from Adams, by a band of music, and a long train of carriages and gentlemen on horseback.

Agreeably to public notice, the Alumni assembled in the College chapel at eight o'clock, Wednesday morning, and Judge Morris of Springfield, the President of the Society, took the chair. Here were brought together the aged, the middle-aged, and the young, — judges, rulers, pastors, teachers, lawyers, and literary men, — who had passed their days of classical pupilage in this delightful valley. Some who met on this occasion had not seen each other for thirty or forty years. Interesting, yet painful, was it for these venerable men to meet and recognize each other again, and exchange mutual greeting and salutations. It was a most delightful family gathering. The children of a common literary parent had come home to acknowledge their "indebtedness for blessings received and hopes fulfilled." They had come to be strengthened in all good purposes and resolutions for the future.

One could almost hear these venerable men, as they looked around upon each other, and on the gorgeous scenery which surrounds Williams College, exclaim, as Wordsworth did on revisiting the banks of the Wye, — a spot endeared to him for its many poetic inspirations and youthful joys: —

"Though absent long,
These forms of beauty have not been to me

As is a landscape to a blind man's eye;
But oft in lonely rooms, and 'mid the din
Of towns and cities, I have owed to them,
In hours of weariness, sensations sweet,
Felt in the blood, and felt along the heart,
And passing even into my purer mind
With tranquil restoration; feelings, too,
Of unremembered pleasure, such perhaps
As have no slight or trivial influence
On that best portion of a good man's life,
His little, nameless, unremembered acts
Of kindness and of love."

How many tears were shed, how many tender associations awakened, how many silent prayers went up to Heaven for the long-continued prosperity and usefulness of our Alma Mater!

A book had been provided, in which all graduates present were requested to insert their names, class, and residence, to be preserved and presented at the centennial celebration in 1893.

Of the graduates of the early classes, there were present: —

1795. Not one (and only one member of the class was then living).
1796. Rev. Thomas Robbins, D. D., Rochester.
1797. Not one.
1798. Judge William P. Walker, Lenox.
1799. Rev. Samuel Fisher, D. D., New Jersey.
" Rev. William Patrick, Canterbury, Conn.
1800. Rev. Jared Curtis, Chaplain in the State Prison, Charlestown.
" Rev. Caleb Knight, Worthington.
" Judge John Dickinson, Amherst.
1801. Judge Morris, of Springfield.
1802. Lieutenant-Governor Childs, Pittsfield.

1802. James W. Robbins, Esq., Lenox.
1803. David Buttolph, Norwich, N. Y.
" Rev. J. W. Canning, Gill.
" Rev. Phineas Cooke, Lebanon, N. Y.
" Jacob Ten Eyck, Esq., Schodack, N. Y.
1804. Rev. Barnabas King, Rockaway, N. J.
1805. Judge David Buel, Troy, N. Y.
1806. Judge Samuel R. Betts, New York.
" Rev. Professor Dewey, Rochester, N. Y.
" Thomas A. Gold, Esq., Pittsfield.
1807. Rev. John Nelson, D. D., Leicester.
" Judge Stebbins, Springfield.
1808. Judge Joseph Boies, Union Village, Washington County, N. Y.
" Noah Ely, Esq., Chenango, N. Y.
" Rev. F. L. Robbins, Enfield, Conn.
1809. Not represented.
1810. Rev. Justin Edwards, D. D., Andover.
" Judge Daniel Kellogg, Rockingham, Vt.
1811. Judge C. A. Dewey, Northampton.
" Rev. Eben L. Clark, Richmond.

After the reading of the minutes, the Society proceeded to the election of officers for the ensuing year, and Judge Betts of New York was elected President. A vote was immediately passed electing his Excellency Governor Morton an honorary member of the Society, and Lieutenant-Governor Childs and Judge Betts were chosen a committee to repair to the house of President Hopkins, and inform his Excellency of his election, and invite him to attend, and take a seat on the stage. In a few moments he entered the chapel, amid much applause and waving of handkerchiefs, and took his seat by the side of Judge Morris, who had not yet left the chair. At this moment, the Rev. Jared Curtis came to the stage to write his name in the book. Judge Morris remarked: "The individual who is now writing his name is the Rev. Jared Curtis; he was a native of Stockbridge, and belonged to the class of 1800. He is a clergyman, and the only Alumnus of our College who hails from the State Prison." (Loud applause.) "And, inasmuch as his Excellency the Governor is now with us, I would suggest to him whether this would not be a favorable time to present a petition, with the signatures of some of his friends, for an unconditional pardon." Instantly the Governor replied: "It cannot be granted, unless his conduct is different from what it has been." (Loud and prolonged applause.) Mr. Curtis is a clergyman of the old school, puritanical in his sentiments and habits, and has been a judicious and faithful spiritual adviser to that unfortunate class of men who for so many years were under his pastoral care.

At ten o'clock a procession was formed in the following order, viz.: Graduates of the College, in the order of their graduation; Trustees and Faculty of the College; Strangers and Undergraduates; — and proceeded to the church, which was filled to overflowing. The exercises were commenced with singing, "Jerusalem, my happy home," etc. Prayer was offered by the Rev. Dr. Justin Edwards. The audience was then addressed by Dr. Hopkins and by Dr. Robbins. The address of the President was marked by strength and originality of thought, and beauty and elegance of language. So touching and true were some of his allusions, in awakening emotions and recollections of the past, that the eyes of many unaccustomed to weep were suffused with tears. After extending a most cordial and hearty welcome to the Alumni, in his own name and in that of their venerated Alma Mater, — "to her quiet seats, to that green spot in the memory of the past, to these familiar scenes, these remembered walks, to the sound of that bell not unwelcome now, to these circling and unchanged mountains, and the scenery unsurpassed," — he briefly reviewed the changes that had passed since the founding of the College. The subject of his address was "The Law of Progress of the Race," and it closed with some remarks on the connection of this College with that progress.

Rev. Dr. Robbins then pronounced an elaborate address, in which he gave a brief sketch of the history of the College, accompanied with many well-digested thoughts in relation to the obligations of students. The benediction was pronounced by the Rev. Samuel Fisher, D. D.

The services being concluded, the Alumni and invited guests repaired to the East College green, where, under a tent erected for the occasion, a collation was prepared. The Rev. Dr. Shepard invoked the Divine blessing. After the material repast, the intellectual feast was again renewed in numerous and spirited addresses. Judge Betts of New York led the way, by a glowing description of the advantages of this institution, and the benefits conferred by it, not only on individuals, but also upon the community at large; and in concluding, called upon his Excellency Governor Morton. The Governor responded in a very happy speech, which was received with the liveliest applause. He was followed by Professor Dewey of Rochester, Lieutenant-Governor Childs of Pittsfield, Judge Dewey of Northampton, Rev. Dr. Nelson of Leicester, Rev. Dr. Edwards of Andover, Hon. Emory Washburn, Rev. Dr. Brigham, Rev. J. N. Danforth, Erastus C. Benedict, Esq., and some others. The company was enlivened by the presence of a large number of ladies, and prolonged this delightful interchange of sentiment until evening.

The remarks made by the Hon. Charles A. Dewey, LL. D.,* of the class of 1811, as they contain some interesting reminiscences, are here inserted entire: —

" The occasion on which we are assembled is one of thrilling interest. How many themes present themselves to our minds that might well occupy the brief space allowed for the utterance of our sentiments. Prominent is the debt of gratitude we owe to the gallant soldier, the true-hearted philanthropist and patriot, whose name our Alma Mater so appropriately bears. The deep

* Hon. C. A. Dewey was a native of Williamstown, and resided there eleven years after he entered on the duties of his profession. He was early elected a Trustee and Secretary of the College. During the protracted and painful controversy respecting its removal, his voice and pen were successfully employed in the defence of the College *as then located.*

solicitude he felt for the welfare of those who were to come after him induced him to make an endowment for increasing the facilities of education. He here laid the foundation for a school of an elevated character, and one promising great benefit to the youth of this vicinity. It soon came to be felt that the cause of sound learning and true piety demanded an institution of a more elevated character, — one which might extend its benefits to the young men, not of this town merely, but embracing a large circle and an extended region. In the true spirit of our republican institutions this College was chartered, and by its establishment the facilities of a collegiate education were widely extended. Here benefits of a practical character were secured. It occupied a space remote from other similar institutions; its expenses were of small amount, and easily brought within the compass of all who desired to obtain an education. In truth, it extended the advantages to a large class of young men who, but for this College, would have been deprived of the advantages of a liberal education; and many who have now a controlling influence in the affairs of National and State governments; many who have adorned the liberal professions; and many who have gone forth to civilize and Christianize the heathen world, would have remained in comparative obscurity but for this institution. The advantages here offered were eagerly embraced. Young men from every quarter here assembled. Those who would have gone to no other institution were here trained and fitted for strong pillars in church and state, filling the learned professions, occupying the highest stations in our universities and colleges, honored by seats in our legislative halls.

"Williams College was peculiarly fortunate in its first officers. President Fitch, that good man, who for twenty-two years, almost the half of the whole period of its past existence, presided over it, brought to the presidential chair those qualities which gave him extensive influence, and attracted the attention of the friends of learning and science. Uniting the urbane manners of the good-hearted gentleman, highly respectable talents, much and long-continued experience as a teacher, and a heart abounding in love to God and towards his fellow-men, he was beloved of all, esteemed of all.

"His associates, as teachers, were men of the highest order. I see there Jeremiah Day, since so long at the head of Yale College; Henry Davis, who has presided over Middlebury and Hamilton Colleges; Thomas Day and Warren Dutton, lights of science and literature.

"The College had indeed its palmy days, and the evidence of its usefulness soon became apparent. If subsequently there have been days of darkness and depression, they have been shared, it is believed, in common with other similar institutions.

"The period emphatically one of depression as to numbers was that of 1813, 1814, and 1815. The question as to whether a new class was to enter at the new college year was sometimes supposed to depend on the state of things in a private classical school in the little village of Plainfield; and what numbers that good and venerable man and minister, the Rev. Mr. Hallock, could send us. There, in retirement, besides his parochial duties, always faithfully performed, this venerable man devoted his time most successfully to the classical education of young men. Mr. Hallock never forsook us, and in the days of our greatest need always sent us from his retired cloister a number of goodly youth, and in one instance, I believe, furnished more than one half of the entire class.

"The accession of Dr. Griffin gave a new impulse to the College. His eminent talents, his high religious character, his ardent devotion to the College as then located, produced the happiest results. The tide soon turned; and from that day Williams College has had a glorious onward march. Its enlargement and improvement have corresponded with the progress of the age. Everything requisite for a thorough and useful education is provided, so that our sons, to our latest posterity, may come to this fount, and drink freely of those waters so well adapted to secure their intellectual and moral training, and to fit them to act well their parts in the great drama of life.

"In taking a retrospect of the past, in looking over the names of those who have been trained within these walls, while we are pained to say that some have faltered in their progress, tempted by the love of ease; some have been the votaries of pleasure, and the victims of dissipation; but many, very many of our number have shone as stars of the first magnitude. It would be pleasant to group in appropriate classes those who have thus honored their Alma Mater. We are fully authorized to say that the names on our triennial catalogue will not suffer in this respect in comparison with those of the most favored institutions in our land.

"Of the sons of Williams, many already sleep with the dead. In recalling the memory of such to my mind, I was forciby struck with the fact, that, among the brilliant lights thus early extinguished, three have been my neighbors and friends in Northampton. Mills, Howe, and Ashmun, all distinguished, all shining lights in the spheres in which they moved. Mills, whose brilliant eye and intelligent countenance bespoke the splendid genius within, that could lead captive his admiring hearers, whether in the senate chamber or the judicial forum. Howe, whom so many of us have seen at the bar or on the bench, an example of triumphant success, accomplished mainly by an ardent devotion to his profession, and whose whole career was distinguished for his love of principle and justice. Ashmun (three years a member of this institution) fell an early victim to disease, but he too lived long enough to acquire the reputation of an accomplished lawyer, and to be counted worthy to fill a professional chair, as an associate with the learned Justice Story, who respected him while living, and honored his memory in an obituary sketch most honorable to our lamented friend.

"But let us return from this digression, and contemplate our personal relations to this institution. As individuals, we owe a debt of gratitude to Williams College, for the advantages here enjoyed, for that early training, moral and intellectual, we here received. But the benefits of education are not limited to the consideration of the advancement of the individual. It is society at large that is benefited by institutions like these. This constitutional government of ours, if it can be sustained at all, is to be sustained by the virtue and intelligence of the people. To this end there must be a general diffusion of education among the masses of the people. They must be educated, but how are they

C. Currier's Lith. E. Valois, lith. 33 Spruce St N.Y.

LAWRENCE HALL
1847.

JACKSON HALL.
1855.

to be educated? Through the instrumentality of those first educated at our collegiate institutions.

"In conclusion, allow me to say that the occasion forcibly reminds us that more devotion is required on our part to the cause of science and literature. Enjoying the blessings of education, and appreciating their value, we ought to be excited to labor that education may be more generally diffused. As sons of Williams, let us arouse ourselves, and buckle on our armor in this great cause. Let us especially exert ourselves to preserve and perpetuate this luminary in our intellectual and moral horizon. Long, long may she remain a beacon light, guiding the young to knowledge and virtue. Here may the standard of scholarship be elevated, thoroughly and practically useful. Here may annually issue forth minds, properly trained for the great purposes of this life and that which is yet future. Thus, and thus only, will she satisfy our wants as rational and immortal beings, and answer the full purposes of her existence."

In January, 1844, while still embarrassed in consequence of its recent loss, the College received an unexpected donation of five thousand dollars from Amos Lawrence, Esq., of Boston. It nearly cancelled the debt which had been contracted in consequence of the fore-mentioned loss. In July following, Mr. Lawrence increased his donation to ten thousand dollars.

At a meeting of the Trustees in August, this year, in view of the generous donations just named, it was voted that one of the professorships shall be called the Lawrence Professorship.

In January, 1846, after consultation with Dr. Hopkins, Mr. Lawrence added another ten thousand dollars to his previous donations. His next gift was the present library building. It was erected in 1846, at an expense of seven thousand dollars; and by vote of the Trustees the building is called "Lawrence Hall."

Soon after, he gave two thousand dollars to establish four scholarships, designed for the benefit, primarily, of students from Groton Academy; a scholarship merely paying the tuition of the student.

For a number of years Mr. Lawrence was in the habit of inviting some two or three individuals in the vicinity of Boston to attend the annual Commencement at Williams, at his expense, and bring him a full report of the proceedings. Never will the writer forget the pleasure and profit it afforded him to be for successive years one of these representatives and reporters.

In 1851, Mr. Lawrence, accompanied by Mrs. Lawrence, made his first and only visit to Williamstown. On viewing the College grounds, and observing their great susceptibilities of improvement, but lack of room, he authorized the purchase of four acres, south of the East College grounds.

His next gift was a telescope, which cost about fifteen hundred dollars.

In addition to these gifts, Mr. Lawrence, at different times, greatly enlarged the library with costly books, the expense of which cannot be ascertained.

In 1845, on Forefathers' Day, he sent to the President a check for one hundred dollars, to be used for the aid of needy students; and he furnished at least one hundred dollars annually for that purpose, and regarded the results with much interest.

Thus, in different ways, Mr. Lawrence gave to the College between thirty and forty thousand dollars; and he had expressed the purpose, should he live, of aiding it still further.

He fully sympathized with the Trustees in the effort, which was commenced just before his death, to raise fifty thousand dollars for a permanent endowment of the institution. During the last thirteen years of Mr. Lawrence's life there is good authority for saying that his various benefactions were not less than five hundred thousand dollars; still, no memorial of his will be more enduring than what he did for this College. By this, "he being dead, yet speaketh."

Mr. Lawrence was once requested to write a few lines in a book which contains, in manuscript, some notice of the principal donors, the Trustees, Presidents, and Professors of Williams College. He wrote as follows: —

"BOSTON, December 17, 1847.

"REV. AND DEAR SIR: —

". . . . . On this day, forty years ago, I commenced business in this city, without property to the amount of twenty dollars, — without any rich friend or any poor friend to speak a good word for me, — and made my first sale to a Cape Cod man, of four cotton handkerchiefs for twenty-eight cents each, on which I made a profit of twenty-nine cents, which is the foundation of my business capital. I told the man my purpose, and if he liked my plan, should be glad to have him call and see and try me again. On a rainy day, about a week after, this same man came peeping along into the store-doors (mine had two doors, and was 31 Cornhill), and as he looked in at the second door, said, 'This is the place, boys,' and was followed in by some half a dozen of his comrades to get 'fitted out' for their return home. I supplied them with such articles as they wanted, and ever after, while I sold goods at retail, these people continued to come to me for what they wanted, because I never deceived them by pretending to keep 'a cheap shop,' but that I would always give them a fair return for their money, and such articles as were not satisfactory might be returned to me, and I would return them the money. In my whole experience of more than ten years with them, they never in any case asked for a return of money. From the 17th day of December, 1807, to this 17th day of December, 1847, I have not inherited or received as my own property to the amount of a dollar that I have not paid out a full equivalent for, thus possessing the fruits of my own labors, 'full measure and running over,' by the blessing of God uniformly on these labors. I desire to use the talents committed to me so as to receive 'THE WELL DONE' when called to an account. If I succeed, it will be through the mercy of the Beloved.

"AMOS LAWRENCE.

"REV. CALVIN DURFEE."

In this connection it may be mentioned, that, in 1856, Mr. Amos Lawrence gave to the College five thousand dollars as a library fund.

In August, 1844, Professor Kellogg resigned his office as Professor of Languages, having been unable for some time, on account of ill health, to attend to all his College duties. He died at Williamstown, October, 1846, aged fifty-seven, having been connected with the institution for a period of thirty years. Professor Kellogg was born at Vernon, Conn., October 25, 1789. He entered Yale College in 1807, joining the Sophomore class, and graduated in 1810, when he pronounced the Salutatory oration. After teaching two years he studied theology at Andover, and was appointed Professor of Languages in Williams College in the spring of 1815.

In 1845 Professor Tatlock was appointed Professor of Languages, as successor to Professor Kellogg, and Mr. John Darby of Georgia was appointed Professor of Mathematics.

The old laboratory being found inconvenient, a new and commodious building was erected at this time, and the chemical apparatus was greatly enlarged.

In January, 1846, the Rev. Dr. Shepard, of Lenox, died, in the seventy-third year of his age, and fifty-first of his ministry. He was born at Chatham, Conn., November 19, 1772; was graduated at Yale College, 1793; was ordained in Lenox, April 30, 1795. He was a man of a quick and vigorous mind; an earnest and popular preacher; an able and judicious spiritual adviser. Many were the seals of his ministry. He was remarkably appropriate and solemn in prayer. There was a rare compass and power in his eloquent voice, the memory of which will long be cherished in the sanctuaries of Berkshire. He was a man of noble personal appearance, and his social qualities were uncommonly interesting and versatile. He was a Trustee of the College thirty-eight years, twelve of which he had officiated as Vice-President.

His name will long be held in grateful remembrance.*

In 1846 Professor Darby resigned his connection with the College, and Professor Tatlock was re-appointed Professor of Mathematics. The Rev. Nathaniel H. Griffin was appointed Professor of Languages.

In 1847 the building known as Kellogg Hall was erected.

At a meeting of the Alumni, August, 1847, the Rev. Dr. Robbins made some remarks, suggesting certain improvements in the Triennial Catalogue. In accordance with his suggestions, a committee, consisting of Dr. Robbins, Dr. Davis, Rev. Mr. Durfee, Hon. E. Washburn, and Professor Griffin, were appointed, and requested to report at the next annual meeting. This committee subsequently made a report, prepared by Professor Griffin, for which they received the thanks of the Alumni, and were continued, and requested to make such other improvements in the Triennial Catalogue as further investigations should warrant. For the great amount of statistical information with which our Triennial Catalogue abounds the Alumni are chiefly indebted to the persevering labors of Professor Griffin.

In 1848 Ebenezer Emmons, M. D., was elected Professor of Natural History. This year, too, he

* The College has a lifelike portrait of Dr. Shepard, a present from his daughter, Miss Lucy A. Shepard.

presented to the College his valuable cabinet of mineralogical and geological specimens; a donation of unspeakable value.

This year the Hon. John Mills and the Hon. Christopher A. Paige received the thanks of the Board for valuable donations of books to the College.

In the fall of 1849, a successful effort was made to unite the Theological and the Mills Society of Inquiry. The former society had existed for about half a century; the latter was organized in 1820. Both societies were small. All the members of the Mills Society were considered as pledged to the missionary work. In connection with this union of the two societies, an effort was made to secure a room for the library. After this organization had taken place, and the library had been greatly enlarged, the number of members was, in a short time, nearly doubled, and much good was accomplished. The leading individuals in this movement were the Rev. P. M. Bartlett and Mr. William D. Porter. The two societies now meet every Sabbath evening at six o'clock, — one evening as a theological society, the next as a missionary association.

At the Commencement in 1850, Dudley Field of New York was graduated, and delivered the Philosophical oration. On the same day, at the close of the forenoon exercises, his father, David Dudley Field, LL.D., of the class of 1825, delivered the annual address before the Society of Alumni.

On the same day, the services in the afternoon were closed with prayer by the Rev. David Dudley Field, D. D., of Stockbridge, father of one and grandfather of the other individual just named. Thus three generations participated in the Commencement exercises on the same day.

In 1852 Professor Edward Lasell died, greatly lamented. He was born at Scoharie, N. Y., January 21, 1809, was fitted for college mostly at home, under private instruction, entered Williams College in 1824, and graduated in 1828, when he pronounced the Valedictory oration. He passed one year as a teacher in a high school at Pittsfield, was elected a Tutor in Williams College in 1829, remained in that capacity four years, and was then elected Professor of Chemistry. He was the founder of the Lasell Seminary, at Auburndale. He lives in the grateful recollection of all who knew him. He married Miss Ruth Whitman, a daughter of Dr. Timothy Whitman; and Mrs. Laura Whitman, widow of Dr. Whitman, contributed six hundred dollars annually towards Professor Lasell's salary during his connection with the College. Mrs. Lucy Whitman, widow of John P. Whitman, Esq., gave to the College one thousand dollars in 1842, which is mentioned by Dr. Hopkins in his Jubilee address. These brothers and their wives were among the early and efficient friends of the College.

In 1852 it was voted that the interests of the College demand that an effort be made to raise the sum of fifty thousand dollars, by the donations of the friends of the College. To effect this, Dr. Peters was appointed financial agent.

At the Commencement in 1853, Dr. Hopkins, in behalf of Dr. Stephen West Williams of Deerfield, presented to the College the sword and watch of Colonel Ephraim Williams, its founder. These relics had been carefully preserved in the Williams family. Their acceptance was accompanied by a motion from David Dudley Field, Esq., to erect a monument to the memory of Colonel Williams, on the spot where he fell, near Lake George; also, if possible, to recover his remains, deposit them in a sarcophagus, and erect over them a monument on the College grounds; and Mr. Field, Mr. Canning, and Hon. Asahel Foote were appointed a committee for this purpose.

At the next annual meeting of the Society this committee reported, through Mr. Canning as chairman, that, shortly after their appointment, they (Professor Griffin taking the place of Mr. Field on the committee) repaired to the place of Colonel Williams's last conflict and fall. They found that Judge Rosekrans, the owner of the land where the remains of Williams repose, entered warmly into the object proposed, and very readily deeded to the Trustees of Williams College Williams Rock, and a sufficient quantity of land around it for all the purposes required, with right of way to the public road running a few rods northward. In the course of the winter following, the committee obtained of Messrs. Fitch and Son, of Alford, in this county, a monument, wrought of the gray marble, of Southern Berkshire, a symmetrical obelisk, ten feet and nine inches in height and eighteen inches square at the base, tapering to ten inches, and resting on a plinth two feet square and nine inches in height; making the whole structure, including rock, about twenty feet in elevation. It is inscribed on three sides as follows: —

ON THE EAST SIDE:

"To the memory of Colonel Ephraim Williams, a native of Newton, Mass., who after gallantly defending his native State, served under General Johnson against the French and Indians, and nobly fell near this spot in the bloody conflict of September 8, 1755, in the forty-first year of his age."

ON THE NORTH SIDE:

"A lover of peace and learning, as courteous and generous as he was brave and patriotic, Colonel Williams sympathized deeply with the privations of the frontier settlers, and by his will, made at Albany, on his way to the field of battle, provided for the founding among them of an institution of learning which has since been chartered as a College."

ON THE WEST SIDE:

"Forti ac magnanimo Eph. Williams, Collegii Gulielmensi conditori, qui in hostibus patriæ repellendis, prope hoc saxum cecidit, grati Alumni hoc monumentum posuerunt, A. D. 1854."

The remains of Williams were not obtained. The committee ascertained that, about twenty years before they visited the place, a relative of Colonel Williams, probably a nephew, Dr. William H. Williams, of Raleigh, N. C., had disinterred and carried off the skull. The committee were directed to the place of Colonel Williams's burial by an aged man, who assisted in the exhumation of his remains, or a portion of them. The disturbed grave was reverently filled, and a large pyramidal boulder was placed upon it, and the initials, "E. W. 1755," were carved thereon. The grave is some fifteen or twenty rods southerly from the monument, by the side of the old military road.

"To a personal visitation of these localities the committee invite every son of Williams. It is a charming region, rife with the memories of the most stirring scenes in our country's history. They cluster about every crag and mountain, in every valley, and around the mouldering walls of the many fortresses, and above the placid mirror of the Horicon. The names of Howe, Abercrombie, Amherst, Johnson, Putnam, Stark, Rogers, Williams, and a host besides, are not forgotten amid the scenes where they recorded their fame. The committee doubt not they utter the feelings of every Alumnus, in expressing their great satisfaction, that, after a lapse of almost a century of neglect, we may now point to an honorable memorial of the founder of our Alma Mater on the field of his last battle, and no longer with a blush exclaim, —

'How sleep the brave, who sink to rest
With all their country's wishes blest!'"

The deeded land on which the monument stands was subsequently enclosed by a substantial iron fence, at the expense of the Alumni of the College.

In the fall of 1853, Dr. Alden resigned the Professorship of Rhetoric and Moral Philosophy, to accept the Professorship of Intellectual Philosophy in Lafayette College, Pennsylvania.

The Rev. I. N. Lincoln was elected Professor of the Latin and French Languages.

In 1853 Mr. Paul A. Chadbourne, A. M., was elected Professor of Chemistry and Botany, as successor to Professor Lasell, deceased.

In 1854 Mr. Addison Ballard, A. M., was elected Professor of Rhetoric. At the same time it was voted to establish a Professorship of History, Political Economy, and the German Language; and Mr. Arthur L. Perry was elected to fill the professorship. Since that time there have been no tutors in this College.

In 1855 Professor Ballard resigned the chair of Rhetoric, and Mr. John Bascom, A. M., was appointed his successor.

The time of holding Commencement was this year changed from the third to the first Wednesday in August. The Rev. Dr. Peters resigned the office of financial agent, and the Rev. Calvin Durfee was appointed his successor. The thanks of the Trustees were voted to Mr. James Orton, of the Senior class, for his aid in the procurement of the means, and for his services in the erection of Jackson Hall.

The thanks of the Trustees were likewise voted to Nathan Jackson, Esq., of New York, for his generous and munificent donation of three thou-

Nathan Jackson

sand five hundred dollars for the use of the Natural History Society, connected with this College.

Mr. Jackson was a native of Berkshire County, and was born in Tyringham, now Monterey, March 16, 1780, and was the fourteenth child of his parents. His father, Colonel Giles Jackson, was born at Weston, February 22, 1733, and came to Tyringham when he was sixteen years old, and afterwards became a leading citizen of the place. He was a magistrate twenty years, and a representative in the General Court fourteen years. He was a member of the first Congress, which met at Stockbridge, in 1774; and afterwards a member of the State Congress, which met at Watertown. He was a commissioned officer in the army of the Revolution, and drew up the articles of capitulation at the surrender of Burgoyne. His grandfather, John Jackson, came from Weston to Tyringham in 1749, and was one of the first settlers of that town, and was the first deacon of the Congregational Church in that place. The mother of Nathan Jackson (once Miss Anna Thomas, of Farmington, Conn.) died in July, 1780, when he was four months old. When he was seven years old his sister, who had had the principal care of him, was married to Mr. David Manning, afterwards Major Manning, of Stockbridge; and he went to reside with her, where he remained about six years. Near the commencement of 1793, he went with a former acquaintance of his father to Poultney, Vermont, where he remained two years. In 1796 he returned to his father's house in Tyringham, where he remained three years. His father's family at this time was very numerous. His mother at her death left eight sons and six daughters. His father, for his second wife, married Mrs. Sarah Orton, widow of Thomas Orton, Esq., who had six children,—four sons and two daughters. By this last marriage six children more were added to the family, making twenty-six in all. At one time over twenty children were living together in the family, and seventeen of them attended the district school.

In 1799, when Nathan was nineteen years old, he left his father's house and went to Boston, intending to go to sea. But the Captain to whom he and another young man applied for employment, utterly refused to employ "two such 'greenhorns.'" Here he remained four years. In 1803, leaving Boston, he went to New London, Conn., where he remained seven years. In 1810, he took up his permanent residence in New York.

When an individual in subsequent life becomes in any way distinguished in the walks of usefulness, we naturally inquire if there was anything peculiar in his childhood. Now, if our limits would allow, we could relate some anecdotes respecting young Jackson, showing what he was, and foreshadowing what he was to become. But we forbear.

The question has often been asked,—"*What first gave Mr. Jackson such an interest in Williams College?*" There are two general reasons. One is, he first opened his eyes on the green hills and fertile vales of Berkshire; and, with his strong local attachments, would naturally cherish a deep interest in the favored institutions of his native county. Another is, the mother of Williams, the founder of the College, was a daughter of Abraham Jackson of Newton. She died when he was three years old, leaving him and a younger son, Thomas (afterwards Dr. Thomas Williams, of Deerfield), to the care of their grandfather Jackson, "who gave them a good education for the times; and it is quite apparent," says a historian, "that the first sprouts of Williams College were germinated in the family of Abraham Jackson." And it is fitting in itself, and interesting to remember, that a lineal descendant of Abraham Jackson, and consequently a near relative of Ephraim Williams, has now personally associated the Jackson name with an institution founded by one of the Williams family.

Another question has often been asked: "*How did Mr. Jackson acquire the means of aiding Williams College so liberally?*" He commenced the acquisition of property in early life, and has been, in the common acceptation of the term, a fortunate man. In the summer of 1792, while residing in Stockbridge, Barnabas Bidwell, a son of the first clergyman in Tyringham, was a law student in that place. He kept a horse; and he told young Jackson if he would catch his horse for him, and turn him out, he might have it to ride home to keep Thanksgiving. He readily accepted the offer, and fulfilled his part of the contract. The day before Thanksgiving, as he was mounted on his horse ready to start for home, Mr. Bidwell said, "Nathan, have you any pocket-money?" "Yes, Sir, I have three ninepenny pieces." Mr. Bidwell then handed him a silver dollar. This was the first dollar he ever had. And what did he do with it? He did not spend it to see shows, nor for rum, nor brandy, nor cigars, nor tobacco. But he bought a sheep with it, and put out that sheep to double once in four years, and kept on letting out his sheep for forty years. In 1832 his flock amounted to one thousand and sixty-four sheep; and he then sold them for fifteen hundred and ninety-six dollars. He knew where he could invest this money to good advantage. Up-town lots in New York had recently been surveyed, and were now for sale at a very low price. He ascertained that a large number of them were to be sold at auction. He attended the sale, and purchased ten lots for two hundred and fifty dollars each. These lots he sold in two years for twelve thousand dollars. Thus, JACKSON HALL, which he erected at Williams College for the use of the Natural History Society, and which, with its fixtures, has cost him near five thousand dollars, has taken only about one half of his Bidwell dollar.

It is always interesting to trace the developments of Divine Providence. Near the beginning of the year 1855, Mr. James Orton, then a member of the

Senior class, prepared a circular, setting forth in strong terms the condition and wants of the Natural History Society connected with the College; and stating that twenty-five hundred dollars were urgently needed to erect a suitable building for the accommodation of the Society; and that whoever would subscribe one thousand might give his name to the edifice. During the next spring vacation, while in New York, at Mr. Jackson's, he showed him the circular. Mr. Jackson made particular inquiries respecting the wants and prospects of the College, and offered to correspond with him on the subject of the projected edifice. On the 17th of May, 1855, the first letter which he wrote touching this matter was addressed to the President and Trustees of the College, and contained the cheering declaration that he would give the whole amount named in the circular. He says: "After mature deliberation, I have concluded to say, that you may consider funds to the extent of twenty-five hundred dollars to be provided by me, for the purpose named in your circular; and you may look to me for that amount whenever it is required.

"There are many inducements which have led me to this conclusion, among some of which are the following. The founder of Williams College — Colonel Ephraim Williams — was the son of a sister of my grandfather, thus throwing around the institution the influence of family association. And the interest growing out of the fact that I am a native of that section of the State in which the institution is situated, descended from one of the oldest and first families there, whose history has been identified with the history of that part of the State since its first settlement; and I would erect a monument that would cause it to live after, perhaps, all those who bear the name shall have passed away.

"And the last, though not the least, is, that I esteem it a privilege, as well as a duty, to devote a portion of the means wherewith a beneficent Providence has blessed me, to the encouragement and promotion of science, in connection with an institution under sound moral and religious influence, as I believe Williams College to be, under the profound conviction that knowledge obtained and accompanied by such influence is to be the future safeguard of our free institutions."

When the building was finished, Mr. Jackson inquired what had been the whole cost of it. He was told, thirty-five hundred dollars; and he immediately sent the College Treasurer a check for one thousand more than he originally promised, "because he could not consent to have others at any expense for a building which bears his name!"

In January, 1858, Mr. Jackson wrote to the agent of the College to ascertain its chartered rights, and to know if the house and land situated between Mission Park and the West College could be purchased for a reasonable price. On the 16th day of March following, — the day that he was seventy-eight years old, — he gave the College the house and land just named, which cost him six thousand dollars, and fourteen thousand dollars besides, "for the purpose of establishing a Professorship of Christian Theology in the College, which is always to be under the control of the President and Trustees, in the same manner and to the same extent as the other professors; and whose duties shall be the teaching of Christian theology, and such other branches of knowledge, in harmony therewith, as the President and Trustees may from time to time prescribe." This was the consummation or accomplishment of a general purpose to do something more for the College, which Mr. Jackson had long entertained.

The grateful manner in which this liberal benefaction was received was expressed by the following appropriate letter of the President, addressed to Mr. Jackson, which we take the liberty to transcribe as a part of the history of the transaction.

"WILLIAMSTOWN, March 18, 1858.

"MY DEAR SIR:—

"I have this morning received through —— a draft from you for six thousand dollars, to pay for the Whitman place, and a deed of the place, to the President and Trustees of Williams College; also a conveyance to the College of fourteen thousand dollars to found the JACKSON PROFESSORSHIP OF THEOLOGY. This is a great, liberal, and most important donation. In my own name — and I am sure I may add in the name of the Trustees, of the Alumni, and all the friends of a collegiate training — I thank you most sincerely. I am pleased with it in every point of view. The conditions are liberal, and I think wise; such as must bring great good to the College, as well as give relief and comfort to the hearts of many friends in other lands, who have left all for Christ. I am pleased that such a thing has been done by a son of BERKSHIRE. It is a credit to the county, and will do its people good. It is fitting, too, as coming from one related as you are to the founder of the College, — and I am happy that your name is to be associated, as it will be, with his.

"And then how remarkable that such a thing should have been done on your seventy-eighth birthday! It is one of those pleasing coincidences, that we can hardly consider accidental. How few live to such an age. Of those how few have the means to do such an act; and of those who have, how very few have the will. While we have cause for gratitude to the Great Disposer of all that you have thus remembered the College, I think you have even greater cause for being enabled and permitted to do an act that has such promise of being a blessing in all time to come.

"The Festival went off finely; we only needed to have you there. You will rejoice to know that there is a deep religious interest in the College, and we hope quite a number of conversions.

"And now, my dear sir, that the promise, 'He that watereth shall be watered himself,' may be fulfilled to you in those spiritual mercies without which all are poor, is the prayer of yours,

"Truly and gratefully,

"MARK HOPKINS.

"NATHAN JACKSON, ESQ."

Mr. Jackson has made many smaller donations to the College, and to those who are connected with it, which are pleasantly remembered, and deserve a grateful acknowledgment.

When Mr. Jackson first came to New York, he attended for a few years on the ministrations of the celebrated Dr. John M. Mason; and for a time was connected with the congregation to which the Rev. Dr. Spring ministers. In 1835 he moved up town, and became connected with the Collegiate Dutch Church. This was a most important period in his history. Now he was led, as he trusts, by the Holy Spirit, to a sense of his lost condition as a sinner, and a cordial surrender of his heart to the claims of the Saviour. At this time it was that himself, wife, and eldest daughter, the late Mrs. De Motte, made a public profession of their faith in Christ on the same day.

In personal appearance, Mr. Jackson is above the middling stature, well-proportioned, and with a countenance uncommonly benignant and pleasant. His portrait in JACKSON HALL does not do him justice. His liberal benefactions to the College, especially his recent establishment of a Professorship of Christian Theology, entitle him to the gratitude, and will embalm his memory in the unfading recollections of all its Alumni and friends. His very name has now become so interwoven with the institution, that it will hereafter stand high on the list of its benefactors, and will go down to the latest posterity by the side of WILLIAMS and LAWRENCE.

The Lyceum of Natural History was founded in 1835, on the ruins of the "Linnæan Society." It was originally a secret society, called the Phi Beta Theta (Phusis Biblos Theou, Nature, the book of God); but dropped its veil in about a year, and assumed its present title. The object of the Society is "the study of the natural sciences, and the prosecution of antiquarian researches." They formerly had a room in South College, where they met once in two weeks, and listened to reports from committees on the various branches of natural history. The room was well stored with specimens, although many were lost in the fire. They had, and still have, a very valuable library.

In addition to the expeditions made by the Society of Natural History, others have been undertaken from time to time upon a smaller scale, commonly accompanied by some one of the Professors.

In February, 1857, the Society of Natural History, wishing to fill the empty cases in Jackson Hall, resolved on chartering a small vessel, which should convey an exploring party to Florida. Aided by the liberality of Mr. Jackson, and other friends of the Lyceum, the requisite expenses were provided for, and Professor Chadbourne, at considerable expense and personal inconvenience, consented to assume the guidance of the expedition. The party was composed of the following individuals: H. C. Allen, Lyman Beecher, G. W. Carlton, W. D. Day, J. E. Darby, S. E. Elmore, W. S. Gilman, C. J. Lyons, Archibald Hopkins, S. H. Scudder, J. M. Nichols, N. B. Sherwin, E. P. Willard, R. H. Ward, E. M. Wight, H. M. Lyman. Not members of the Society, Dr. Kerr of Franklin, N. Y., Mr. John Blackinton, D. C. Eaton of Yale College, and J. V. Lauderdale of Geneseo, N. Y. The expedition was in a high degree successful.

As the year 1855 completed a century, from the founding of the College by Williams, it was voted the year previous to have an oration and poem this year, commemorative of the life and character of Colonel Williams. The oration was delivered by the Hon. Joseph White, and the poem by E. W. B. Canning. As an abstract of the oration is inserted in the first part of this volume, we here insert some extracts from the poem: —

"See Williams' children, from their various homes,
By various fortune scattered, rallying come,
To take again their foster-mother's hand,
As when in days 'lang syne' she led their feet
Up Learning's mazy paths; her blessing laid
Upon their laurelled brows, and said farewell.
Fratres Alumni! ye are not the men
Whose names ye bore when college days were young;
I see the silvered lock, the look of care,
And labor's furrows on your manly brows;
And yet, methinks, the comely grace of youth
Hath comelier aspect now, that ye have met
The shock of life's great battle, and have proved
Your stalwart arms, and the tried steel they bear.
The stripling soldier then — the veteran now —
Mayhap with armor dinted, but with hearts
Strong for the conflict ye must finish yet.
Ye 've seen, in fields of honorable toil,
Full many a comrade fallen, and your van
In shattered columns stands; but there is still
A baptism for the dead, — ye 're not alone.
Along their honored path, and up to heaven,
Like pilgrims pass the venerable men
Who watched our wayward youth: wisely they build,
In life, their monuments of living hearts,
And multiply themselves in those to come.
Fathers,* we greet you! Here our *Lares* are, —
Our *penetralia;* here the altar-fire
Of love burns ever brightly, and we lay
Fresh incense on it now. And, honored sire, †

* The Trustees. † The President.

Whose is its sacred ministry, accept
The prayer engraven on our heart of hearts
For thee, — 'Ad cœlum serus redeas,' —
And, like the Prophet, leave thy mantle here!

. . . . .

Brethren Alumni! pleasant hours
Were those we spent in Learning's bowers;
And pleasant now, though older men,
To tell the tales of youth again.
As on we tread the path of years,
Farther the vista'd Past appears;
But there are spots in Memory's dream
Whose green and beauty never dim.
Such we recall with joy to-day,
And as we erst were taught to say, —
'Est bonum amavisse,'
Let Mantua's bard still ride our wreck
Of Latin, — 'forsan olim hæc
'Juvabit meminisse.'
Dear Alma Mater, long as stand,
Like pillars of our native land,
These everlasting hills,
Thy grateful children shall proclaim
In every clime thy growing fame,
And deathless glory yield the name
Of Williams and of Mills."

A letter from Dr. Abner Phelps, of Boston, who was graduated at Williams College in 1806, may without impropriety be here introduced.

"BOSTON, July 9, 1856.

"DEAR SIR: —

"In reply to your inquiries respecting the Rev. S. J. Mills, and his efforts in the missionary cause, I very cheerfully state that I became intimately acquainted with him during my residence in College [I graduated in September, 1806]. I perfectly recollect conversing with him on the deplorable condition of Africa, and the slaves in this country, at different times; and once on a warm evening we sat down in the East College yard, when he told me his plans of future operation, and what he intended to undertake. His thoughts were new to me, and were uttered with so much self-devotion and piety that they made such a lasting impression on my mind, that I doubt whether I have ever since seen his name in print, or heard it spoken, without calling to mind his conversation with me that warm evening.*

"Respectfully yours,

"ABNER PHELPS."

---

* "P. S. While I was at Williams College in 1806, I met with a small book, describing a railway in Wales, one and a half mile long; made to carry slate from the quarry down to the landing; in which it was stated that one horse could take down as many as eight horses could in the common road, and bring the empty wagons back. The moment I read that, I said, 'If one horse can do that for a mile and a half, why not for a hundred miles? and if he can do it one way, why not the other way? and why not make it a road for general travel? No such work existed at that time on the globe. But this thought, simple and natural as I should think to every one, has cost me more than a thousand dollars cash, and four or five years' labor of all the time I could spare from my profession, and for which I never received anything but compliments as 'the first projector of railroads.' For more than twenty years I tried to induce some member of our Legislature to propose the construction of a railroad from Boston to Albany, without success, till in 1826, when I brought the subject forward myself, as a member of that body from this city.

"On the twenty-eighth page of the fourth Number, Vol. I., of the Christian Library Report (which I send), you will see it stated (by whom I know not), that 'Dr. Abner Phelps made the first proposition for the opening of a railroad from Boston to the Hudson River,' whereas I had made the proposition twenty years before. True, the measure was first proposed in our Legislature in 1826."

We add a word of explanation. In 1808, Colonel Phelps of Belchertown was a prominent member of the Legislature of Massachusetts. He wrote a letter to his son, saying that the subject of constructing a canal from Boston to Albany had been mooted in the Legislature. The son, now Dr. Abner Phelps, wrote a letter back, urging that a railroad, instead of a canal, should be constructed. That letter is now in existence.

For more than thirty years the precise spot where the haystack stood, under which the first proposal was made to send out foreign missions from this country, was known by no one in Williamstown. Inquiry was often made by strangers, and a desire expressed that it might be designated in some appropriate way; but the hope of being able to do this had been nearly abandoned. As illustrating the general state of feeling, the following extract from a letter, by an entire stranger, then and afterwards, to all connected with the College, may be given: * —

"In making inquiries, this afternoon, on my first visit to Williamstown, in relation to the spot where the *haystack* stood, so famous in the history of missions as the one behind which Mills and his associates prayed for the Divine guidance and blessing while maturing their plans for preaching the Gospel of the kingdom to the heathen world, — plans which were carried out so successfully, — I regretted to learn that the place was unmarked by tree, shrub, stone, or monument of any kind.

"Having learned that there had been among some ladies — who are, the world over, always ready to every good work — some desire manifested to mark the sacred place before it was entirely forgotten, with some memorial, will you please take charge of the enclosed dollar (a gold one), and apply it in any way you may deem best suited to effect the object. It is little, but rain-drops make the shower. If it does no more than purchase a cedar stake to mark the spot, it will not be in vain; for long ere that will have time to moulder, wealthy ones will have marked with marble the place where American missions had their birth, and from whence went forth those who were chosen of God to commence the work of making every heathen heart bow at the blessed name of Jesus."

* It was dated South Williamstown, April 26, 1852.

This dollar remained as buried seed for more than two years, in the care of Professor Hopkins, and might have continued so; but in the spring of 1854, Hon. Byram Green of Sodus, N. Y., visited Williamstown, and it was ascertained that he was present at the prayer-meeting under the haystack, and could identify the spot. This he did, sticking a stake with his own hand. The circumstances attending the meeting were then stated, and are contained in the following communication which he afterwards furnished: —

"You request a statement of the facts in relation to the prayer-meeting which was held under the haystack, by some students of Williams College, in July or August, 1806. That prayer-meeting becomes interesting to the Christian community, because it was then and there first proposed to send the Gospel to the pagans of Asia, and to the disciples of Mohammed. The stack of hay stood northerly from the West College, near a maple grove, in a field that was then called Sloan's meadow.

"Samuel J. Mills, James Richards, Francis L. Robbins, Harvey Loomis, and Byram Green were present. The afternoon was oppressively warm, which probably detained all those from the East College that usually attended, and some from the West. We first went to the grove, expecting to hold our prayer-meeting there, but a dark cloud was rising in the west, and it soon began to thunder and lighten, and we left the grove and went under the haystack to protect us from the approaching storm, which was soon realized.

"The subject of conversation under the stack, before and during the shower, was the moral darkness of Asia. Mills proposed to send the Gospel to that dark and heathen land; and said that we could do it if we would. We were all agreed and delighted with the idea, except Loomis, who contended that it was premature; that if missionaries should be sent to Asia they would be murdered; that Christian armies must subdue the country before the Gospel could be sent to the Turks and Arabs. In reply, it was said, that God was always willing to have his Gospel spread throughout the world; that if the Christian public was willing and active, the work would be done; that on this subject the Roman adage would be true, 'Vox populi, vox Dei.' 'Come,' said Mills, 'let us make it a subject of prayer, under this haystack, while the dark clouds are going, and the clear sky is coming.'

"We all prayed, and made Foreign Missions a subject in our prayers, except Loomis. Mills made the last prayer, and was in some degree enthusiastic; he prayed that God would strike down the arm, with the red artillery of heaven, that should be raised against a herald of the cross. We then sang one stanza, as follows:—

'Let all the heathen writers join
To form one perfect book:
Great God, if once compared with thine,
How mean their writings look!'

"The prayer-meetings were continued during the warm season of that year, in the groves somewhere between the village and the Hoosac, and the subject of Foreign Missions was remembered in our prayers. The following is a list of names that usually attended, to wit: John Nelson, Calvin Bushnell, Byram Green, Rufus Pomeroy, Francis L. Robbins, Samuel Ware, Edwin W. Dwight, Ezra Fisk, Harvey Loomis, Samuel J. Mills, and James Richards. Others attended occasionally.

"The next summer, 1807, the prayer-meetings were again held in the grove; two were added to our number, to wit, Luther Rice and John Whittlesey. I have several times seen the names of Hall and Rice numbered among those who were at the prayer-meeting under the haystack. That is an error. Rice was not a member of College until October, 1806. Hall was not a professor of religion at that time, and did not attend our religious meetings. He was made a subject of grace in the year 1808, about six or eight months before he graduated. After that he was active in the cause. . . . . .

"Nothing can be more certain and direct than the connection between this prayer-meeting and the subsequent movements in this country respecting Foreign Missions. They continued to be the subject of prayer, of conversation, and discussion, until, two years after, the first Foreign Missionary Society in this country was formed in this College, — a society for the purpose, not of sending others, but of GOING to the heathen.

"This society, with a modified constitution, has been continued here from that time. A similar society, still flourishing, was founded by Mills, and those who went with him, at Andover; and from that the proposition was made to the General Association of Massachusetts, which resulted in the formation of the American Board."

At a meeting of the Society of Alumni of the College in August, 1854, the following resolution was passed: "That the grounds north of the West College, where Mills and his associates used to meet for prayer, and where the first American missions were projected, be purchased by the Alumni of the College, and be called the Mission Park or Grounds." A committee was chosen to effect the purchase, to receive subscriptions for that purpose from the Alumni and others, and to lay out the grounds.

When the report of these proceedings appeared in the papers, John Tappan, Esq., of Boston, expressed his apprehension that the land would not be obtained unless some one should assume the whole responsibility of the purchase. Accordingly he wrote to Dr. Hopkins, requesting him to buy the land, and look to him for the funds to pay for it, in case the Alumni should fail to do it. Thus encouraged, the land was secured, and the deed was given. Funds, however, came in slowly.

At the Commencement in 1855, it was ascertained that only a small portion of the funds needed had been obtained. A proposition was then submitted to the Alumni by the Rev. J. E. Woodbridge, that the classes in lustrums, or divisions of fours, engage to contribute two hundred and fifty dollars each; and in a short time an amount more than sufficient to pay for the land was pledged. As there was some delay in making the last payments, Mr. Tappan readily paid the price of one acre of the land — two hundred and fifty dollars — in addition to what he had previously given.

At the same meeting it was voted that, "inasmuch as the year 1856 will complete half a century since the first personal consecrations to the work of effecting missions among the heathen took place on this spot, it appears proper that there should be a general Missionary Jubilee in this Park on the day preceding the next annual Commencement." A committee, consisting of David Dudley Field, Martin I. Townsend, George N. Briggs, Albert Hopkins, and Henry L. Sabin, was appointed to make the necessary arrangements. Professor Hopkins was chosen to deliver the address.

In accordance with this resolution, a Missionary Jubilee was held in Williamstown, August 5, 1856. "Preparations had been made for the exercises in the Park, where seats were arranged in the grove, a bungalow for missionaries, and a haystack were prepared; but a severe and almost unprecedented storm, forcibly reminding us of the storm that drove Mills and his associates to the haystack, rendered it necessary to take shelter in the church, where the exercises were held." *

Hon. David Dudley Field presided, and made the introductory address. The stanza, sung at the close of the prayer-meeting under the haystack, was then sung to the tune of St. Martin's, all the congregation joining, "Let all the heathen writers join." The Rev. Isaac Ferris, D. D., Chancellor of the University of New York, then read the 67th Psalm. The Rev. Timothy Woodbridge, D. D., of Spencertown, N. Y., the chaplain of the day, offered prayer. All then joined in singing the hymn, "Saw ye not the cloud arise?" The address was then delivered by Professor Albert Hopkins. Taking the haystack for his theme, he spoke, first, of the times of the haystack; secondly, of the men of the haystack; thirdly, of the relation of those times and men to the problem of the age; and, fourthly, of the position in which we stand, and our duties with reference to the same problem. The address occupied about an hour and a half in the delivery, and was well received. The hymn, to the tune of Lenox, was then sung, "Blow ye the trumpet, blow."

---

* See the pamphlet which contains a full account of the proceedings on that memorable occasion.

A recess was then taken, of fifteen minutes. Very few left the house. The afternoon exercises were inaugurated with singing, to the tune of Coronation, "All hail the power of Jesus' name." After which Dr. Chester Dewey of Rochester, N. Y., led in prayer.

The chairman remarked, that the speakers who had been invited to address the audience were representative men. The meeting was then addressed by President Hopkins, the Rev. Rufus Anderson, D. D., Senior Secretary of the American Board, Hon. George N. Briggs, LL. D., of Pittsfield, President of the American Baptist Missionary Union, the Rev. I. N. Wyckoff, D. D., Albany, of the Dutch Church, the Rev. Stephen H. Tyng, D. D., New York, of the Episcopal Church, the Hon. Emory Washburn, LL. D., of Worcester, the Rev. Elias Riggs, D. D., of Constantinople, the Rev. Myron Winslow from Ceylon, the Rev. Gordon Hall of Northampton, and some others, mostly returned missionaries, made short and appropriate speeches. At four o'clock in the afternoon, the audience having been in session six hours (and many would gladly have continued longer), all joined in singing, to the tune of Old Hundred, the 72d Psalm, "Jesus shall reign where'er the sun." The Rev. Samuel H. Cox, D. D., pronounced the benediction.

The address of Dr. Anderson contains so many interesting reminiscences that we have concluded to insert a portion of it.

"Less than a year ago, it was my privilege to stand on the site of Antioch, where the first foreign missionaries received their special designation from the Holy Ghost. This historical association was to me the principal charm of that beautiful and interesting spot. Next to Jerusalem and the Sea of Galilee, I have most pleasure in the recollection of Antioch. But where am I now? The mountains yonder are not ranges of Lebanon, nor is yonder stream the Orontes. We are met in the New World. The historical events we commemorate occurred within the memory of some of us. Nevertheless they are important, and have, and will have, a place on the historic page. And they make this, rather than any and all other places, the *Antioch* of our Western hemisphere.

"We may not claim, that the *foreign missionary spirit* in our American churches had its first development here. The proof is ample that it had not. But, so far as my own researches have gone, the first *personal consecrations* to the work of effecting missions among foreign heathen nations were here. Here the Holy Ghost made the first visible separations of men in this country for the foreign work whereto he had called them. The first observable rill of the stream of American missionaries, which has gone on swelling until now, issued just on this spot; and I am thankful the spot has been so well identified, and is so convenient of access, and withal so beautiful; and that it has now been secured and consecrated as a permanent memorial.

"The development and result of this movement meet our reasonable wishes. Samuel J. Mills rests near the shores of Africa. The grave of James Richards I saw in Ceylon. Gordon Hall sleeps among the Mahrattas of Western India. Hall died young; but a life of rare and consistent devotedness, illustrated by noble exhibitions of talent, give him a place in the highest rank of missionaries.

"The AMERICAN BOARD OF COMMISSIONERS FOR FOREIGN MISSIONS had its origin in the desire and request of young men of the Andover Seminary, including those just named, to be sent abroad as missionaries. These two things stand in the immediate relation of cause and effect. I am also persuaded, that the forming of the '*Society of* BRETHREN' here in this College, in September, 1808, — before even the *conversion* of Dr. Judson, — and its removal to the Andover Seminary early in 1810, or sooner, had much to do, by its weekly conferences and prayers, in maturing the plans of its members. Its leading object, indeed, as we are assured, 'was so to operate on the public mind as to lead to the formation of a missionary society.' And its members corresponded on this subject with the men, who actually became the founders of the American Board."

At the Commencement in August, 1856, the Trustees voted that the agent of the College may solicit donations, on the ground that a new building is one of the wants of the College. A subscription was at once opened, and donations solicited with reference to a new chapel and Alumni Hall. Twelve thousand dollars were secured in one year, and these buildings were soon after commenced. Five thousand dollars were subscribed on the morning of Commencement day, in 1857. Towards this enterprise David Dudley Field subscribed eleven hundred dollars, and Mr. Jackson one thousand.

February 24, 1857, at the suggestion of Mr. Jackson, who furnished the entertainment, the anniversary of Colonel Williams's birth was celebrated at the Mansion House by the Faculty and students of the College, and other invited guests.

In 1857 the Rev. Professor Griffin resigned the Professorship of the Greek Language and Literature. The following vote was passed by the Trustees: "That this Board have received with sincere regret the resignation of Rev. N. H. Griffin, and that, in parting with him after a service of eleven years, we bear our cordial testimony to the marked faithfulness and ability which have characterized his labors as an officer and instructor in this institution, and express to him our heart-felt desires for his continued usefulness and success in whatever sphere of labor he may be called to engage."

Mr. John L. T. Phillips, A. M., was elected Professor of the Greek Language and Literature.

Voted, that the examination of the Senior class hereafter commence on Tuesday of the sixth week previous to the Commencement; and the Senior appointments be made as soon as may be after the close of the examination. The appointments had previously been given out at the close of the spring term.

In August, 1858, Professor Chadburn resigned the Professorship of Chemistry, and Mr. Thomas Edwards Clark of New York was appointed his successor in that department.

Hon. Daniel N. Dewey died at his residence in Williamstown, January 14, 1859. He was born in Williamstown, April 4, 1800. He completed his college course at Yale College in 1820. His legal studies were pursued in the office of the Hon. Elisha H. Mills of Northampton. Soon after he was admitted to the practice of his profession he became a permanent resident in his native town. He was a representative to the General Court, a member of the Executive Council, and was a Judge of Probate from 1848 until the time of his decease. He held the responsible post of Treasurer and Secretary of Williams College for twenty-nine years, managing its financial affairs with care and economy. He was a man of unbending integrity and uprightness. Though a lawyer by profession, he very much discouraged litigation. Judge Dewey was a religious man, deeply interested in the welfare of the Church, of which he became a member in 1838, and was liberal in his contributions for the support of the institutions of religion at home and abroad.

At a special meeting of the Board of Trustees in April, 1859, the Hon. Joseph White was elected

Treasurer of the College. Mr. White was a native of Charlemont, was graduated at Williams College in 1836; had been a Tutor in College two years, and for eleven years a Trustee, and during most of that time had been Auditor of the Treasurer's accounts. This appointment was in accordance with the general expectation and wishes of the friends of the College.

The Society of Alumni, according to adjournment, met in their new hall, at half past nine o'clock, A. M., Tuesday, August 2, 1859. Hon. Abraham Olin, M. C., of Troy, in the chair. Mr. Olin called on the venerable Dr. Field of Stockbridge to open the meeting with prayer. Hon. H. H. Childs was elected President and Hon. James D. Colt, Vice-President. Professor Griffin then read the list of Alumni who had died during the past year, —*fourteen.*

The President then proceeded to call on the gentlemen who had been invited to speak in honor of the occupation of the new hall.

The first speaker was the President of the College, who now extended a most hearty welcome to the Society of Alumni to their new and commodious hall.

The next speaker was the Hon. James D. Colt of Pittsfield, who could make "no apology for asking a few moments' consideration of the influence which this College has had upon the growth and development of this good old County of Berkshire."

William Pitt Palmer, Esq. of New York, who

has won so many poetic laurels for himself and his Alma Mater, then read a spirited and witty poem, which needed no apology.

Hon. Stephen J. Field of California not being present, as expected, his brother, the Rev. Henry M. Field of New York, was called out, and his wit and pathos were duly appreciated.

Samuel B. Sumner, Esq., of Great Barrington, added to his growing reputation as a true poet, by a glowing tribute to his Alma Mater, and to the memory of Colonel Williams.

The President, Dr. Childs, here called for volunteer speeches, when the writer came forward, and spoke of the portraits on the wall; all but one he had obtained. Pointing to the remotest one, without mentioning the name of the original, he charged his own son, and Archibald Hopkins, and Edward H. Griffin, and those of their age, to keep bright the memory of the original of that portrait, as they should meet in this hall in future years. He then announced a donation to the College of ten thousand dollars, from Dr. Philip Van Ness Morris of Cambridge, N. Y. Dr. Morris was then conducted to the platform, and introduced to the President amid cheers sufficiently loud and hearty for any assembly. Dr. Morris declined speaking.

Hon. David Dudley Field then arose and proposed a vote of thanks to Dr. Morris, for this, the largest donation ever made to the College by one of its graduates. The vote was passed with acclamation, which it seemed impossible to exhaust.

Governor Washburn was then called on for the closing address. He gave a rapid and glowing sketch of the history of the College, and closed by an eloquent allusion to the death of some of the patrons and friends of the institution. "We are falling," said the speaker, "like the leaves of the forest, leaf by leaf, each to its own resting-place, while our Alma Mater stands like the trees of the same forest, renewing and enlarging her life year by year, in perennial verdure and strength."

At half past one o'clock the Alumni dined together at the Mansion House. The blessing was invoked by the Rev. J. E. Woodbridge, the chaplain of the day. When the physical man had been feasted the intellectual repast was resumed, and the following toasts were given: —

"*Our Alma Mater*, — Her jewels are her children, and her children are men."

Hon. David Dudley Field of New York responded.

"*The Memory of Colonel Williams*, — His blood was the ink wherewith the charter of Alma Mater was written."

Hon. Joseph White, the new Treasurer, spoke to this sentiment, recalling some of the leading incidents in the life of the founder of the College.

"*The Old Commonwealth*, — She has at last remembered her neglected child."

Governor Briggs was called to respond, and did so with an eloquent tribute to old Massachusetts, as the liberal patron of learning, and of all benevolent institutions.

"*The departed Alumni of Williams*, — Forever green be their graves in our memories."

Responded to with deep feeling by Judge Bishop of Lenox. He alluded, particularly, to the late Judge Walker of Lenox, who, full of years and honors, had been called home during the past year, sketching the perfections of his character, and paying a tribute to the integrity of his administration of the office of Judge of Probate during the long generation that he held it.

At three o'clock the Alumni marched to the Congregrational church, where prayer was offered by the chaplain, and the annual oration was delivered by Hon. M. I. Townsend of Troy, which was an able advocacy of the duty of labor, and a poem by the Rev. Amos D. Wheeler of Topsham, Maine.

Thus closed the exercises of one of the most interesting and memorable days ever witnessed by the Alumni of Williams College.

The following letter, bearing date July 30, 1859, may, without impropriety, be here introduced.

"DEAR SIR: —

"You know that for several years I have kept by me an instrument, by which a portion of the pecuniary means, which God has given to me, would, when I had done with them, be carried to certain benevolent societies, to the support of which it has been my privilege to contribute for many years past.

"You first suggested, what I have adopted as a better way, to embody these in one sum, add to them somewhat, and bestow the whole upon Williams College for the purpose of founding a professorship in that institution."

After describing the manner of paying the ten thousand dollars pledged, he adds: "While I hope by this procedure to prolong the memory of the name I bear, I wish it might, like a monument, record still more prominently that of an ancestor (Thomas Morris), who, in 1639, signed the plantation covenant of New Haven, and those of his descendants, particularly a grandfather (Amos Morris), who, for his ardent patriotism, was, in our Revolutionary struggle, taken from his bed to the prison-ship, and was released because he was an unarmed citizen; who gave to his son (Amos Morris) the ancestral acres still occupied by his posterity, each of whom has held in succession, in an evangelical church, the office he did, to the fourth generation." All deacons.

"Not less dear to memory, nor less worthy of record, are the virtues and excellences of a maternal grandfather, whose name was given to me, whose old Dutch Bible gives evidence, in the note on its margin, in his own hand, of the interest he had in the sacred volume; who, with his neighbors, at an early day erected a house for the worship of God, where for years it was maintained in the Dutch language. In that house I have stood in a row of children and recited the catechism; and from that spot came the influences which, in later years, brought about the decision to 'seek first the kingdom of God and his righteousness.'

"Still dearer is the memory of a father, who chose for himself to become an Alumnus of Yale College, and labor in a profession, rather than share in an inheritance of land; and whose children had given to them, first and foremost of all, the means of education; and the mother, who sent me to college wearing fine linen and clothing of her own make.

"If it be permitted to add to these the names of my roommate, Charles Jenkins, of cherished memory, of the sainted Larned and the living Bryant, all members of the same class (1813), then will all the expectations which could spring from this step be satisfied and fulfilled.

"PHILIP VAN NESS MORRIS.

"REV. CALVIN DURFEE."

Dr. Morris has an extensive practice as a physician, and a farm of three hundred and twenty acres, beautifully located, and under a high state of cultivation. He has no family.

In Professor Hopkins's narrative of the revival of religion which occurred in 1812, he mentions, in particular, the conversion of Charles Jenkins, who was Dr. Morris's room-mate at that time.

This donation of Dr. Morris's was peculiarly timely and acceptable, as the Legislature had, a few months before, passed a resolution to give the College twenty-five thousand dollars; but not until the College had secured a corresponding amount.

On Thursday, September 22, 1859, the new College chapel was dedicated. Invocation by the Rev. Mr. Ballard. An anthem, "Peace be within thy walls," was sung by the College choir. Dr. Todd then read select portions of Scripture, and led in prayer. The sermon was preached by Dr. Hopkins, from Matthew v. 25: "And it fell not; for it was founded on a rock." From this discourse we insert a single paragraph: "From the form of this building, its parts have a relation that may be said to symbolize, not inaptly, the proper relation of ideas and ends in a college. In front, prominent and beautiful, is the chapel, which represents the great ideas of religious instruction and worship. Separate from this, yet connected by the tower and spire, heavenward pointing for both, are the rooms for the instruction of the two upper classes; and over these, united with each and all, is the Alumni

Hall. So, through worship and instruction, religious and secular, but both pointing to heaven, would we raise our Alumni to their own place, and send them thence into the world." The dedicatory prayer was offered, and the benediction pronounced by the Rev. Dr. Davis. At the close of the service there was a meeting of a number of the Alumni, in their hall, and it was unanimously voted to request a copy of the sermon for publication.

It has been customary at this College for the President to suspend the recitations of the classes for one day in each year, — commonly the second Monday of the first term, — to give them an opportunity to re-gravel the College walks. This has always been called Gravel Day.

The graduates of this College will not fail to remember the man with whom, since 1817, they have been familiarly acquainted, as he has daily performed the duties of his vocation. His daily visits, his interesting recitals of anecdotes and scraps of history and biography, his amusing statement, that he has seventeen times saved the old West College from being burned up, his genuine simplicity and kindness of heart and conscientious Christian deportment, have earned for Mr. Thomas Cox a place in the sincere regards of more than forty successive classes of students, and rendered his name not unworthy of an honorable place in these College annals.

Our readers would deem it a painful omission if

we should fail to make grateful mention of the venerable Vice-President of the College, the Rev. Timothy Mather Cooley, D. D. He was born in Granville, Mass., March 13, 1772; was the sixth in descent from Benjamin Cooley of Springfield; and the sixth in maternal descent from the Rev. Richard Mather of Dorchester. At the age of sixteen he entered Yale College, and was graduated in 1792. He taught school one year in New Haven, and one year in Litchfield, Conn. He studied theology with the Rev. Dr. Charles Backus of Somers, and was licensed to preach the Gospel in 1795. He preached one Sabbath in Granville, and eighteen in Salisbury, Conn., and received a call for settlement in both places. He was ordained in Granville, his native place, February 3, 1796. In May following, he was married to Content Chapman; and sixty years from that day, their bridal anniversary, by vote of the parish, was celebrated as a donation visit, by appropriate addresses and religious services. Dr. Cooley has devoted much time to the cause of education; has been on the school committee forty-five years; over fifty years has been a Trustee of Westfield Academy; forty-six years a Trustee of Williams College, and since 1846 its Vice-President. He has been uniform and punctual in his attendance at the meetings of the Board. He has fitted many students for College, some of whom have occupied high places of usefulness in church and state. In the retired parish of East Granville, Dr. Cooley has passed a peaceful and prosperous pastorate of more than threescore years. In 1845, by vote of the parish, his jubilee was celebrated, when it was stated that the Church had enjoyed ten years of the right hand of the Lord. On his eighty-fifth birthday (March 13, 1857) he preached a sermon from Joshua xiv. 10: "Lo, I am this day fourscore and five years old." *

We have now traced the history of the College from its origin to the present time. Sixty-seven years have elapsed since its incorporation. It came into existence at the commencement of a new era, when society was beginning to advance with bolder and more rapid step, and was adopting new views concerning the nature and rights of man; at a time when that "series of revivals of religion commenced in this country, which has never since entirely ceased, in connection with which this College has been so largely blessed, and in consequence of which alone it has been sustained."

"The Trustees of this College have always been men who appreciated the necessity of moral and religious training, and have appointed, from time to time, those men to instruct who would carry out their views, — men of principle and of an active piety, — men who would labor for the spiritual welfare of those committed to their charge. Under such auspices, it might have been expected that the

* The College has a portrait of Dr. Cooley, a present from his children.

influence of the College would be as good as it was great."

There is abundant evidence that a strong desire has been felt, and corresponding efforts made, from the earliest days of the College, to preserve the students from vice, and to promote their moral and religious, as well as literary and scientific improvement. The ultimate end of their existence has not been overlooked, but their spiritual good has ever been regarded as paramount to all other considerations. They are all required to attend public worship on the Sabbath, and to be present at morning and evening prayers in the chapel. The early graduates will recollect the Saturday evening prayer-meetings, which were conducted by members of the Senior class, in rotation, who were professors of religion, and occasionally by some one of the College Faculty. Class prayer-meetings are frequent. In the early days of the College, prayer-meetings were held every evening. For a quarter of a century prayer-meetings have been held four days in the week, at one o'clock, P. M. On Saturday forenoon, the Senior recitation, always conducted by the President, is theological, — the Assembly's Shorter Catechism being the text-book. On Saturday evening Dr. Hopkins has uniformly appeared in the conference-room as the College pastor. His exercises on these occasions have comprised a series of familiar lectures, in which are happily blended doctrinal discussions with close and affectionate appeals to the heart. And they have contributed in no small degree to promote the religious interests of the College.

From 1818 to 1825 the condition and prospects of the College were sufficiently dark and discouraging to shake the confidence and paralyze the efforts of ordinary men. But since the question respecting its permanent location has been put to rest its number of graduates has been annually increasing, and its future prospects annually brightening. The following statements will show the average number who have graduated under the several Presidents. The whole number who graduated during the twenty-two years of Dr. Fitch's presidency amount to 460, averaging nearly 22 annually. The six classes under Dr. Moore contained 90, averaging 15 annually. The fifteen classes under Dr. Griffin contained 311, annual average about 21. The twenty-three classes under Dr. Hopkins contained 896, annual average 39. Such has been the prosperity of the College, that for ten years past the annual average of graduates has exceeded 50. The whole number up to 1859 is 1756. Not far from one third of these have entered the ministry. In looking over the history of the College, it will appear that the early classes were small. Yet from each of these some are known to have been more or less distinguished in the walks of usefulness. And it must occur to every reflecting mind that it is a good investment to educate a number for the sake of even a few whose influence is extensively felt for good.

A glance at the history of the College shows that for many years it received no very considerable benefactions, except a few grants from the State. Wealthy men have not heretofore been numerous in Western Massachusetts. One of them, the Hon. Woodbridge Little of Pittsfield, early rendered the College essential aid. Men of moderate fortunes have aided it to some extent. More recently the College has received munificent donations from Mr. Lawrence, Mr. Jackson, and Dr. Morris. Benefactions like theirs to a college are among the most useful acts of charity ever performed by man. The beneficial influence of their various donations upon a perpetuated circle of two hundred and thirty ardent, aspiring young men, no human arithmetic can compute. Our Legislature, our courts of justice, our churches and congregations, our common schools, our happy firesides, all daily share in these benefits, and will for generations to come.

This College has not been sustained, hitherto, without an effort on the part of its guardians and friends. The bounty of Heaven never descends on soil which is not prepared to receive it. To keep the growth of a college, especially at this day, on a level with that of our country, requires not only the fostering munificence of the Legislature and of wealthy individuals, but the wisdom, zeal, and energy of well-qualified teachers, and of those who have the care and management of its concerns. In these respects this College has been highly favored.

How far Williams College has answered the end of its enlightened and patriotic founders, and for which it has been hitherto patronized and sustained, would be an interesting and useful subject of investigation. But to do full justice to it would require an induction of particulars which would extend this work beyond its anticipated limits. In reflecting on her past history, on what, with scanty means, and even struggling at times for her very existence, Williams College has accomplished, we reasonably anticipate that, with increased advantages, and more than double her former number of pupils, a high and even glorious career of prosperity and usefulness is yet in reserve for her. "SEMPER HONOR NOMENQUE SUUM, LAUDESQUE MANEBUNT."

CHAPTER XIV.

RELIGIOUS HISTORY OF THE COLLEGE FROM 1836-1860.

From the fall of 1836 there was nothing of marked religious interest in Williams College for two years. The regular means of grace were well sustained. There was considerable private fasting and private labor, and several interesting cases of conversion occurred. In 1838 the attention to religion was more general. At a noon meeting, held on the 14th of February, soon after the commencement of the spring term, it was proposed to have a meeting in the evening, and to have preaching. The meeting was held in the West College. About the middle of the afternoon, uncommon seriousness appeared to manifest itself in the north hall of the East College, mostly in the Senior class. At the evening meeting every member of the class was present. The prospect seemed fair for a great work. Satan, however, took occasion to distract the public mind. An unhappy case of litigation came up, growing out of some things which had occurred in town the term previous. As the College fast was approaching, the Faculty of College, and those among the students who were favorably disposed towards religion, were anxious that a legal process should, if possible, be avoided. A compromise was proposed, and mutually assented to by the parties the evening before the fast, and high hopes were entertained in reference to the day. When the morning came, however, it was found that some unquiet spirits had been successfully busy in undoing all that had been done in the way of compromise, and probably a more stormy morning had not been known in East College for years. Everything seemed to be in a complete ferment. The religious part of the College went, as our custom is, in the forenoon, and united with the people of the town, in a meeting for prayer and conference. The usual noon-meeting was held at one o'clock, and knowing the turbulent and angry state of College, and feeling the utter hopelessness of the case, without Divine interference, it is believed that the cause was laid over upon the arm of Him who holds the hearts of all men in his hands. At the afternoon exercise, in the conference-room, all College are required to be present. On this occasion there was no preaching, but brief remarks were made by individuals. It began to be evident, before the meeting had proceeded far, that a Divine influence had pervaded the assembly. The room became still and solemn. Many were affected to tears. Scarcely a member of College but that felt a kind of awe from God, which lasted several days. With others impressions were more permanent. The work went on, and several, particularly in the upper classes, professed submission to Christ. This was a good work, more powerful than any since 1831. It was, however, wanting in depth and thoroughness. The ensuing year passed in general quiet, but with no special religious interest. This brings us on to the year 1840, — a year somewhat memorable in the religious annals of the College. Before proceeding directly to an account of what took place during that year, I wish to make some general statements. I have run over very briefly the eight years previous, confining myself simply to facts. Let me observe them more generally. 1. That since the year 1831 there has been a general improvement in the order of College, petty annoyances have become less frequent, and cases of discipline have been rare. Except one or two 4th of July occasions, there has been next to nothing of an outbreaking character. I have lived during all these years in the East College building, and could not wish in general for a more quiet habitation. This statement cannot be made, with equal truth, in reference to the West College, occupied by the two lower classes. The order there has been, however, generally good. 2. The moral tone of College has been elevated. Drunkenness, in the daylight, and open profanation of God's name, do not show themselves boldly as they once did. Avowed infidelity is extremely rare, and those who have opportunity to know, speak of it as an occurrence extremely uncommon to hear the Christian religion and Divine institutions spoken of contemptuously or disrespectfully.

It would not be easy, perhaps, to trace this gradually favorable change to all its causes. Indirectly might be mentioned a system of exercise of a somewhat rural character, which has been introduced amongst us. The occupying of the mind during the warm and open season, when the avenues to temptation are more open, with tasteful arrangements about the College grounds, spending leisure hours in laying out better plots, cultivating shrubbery, flowers, &c., instead of lounging about in idleness, as was formerly the case, smoking and indulging in various kinds of things not very favorable to good health or good morals. We do not believe, with Combe, in converting men by beginning with the skin. There is no doubt much religion in nature, if we have grace to find it. It is not easy to be familiar with her forms, without owing, though unconsciously, an influence to a certain extent humanizing, softening, and even purifying. Natural history, also the study of atmospheric laws and of celestial phenomena, to which numbers are beginning to devote themselves assiduously, all come in aid of sound virtue and the peaceful and happy pursuance of those ends for which youth ought to be associated in an institution like this.

Of those causes which have operated *directly* in the way of bringing about the change above alluded to may be mentioned the temperance reform. The evils arising from the use of strong drink in our literary institutions, as strange and incongruous as such a mixture may seem, have been among the most appalling which they have had to contend with. These evils are not done away, but they are moderated; they have taken their place among those evils which are committed in the dark, and do not receive the countenance, as formerly, of men of respectable moral character. Another direct cause is that already adverted to, namely, the uninterrupted use of a system of means intended to bear directly on the religious character. Recognizing the Gospel as the only adequate moral purifier, this system bears directly upon the conscience. It is like a wheel in constant motion, which proves the existence of a secret power, and reproves men silently for their vain practices and worldly course of living, to say nothing of outward vice.

With all these helps to a pure state of things in a moral and religious point of view, and especially after what has been said of the general quiet which has reigned among us for several years, those who read this account will doubtless be surprised at some statements which I am presently to make. Let it be remarked, however, that all these helps are of voluntary application; we cannot compel men to prefer the cool outward air of a summer's morning and the odor of a flower-bed to a pent-up room filled with the fumes of tobacco. We are obliged to say, however reluctantly, on these points, "De gustibus nil disputandum." In respect to the daily meetings, they have never embraced much over seventy; about half of College, in the best times, and this only for a brief period, leaving the rest, ordinarily by far the majority, unaffected by them, except indirectly and incidentally. What has now been said will relieve some statements which I am about to make.

The College year of 1839 and 1840 opened with no very favorable omens for good. The Senior class, which always gives tone more or less in College, both to opinion and feeling, embodied but little vigorous, active piety. There was no particular deficiency in respect to profession, but the profession of many set so loosely upon them that piety itself came to be greatly depreciated in the estimate of others. There were also various causes of intestine difficulty. About the middle of November several began to feel that they could not live longer without making an effort to interrupt the prevailing apathy, and lay a check on those influences which were sapping the foundation of all that was vital in Christianity amongst us. As the way did not appear to be open for any direct effort, it was determined to hold meetings, several evenings successively, in a private house near by; these meetings were attended both by Christians and sinners from College, and it is now known that one individual was, about that time, under very deep conviction. These meetings were continued, with more or less frequency, till the close of the term. When College assembled at the 1st of February, there was an uncommon degree of wakefulness among several Christians. The noon meetings were more full and solemn than had been usual. The Methodists were holding a meeting near by, the influence of which was to deepen the feeling in College, the students attending without restriction. About the time of the College fast, two or three meetings were held at the conference-room in the chapel. There was preaching at these meetings, which seemed to produce an awakening influence upon the church, to whom it was mainly directed. After this time the noon meetings thickened, almost all the church being now gathered into them, and some of the impenitent, taking covert under increasing numbers, came in also. In this state of painful and solemn suspense things remained for several days. Having been brought up before, on more than one occasion, nearly to the point where we were at present standing, there was ground for alarm lest this might prove the case now. Prayer was offered "without ceasing," and it would be no exaggerated statement to say of some, that they appeared to be willing to die, rather than not to see God glorified in the salvation of souls. It was with us, indeed, a great day, "even the time of Jacob's trouble." There was, however, strength in the church to lay hold on the promise, "he shall be saved out of it." God also encouraged some of his people by gracious intimations, which he was pleased to give them, that he would work "for his great name's sake that his name might not be polluted." There was no movement, outwardly, which went to relieve this suspense, till the 16th of March, which was town-meeting day, or rather the evening of the day before, which was Sabbath. At that time, numbers of the impenitent had their attention arrested in a more sensible and lively manner. Two or three conversions had occurred before this, but now there seemed to be a breaking away and lifting up of the cloud. That kind of false shame which had hitherto prevented sinners from resorting to little prayer-meetings, and seeking the company and conversation of the pious, was all done away. They began now, indeed, "to flock like clouds, and like doves to their windows."

The increasing tide of feeling which, up to this point, had flowed harmoniously in the channel of our daily meetings, began to overflow, and require more expansion; it not being thought best to alter the form of these meetings, which are devoted, in part, to repetition of the Scriptures, and which, therefore, did not give sufficient time for expressions of feeling. This will be readily understood, when we observe that the Sophomore and Junior recitation-rooms, where these meetings are held, were both much crowded. Meetings, accordingly, began to be held at nine o'clock in the evening. These were, many of them, very happy meetings. There was a great deal of freedom in them. Almost every one had something to say. Some, who were older, a word in the way of experience; some had an invitation or a promise; some a sigh or a tear. Many had confessions. This was true of the most conscientious among us, whose walk had been irreproachable. Under the strong impressions of the Spirit, and the clear light which was now shed upon eternal things, their best services appeared defective, either in motive or in measure. Lukewarm persons, who had been living loose and encouraging in wickedness those whose countenances they now saw in the solemn meeting, felt called upon to do something more than confess. Not a few of this description became convinced that they had been building on the sand, renounced their hopes, and took their place among inquirers. Anxious sinners stated their case, and asked for prayers. And those into whose minds light had begun to break bore testimony to this. In brief expressions of feeling, from individuals in almost every variety of mental frame, time would pass away unconsciously. I was struck, one evening, with a remark. It was at a late hour, numbers had expressed their feelings, and the meeting was exceedingly solemn and still. One spoke and said, "I have forgotten what day it is." Such a contrast with the dark and wintry days which had preceded might well throw a transient doubt about the reality of those scenes which were now passing. This meeting will not soon be forgotten. It closed by singing the words, "O, there will be mourning at the judgment-seat of Christ." The following language of Watts was well suited to this time, and found involuntary utterance from those who had long "waited for it": —

"When we review our dismal fears,
'T was hard to think they 'd vanish so;
With God we left our flowing tears,
He made our joys like rivers flow."

From the period before alluded to, when the West College set up for themselves, it had been our custom to have a joint meeting on Friday, at one College and the other, alternately. The recitation-room being too strait, we adjourned, this week, to the conference-room, in the chapel. Many were affected at this meeting. I may mention, too, in this connection, the existence among us of what are termed class-meetings, on Friday evening, — meetings for the individual classes, — an important means of grace, which originated some time during the dark period between 1827 and 1831. The meeting in the Senior class, on the evening of the Friday above referred to, appeared to be accompanied with a remarkable effusion of the Spirit. On the evening of the succeeding Wednesday, the two literary societies adjourned for prayer, and after a season came together to hear the Word of God. The same evening a spirit of confession appeared to break out anew in the nine o'clock meeting, at the East College. Some confessions of rather a startling character were made by individuals who had confessed before, but it seemed that their confessions did not go sufficiently deep to satisfy conscience, with the amount of light and of the spirit now enjoyed. Statements were made which involved, more or less, the lower classes in College.

At least, transactions were confessed to, the influence of which upon members of these classes had been injurious. It now began to be evident that things were coming to a crisis, — that pride of character, in the two upper classes, was likely to be severely tested. Christianity was getting sufficiently deep hold to make men *honest,* — a point to which it comes more rarely than is often imagined. Feelings and frames and experiences and happy modes began, at this moment, to look rather dim. The great practical question came up now, Are you willing to turn about, and become an *honest man?* Throw off all disguises, make confession of the whole, take high ground, and start anew. Had it not been for this meeting, things might have ran along. The happy state of feeling before described might have continued, and men have blessed themselves in the enjoyment of it. As it was, it became evident that a new page must be turned over in the history of the revival. It says in the Bible, "that man perished not alone in his iniquity." So, now, it was obvious that the sins of individuals were so linked in with those of others, in both buildings, that a general meeting was needed for confession. Such a meeting, accordingly, was agreed upon at the conference-room the next night. Every member of College, it is believed, was present; and after some remarks in relation to the duty, to attend to which, especially, the meeting was convened, the work of confession went forward. It is not necessary to specify all the things which were confessed to in this meeting. Among those things which weighed most heavily, were neglect and abuse of the Sabbath and the Bible, lying to officers of College, stealing, card-playing, drinking, keeping liquor at their rooms. The disclosures of this evening were deeply humiliating, not only to individuals, but to human nature; and probably few scenes are witnessed on earth, ante-dating and foreshadowing more significantly and solemnly the day appointed for the revealing of secrets, when God "shall both bring to light the hidden things of darkness, and make manifest the counsels of the hearts." Their confessions, as might be supposed, were cruel darts to the companions of those who had made them, who now stood revealed as guilty of the same things, but without sufficient moral honesty to make confession of the wrong which they had done. Some of those who confessed this evening had had a good deal of pride of character, and a very fair reputation for honor and integrity. Between these and others, when the scales of the sanctuary were applied as now, there appeared no radical difference, and no one, probably, left the meeting without being convinced of the total depravity of unsanctified human nature. It seemed for a while as though there were about to be an entire upheaving and overturning, and a coming out, from the dark and guilty chaos, of order and moral honesty. There began to be a glimpse of what is implied in a pure community, and a hope that such a condition was about to be realized by us.

The meeting referred to did not on the whole interrupt the solemnity of College; the work went on with interest and power, conversions occurring from time to time, nearly to the close of the term. Boisterous sports, such as ball-playing, &c., were not resumed this year, as has been usual at the opening of the season. The planting of trees, gardening, and going off, evenings, to a distance, in the outskirts of the town, where a protracted meeting was in progress, furnished exercise well suited to the time, and to any time. As in 1812 and 1825, so now, the exhibition at the close of the term was suspended, and a religious exercise took its place. It deserves, perhaps, to be mentioned here, as evidencing the fact that nature and the Christian religion are not unfriendly, that the day after the close of the term, an expedition started under the auspices of the Natural History Society, consisting of about twenty individuals, most of whom had been affected more or less by the awakening. Indeed, had it not been for the awakening, I question whether the expedition would have moved at this time. There was a disposition to blow the Gospel trumpet around the land, and as news of what the Lord had been doing for us had gone before, it seemed to be taken for granted, that we would hold meetings as we travelled; which we did, much to our own gratification, and we have reason to believe, in some instances, not without special benefit to others.

The summer term was one of quiet and religious

activity. A kind of Home Missionary Society was formed, consisting of twenty or more, the object of which was to cultivate the waste ground in the vicinity. The 4th of July, which has sometimes been boisterous, and into the celebration of which cannon, powder in other forms, and fireworks, were introduced in the turbulent period between 1827 and 1831, was this year very quiet. I shall not soon forget the impression made upon my mind as the young men were assembling to form their usual procession. The place of rendezvous was near the West College garden. Not a discordant sound, unless it might be from neighboring villages, had occurred to interrupt the stillness of the morning. The sun shone bright, and the atmosphere seemed to sympathize with the inward serenity which reigned. When all had come, the music struck up and the procession moved. So deep upon my mind was the impression of moral order, and so strong the conviction, that many pure hearts were beating in unison with the soft but lively air, that I seemed to see, in miniature and in type, and obtained, through this outward sign, a more vivid view than ever before, of that purer and longer procession, which will be formed on the morning of a brighter day, before which will be uttered the proclamation, "Open ye the gates that the righteous may enter." I felt an involuntary impulse to go and join myself to the procession, which conscience had never before permitted me to do.

A little before this time about twenty were admitted to the College church, among whom was one of the officers of College who had shared in the awakening. In respect to those whose minds were deeply affected, but who either hoped not at all, or only faintly, and that for a time, I should say that some of them, so far as human judgment can decide, stand on higher ground in reference to the Gospel than before. I am aware that the prevalent theology will not bear me out in such a supposition. I am compelled, however, to believe, judging from the walk of numbers, which is the best criterion, that an impression was made, at that period, upon their minds, which if it does not issue in conversion, will be favorable to Christianity, and ever prevent them from lightly speaking evil of Christ or of his cause. I do not think there are any flagrant cases where a revulsion of feeling has taken place such as we sometimes witness, though our God has humbled us and left us "to bewail many who have sinned already and have not repented."

The first term of the College year 1841 furnished melancholy, though not unexpected proof of the soundness of those views which were entertained by many, in the spring, in relation to what might be expected to occur if the causes of moral infection were not then thoroughly sifted. Many were grieved, though none probably were surprised, on the entrance of a new class, and the commencement of an electioneering campaign for members of the various associations, to witness a recurrence of old jealousies and old feuds. To such an extent did this feeling arise before the close of the term, that on one occasion the quiet of midnight was disturbed by bands of students walking the streets, with loud vociferation and clubs, either for purposes of attack or of self-defence. It is not necessary to say, that numbers in College, I believe I may say with truth the mass, shook their hands of all participation in such disgraceful occurrences. The general good feeling of College interposed a barrier against any permanent and spreading excitement, and so the matter was hushed for a season, and has been kept still by a prevailing spirit, which there is reason to know is nothing less than the Spirit of God. A pretty uniform solemnity, a kind of awe from God, has been among us since the opening of the term in February. One or two hopeful conversions occurred early in the term. The College fast was solemn. Some were awakened then, a few expressed hope afterwards. The noon meetings on Friday were adjourned to the chapel, for the want of room. One or two meetings, held at nine o'clock, were crowded. As fast as the stumbling-blocks were removed, the chariot rolled forward, and souls flocked to the standard of the Redeemer.

The year 1841 likewise furnished some evidences of the special presence of God among us. A few conversions occurred in the spring, and towards the close of the year there was a manifest increase of interest in the daily meetings, and generally a more hopeful state of things. An event occurred at this time, apparently untoward, but which was evidently overruled for good. I refer to the burning of the East College. This building, erected about the beginning of the century, had witnessed many scenes of deep religious interest. Many of its private rooms had been bethels, and here, especially, the daily meetings had long been attended in the Junior recitation-room. The day after the fire we rallied around the spot. It was a desolate place, but the feelings of those who had been wont to gather there seemed rather quickened than depressed.

> " Those ruins shall be built again,
> And all that dust shall rise,"

were words which seemed to have a spiritual significance. It was determined not to abandon the meeting, but to adjourn to the Sophomore recitation-room. We accordingly went over, and the step had a good effect. The lower classes were encouraged by seeing so many, and among them not a few zealous Christians, coming to their support. The meetings became more interesting, and at the close of the term there were some evidences of the special presence of God.

This state of things continued into the next term; but during the early weeks of the term no sensible advance was made. Indeed, nothing more hopeful was witnessed till after the midde of March. At that time a death occurred in the neighborhood which was overruled to the awakening of some young persons. The funeral, by request of the deceased, was attended in the church. Numbers from the College went in, and an unusual solemnity was visible in the audience. It was felt, both in town and College, that the time was critical, and called for special effort. A private house near the College was opened for preaching. Several students attended, and some were awakened. The Sabbath evening following, a somewhat extraordinary meeting was held in an adjoining house, the members of which were all impenitent, some of them standing up in the entry, and nearly all, to some extent, anxious. The words of the prophet seemed strikingly verified, — "The children are come to the birth, and there is not strength to bring forth."

Under these circumstances, the pastor of the church, after consultation, wrote to Dr. Bemen of Troy, requesting him to come out. This request was complied with. Several sermons were preached, but with no very marked effect till the day of the State Fast. On the morning of that day the Doctor read that striking chapter in the prophecy of Zechariah, toward the close of which it is said, "The fast of the fourth month, and the fast of the fifth, and the fast of the seventh, and the fast of the tenth, shall be to the house of Judah joy and gladness and cheerful feasts. Thus saith the Lord of Hosts, it shall yet come to pass that there shall come people, and the inhabitants of many cities, and the inhabitants of one city shall go to another, saying, Let us go speedily to pray before the Lord, and to seek the Lord of Hosts. I will go also."

These and the following verses were the basis of a discourse in which the speaker aimed to set forth the characteristics of a genuine revival of religion. And when, at the close, all anxious inquirers were invited to a neighboring hall, the place was literally thronged. It is rare that such an impression is made upon the young of any community as was visible on that Fast day. The awakening became general, both in College and town. Not many days after, at a meeting in the Sophomore recitation-room, greatly thronged, Dr. Bemen, being present, said, "That if Williams College could always remain in such a state, it would be a little heaven, and he should want to come occasionally over the mountains to get into it."

A religious meeting at the close of this term took the place of the Junior exhibition. On the whole, the revival of this year was an extraordinary work. Still, in depth and power it fell short of that which preceded it in the spring of 1840.

The following year, 1843, was marked by no special seriousness till about the middle of the fall term. At that time there were some cases of inquiry. A sudden death, by accident, in College served to deepen the interest. Meetings filled up, and the term closed with a good deal of seriousness. A few dated their conversions from this time.

The year 1844 was not one of revival; but late in the fall, as in the year preceding, several in the church were stirred up to greater earnestness. This feeling passed over into the spring term. A meeting for scriptual exposition and conference, hard by the College, was attended by many students, some of whom were deeply interested, and before the close of the term expressed hope.

Towards the close of the spring term of the following year, 1846, a few cases of inquiry occurred. This was also, and more markedly the case, near the close of the fall term. Quite a number were more than usually impressed. One member of the Junior class seemed to be affected and brought under deep distress of mind at the last recitation.

The religious history of the four years terminating with the year 1846 occupies but a brief space in this narrative; it was a time of general apathy in the churches, and no marked revival occurred in College during this period. There was not, however, during these years, an entire suspension of divine influences. Whilst the mass of professors, wandering by the "cold streams of Babylon," had hung their harps upon the willows, a few were earnest, prayerful, and anxious to do something for the upbuilding of the church. Sense and sight furnished them but little encouragement; but they labored on in hope, and gathered some precious sheaves, though no abundant harvest rewarded their toils. "Blessed," says our Saviour, "are they who have not seen, and yet have believed." This blessing no doubt will rest upon a faithful few, who, during these years of comparative barrenness, continued to till the moral vineyard. The name of one may be mentioned, as he has gone to his reward, — the beloved Brewster, whose bones are mouldering in the soil of China. Rarely, if ever, did he enter a meeting, in those days of discouragement, without some word of exhortation to encourage the hope and strengthen the faith of his brethren. Another of like spirit, contemporary with him, is now reaping a spiritual harvest in the mountains of Oroomiah.

In the year 1847 another revival was experienced. Professor Lincoln, then a member of College, has given his recollections of that work in the account which follows.

"This revival was intimately connected with a general work of grace in the town, in which more than one hundred persons hopefully shared. There were some favorable indications in College before the fall term closed, but the revival proper commenced in town during the winter vacation of the College. When the term opened, the pious students, who had long waited and prayed for such scenes, hastened gladly back and mingled in them. They found several in town already rejoicing in hope, others anxiously inquiring what they must do, and the church generally coming up to the help of the Lord.

"Gradually, silently, the work progressed in town and spread in College. One after another felt the presence and power of the Holy Spirit; heart after heart glowed and melted under the sacred flame, until few, if any, Christians remained in College who were not awake and at their post. There was much secret and social prayer; much religious conversation among Christians; much faithful, personal effort with the impenitent. Public meetings were frequent, solemn, and crowded. There was also much heart-searching and trembling, confession and contrition on the part of the church. Several professing Christians, becoming convinced of the worthlessness of their hopes, renounced them and sought again, and found, we trust, the pearl of great price. As the fruit of this revival, some thirty or forty persons indulged hope in Christ. And, so far as my knowledge extends, their lives since have given credible evidence that their professions were sincere, and their convictions that they then passed from death unto life genuine. Some of its subjects are preaching Christ; others have set their seal to the faith they then professed by peaceful and happy deaths; others still, then and there impressed, but not expressing hope, have since been led, as they trust, by a sacred chain of influences, in which those impressions form well-remembered links, and by a way which they knew not, to the Lamb of God. No period in this revival was characterized by great manifest excitement; it was, on the contrary, eminently a quiet and thoughtful work. It was most powerful, perhaps, about the time of the College fast, though it continued with great uniformity of interest through several months. Some scenes occurred of very marked and thrilling interest. Some instances of conversion very signally illustrated the power of prayer and the sovereign grace of God. The spirit of harmony and of brotherly love which prevailed was wonderful. There was great joy in our hearts. The watchword of the revival, that with which Christians met and parted, was, 'Hold on, brother,' hold on in prayer and in effort; hold on to the promises; hold on to God."

In the spring of the year 1848 there was unusual religious interest in the College. Before the College fast, there were some cases of awakening. The exercises on that day were solemn, and at a prayer-meeting in the evening it became evident that the Spirit was present, not only in his quickening, but in his awakening influences. Several of the impenitent rose and asked the prayers of the church. Next day, at noon, the recitation-room was full, and the meeting, instead of adjourning over till Monday, as had been usual, was appointed at half past one the succeeding day, — Saturday.

Numbers of the impenitent were present at this meeting, — some scoffers, — some were in deep distress; these found their way, after the meeting, into a private room hard by, where several engaged Christians without any previous concert had assembled. The place was solemn as the birthplace of souls. Very rarely has there been a Saturday afternoon more still and serious. It is believed there was much ejaculatory prayer, and the watchword seemed to be, "Sanctify yourselves, for to-morrow the Lord will work wonders among you."

On Sabbath morning, at nine o'clock, the meeting for prayer and conference was crowded. Christians expected this. They had prepared themselves for a solemn day, and were not disappointed when numbers thronged to the place. One who had just obtained hope arose. He seemed to enjoy great peace, — he inquired where the cross was. Another then rose, and, said he, "Something holds me back." He then dropped on his knees and prayed most earnestly, first begging his friends to aid him while he endeavored to consecrate himself to God. I believe he rose a new man. At least, from that time, and since, his course has been onward, and his praise is now in the churches.

On the afternoon of the same day the President preached; his subject was the flight of Jonah to Tarshish from the presence of the Lord. This sermon produced a solemn impression. A young man of fine talents, who, before entering College, had indulged hope, but had since abandoned his

Christian hopes and professions, was powerfully wrought upon. Like the prophet, he felt himself to be a fugitive from God, and after service, in deep distress and consternation, he was led by one of the brethren to the room of a friend, where he gave vent to his uncontrollable emotions. He seemed to be crushed and subdued, and before he left the place consecrated himself, it is believed, to the service of God.

About this time there began to be much excitement in the lower classes. Meetings were multiplied at the West College. Several there expressed hope. Time, however, showed, in the case of many, that their goodness was "like the morning cloud and early dew." It soon passed away. The work seemed not to be characterized by the genuineness and permanence which marked its progress in the upper classes. Here the work, though not very extensive, was deep. I might mention that the individual whose conversion was last referred to not only illustrated and adorned his profession by a devoted life, but experienced, in a happy death, the sustaining power of his hope in Christ. He devoted himself to the ministry, and was called away suddenly, while pursuing his studies at Andover.

The year 1849 was more than commonly barren. Wickedness abounded in the lower classes. Nearly half the professors of religion left at Commencement. The class, however, which then entered contained two or three devotedly pious persons, whose influence was like leaven, leavening upwards. Some Christians were powerfully wrought upon during the fall of this year, and in the ensuing spring a few conversions occurred, not in connection with any general awakening, but as the result of individual effort. On the whole, religion was at a low ebb during the year 1850.

The spring term of the ensuing year, 1851, opened with some evidences of the special presence of God. This appeared in the noon meetings, though the number in attendance was not larger than usual. On the evening of the College fast, a stated meeting at the study of one of the Professors was considerably thronged. Some of the impenitent were present, and appeared wakeful. The next day, at noon, the meeting was at the West College. It was fuller than was expected. There was also something, aside from numbers, which indicated the immediate presence of God. "I remember well," says a correspondent, "my surprise, on reaching the door, to see the room all black with the crowd. I had never seen anything of the kind before." In the course of this meeting two or three of the impenitent arose and requested prayers. Preaching was demanded, and public meetings, during many successive evenings, were held at the conference-room. A crowd attended these meetings. Divine truth was armed with power. Some of the most devoted Christians were quite broken down, and their confessions alarmed those who had looked up to them as examples and leaders. A very deep work was wrought in the Church, and out of it the impression became deep and general.

Just four weeks after the Friday noon meeting above referred to, — the meeting occurring at the same place, — one of the converts, referring to that meeting, said that just thirty days had elapsed, and there were thirty hopeful converts, — a convert a day, — eventful and solemn month! "It took," writes one, "all the most diligent and industrious members of our class."

This work was remarkable for its permanence. Meetings abated not much in number during the summer term. The last Friday noon meeting attended by the Senior class was particularly solemn. The limits of this sketch forbid much detail, but in general it may be said the work, of whose commencement some account has been given, extended into the following years, with some alternations of interest and power, but retaining its identity as part of the same movement. The noon meetings were meetings of experience. They continued full. Conversions were not infrequent, though not multiplied as at the beginning. During the spring term of 1853 the average attendance at noon, in the two upper classes, was about fifty, — and eternity will show how many were the sanctifying and saving impressions connected with those means of grace. A member of the class graduating this year writes: "Our class, when we entered, numbered twenty-seven. Four were professors of religion. We graduated thirty-seven, and all but five or six were indulging hope."

It was in the course of this revival that the idea of missionary colonies came up, and gave rise to a good deal of animated discussion. The question was raised whether the methods hitherto adopted of evangelizing the world, by the aid of missionary societies, was as well adapted to the end proposed as limited associations of individuals, embracing the different trades, locating at various points, and carrying with them the appliances of Christian civilization, — planting the Church and family at once at points which might be selected as suitable for the experiment. It was proposed to test this idea, at once, in one of the South American States. The field is open, and it is believed that some movement in this line will speedily be realized.

Subsidiary, in part, to the scheme just referred to, and suggested by it, was the plan of a missionary institution to be connected with the College, where all the living tongues should be taught, and facilities furnished for training young men to be teachers and preachers in the missionary colonies.

While these questions were being discussed, the site of the haystack, so long veiled in mystery, was providentially discovered. This, in connection with the jubilee, gave a new impulse to the missionary spirit. The Society of Inquiry gained strength, and the second half-century, in the history of the missionary enterprise amongst us, is opening with renewed hope and promise.

It only remains to speak of the revival of 1858, designated, now, as the *great revival* throughout the land, and in which the College has largely shared. This work appeared early in the winter term. The noon meetings opened with more than usual solemnity. There seemed to be in the church an earnest desire for a more intimate union with Christ. The weighty words of Luther were impressed deeply upon some, — "If Christ and I are two, I am lost."

Towards the last of January those who had been teaching began to return, — some of them from the midst of revival scenes. Indeed, the land began now to be extensively shaken. One brother rose in the meeting, and said that out of twenty-nine scholars in his school, twenty-one had been hopefully converted. He had established a noon meeting in his school. Interesting details were given. Several were affected to tears. On the evening of the same day was the monthly meeting of the College church. The exercises were impressive. It was said, and seemed to be felt, that we needed a baptism of the Holy Ghost. On the ensuing day, at noon, a brother repeated and dwelt on the passage, "It is expedient for you that I go away." Another said he had never felt under so great a pressure, but never had greater hope. In the evening one of the impenitent was found to be under deep impressions.

The Friday noon meeting of this week was at West College, and was very full. As an encouragement to faith, it was urged that Christ did not say to the Syro-Phenician woman, "Ask what thou wilt, and it shall be done unto thee;" but this he says now to his Church. The pastor of the church in town was present, and dwelt on the necessity of being humbled if we would be exalted. It was evident that several of the church, particularly in the Senior class, were much roused.

During the ensuing month of February no abatement of interest was perceived. Conversions occurred from time to time; in one or two cases of individuals who had given up all hope for themselves. They had seemed like barren trees, against which the sentence had gone out, "Let no fruit grow on thee henceforth forever;" but now they were softened, humbled; their despairing thoughts left them; they were led to feel that a spiritual harvest had come, and it became them to make no delay. Some, after resisting the influence for weeks, came forward, confessed their pride, and owned the dealings of the Spirit with them. Some were impressed with alarming apprehensions lest the Spirit might suddenly leave them. Some were convicted under sermons, and brought to feel that they were barren, fruitless trees, exposed to the just judgment of God. Providences alarmed some. A member of the Senior class died at a distance, about this time. This event deepened the impression of the revival, and was the means of awakening some. One was called away by sickness, and thus cut off from the ordinary means of grace, but God met him in his retirement. He read through the four Gospels, and in the light of what he read became convinced that there was a radical defect in his life. He saw that here a remedy was provided, and that the condition of receiving it was *asking*. It was a solemn day when this individual, having returned, came into the prayer-meeting and gave in his testimony. The calmness and decision with which it was rendered, added weight to it. Others felt that they were standing on unsafe ground, rose and asked for prayers.

It was now the middle of March, up to which time the interest had not been confined to the upper classes, but had been most visible there. Now, however, the other classes became greatly moved; the West College meeting rose in attendance and interest. Several conversions took place in these classes; and yet time has shown that the goodness of numbers who then professed hope was like the morning cloud and the early dew which passes away. In the two upper classes I think about twenty conversions were numbered in the course of the work, embracing some of the leading minds in College.

The meetings at noon were perhaps never more thronged than during this revival, and were an important means of grace both to Christians and others. Before closing these sketches it may not be out of place to refer a little more particularly than has been done to the origin of these meetings among us. They were not the fruit directly of a revival, though perhaps indirectly so. It will be recollected that the year 1831 was one of extensive awakening in New England, and indeed in the land generally. In connection with this work of grace, numbers had their attention directed to a higher standard of Christian attainment, or something which might be reasonably hoped for and sought for. It was felt that our religion had been too vacillating, — too much a matter of times and seasons. It was felt especially that it did not permeate as it ought to our every-day life, our secular duties and studies. It was believed that something better was not only attainable, but was actually about to be realized. This view was confirmed by the experience and anticipations of holier men. The life of Dr. Payson, then recently published, fell into the hands of one of the brethren, in which a passage occurs to this effect, — that there is a day coming when the ordinary transactions of life will be performed with seriousness of religious duties, when every day will be like the Sabbath, every grove a temple, and every meal like the Sacrament. This view had something elevating and sanctifying in it; it also tallied strikingly with our own experience, and the unconscious prophesyings of at least some in the midst of us. With a view to ante-date such a day, it was determined to assemble at noon. A few, perhaps six in number, assembled accordingly at that hour. This was in the year 1832, on a pleasant day in June, which will no doubt be vividly remembered by those who were present, and who yet survive. Numbers were on the College green, and under the shade of the maples, as these brethren, with hymn-books in hand, passed through on their way to the conference-room. By some professors of religion the movement was looked upon with disfavor; most supposed, no doubt, that it would be ephemeral. But not so. God was evidently in it. Little was said, but the meeting by degrees increased. From that time it has not been intermitted, but has been on the whole a growing power till now.

After toiling on thus for more than a quarter of a century, reaping present good from the appointment, but still not abandoning the original thought of a better day coming, it may well be supposed that the announcement of last winter's *noon meetings* in Philadelphia and New York was hailed with deep interest. They were regarded, not as mere local means of grace, but as significant of something beyond themselves, as at once the fulfilment of unconscious prophesyings, and as themselves prophesying of a brighter day about to dawn. And when these meetings spread, as they did, immediately, almost with lightning speed, through the land, it seemed as though the voice of the "living creatures and of the wheels" could be heard in the movement.

It would be premature, certainly at the present moment, to assume that these means will be permanent; but in the light of our experience here we may hope that they will be so, — that they will prove, what numbers are beginning assuredly to regard them, significant tokens and harbingers of a better era soon to appear. This College has borne no subordinate part in those movements which are now undermining the superstitions of the world, and hastening a moral crisis in its affairs. Let her not be recreant to her high calling now, when Providence and prophecy unite in pointing to some great event as nigh, "*even at the doors.*" *

While this work is going through the press, a letter has been received from an alumnus in Virginia, dated February 7, 1860, which is so much in harmony with what is above written, that the following extract seems to be a fitting close to this chapter.

"It grieves me to hear that religion is not as prosperous with you as it has been at some other times. Perhaps I may be misinformed, the persons from whom I hear may not be able to judge rightly; but from all I learn, I should judge that there was nothing like a revival of religion among the students. If this is so, I know how it is filling your own heart with sorrow, and I am impelled to say that I feel the sincerest sympathy with you, and if it will be the least encouragement to you, you may know, sir, that I pray with you for the renewal of those blessed and precious scenes which were witnessed eight and ten years ago. You remember that during the three years preceding August, 1853, there was almost a continuous revival. O, sir, were not those blessed days! My own class I think of, almost all converted, and many who entered godless, left to preach the Gospel. I shall never forget coming into the Sophomore recitation-room one Friday, to the noon meeting, and finding it *perfectly full*, not an empty seat; for months we had been praying there — scarcely a dozen of us; but then God's Spirit was poured out, and on every side sinners rose to ask for the prayers of God's people, to confess their sins, and soon to tell us that they had found peace in believing. Daily meetings were scarcely sufficient. Professors of religion renewed their covenant with God, and came up to a higher Christian life; the dissipated and profane rose with streaming eyes to acknowledge their guilt, and beseech God's people to pray in their behalf; passing through the halls of West College at such times, I have sometimes heard the voice of prayer from almost every room as I went along. The whole College sent up incense to God, and it appeared as if it were about to be presented as a whole burnt-offering to Him.

Vacations came, and we bade farewell with regret to these heavenly scenes. O, sir, I love to think of those times! I went to Williams thoughtless and profane, but I left it, through the grace of God, with some experience of the unsearchable riches of Christ in my heart, and a commission, as I trust, to declare them to others. I do not recount these things because I imagine that they are in the least degree fainter in your memory than in mine; but because I *delight* to recall them. Williams College seemed then like a suburb of heaven. The walks, the buildings, the trees, the mountains, the skies, seemed full of God. We thought He had taken up his abode there, and would never go away. O how I wish that the dear brethren who are in the classes now could go back eight years and breathe that air! Perhaps I am in error, but I feel as if it is not so now. How glad I should be to know that I am wrong, but I must ask the brethren, Are you crowding the daily meetings for prayer? Do you watch for souls, and esteem their conversion of more importance than anything else, or than all things else?"

CHAPTER XV.

BUILDINGS, LIBRARIES, AND APPARATUS.

In the biography of individuals we have not only the description of the qualities of the mind and heart which make the man, but also of the personal appearance of the house in which the mind lived.

In the history of a college we wish to know something of its buildings, — the places where the student passes his college life, — places always associated in his mind with that life. It must be confessed, that in the buildings connected with this institution economy rather than elegance has been the leading policy.

The College began its career in the building now known as "West College." In 1788 the Trustees voted to erect a three-story brick building. The town raised a sum (about $2,000) to put on a fourth story. It was erected in 1790, but the rooms in the fourth story were not finished till after the school was opened. It is strongly built, is eighty-two feet long and forty-two feet wide, and cost about $11,700. The rooms were single, large, and intended for the use of two students. The south end of the second and third stories was used for the chapel. The library was the end of the hall of the third story. The Librarian could stand in the middle of the library and reach any book which it contained. The northeast corner room on the first story was the Freshman recitation-room, and the corresponding room on the third story was the Sophomore recitation-room. In 1832 the old chapel was made into recitation-rooms and students' rooms. The building stands in the highway, and the footpath passed through its centre, and all who walked on the south walk from the church to East College "went through College." It stands seventy-five rods east of the village church, and fifty-three west of the chapel. In 1855 this building was remodelled. The interior was taken out, a wall was built through the centre, east and west, and entrances made at the north and south ends. The rooms were made with two bedrooms and closets to each. This old building now stands as high in College estimation as any of the more modern additions, and promises to outlive them all.

The next building erected by the Trustees was the President's house. It was built in 1794. David Noble, Esq., gave one acre of land for the house, and sold five acres more for forty dollars per acre. The cost of the house and land was $ 2,400. In this house have all the Presidents of the College lived, and in it not one of them has died.

In 1798 the old "East College" was built, standing on the eastern eminence, sixty rods east from the West College. This was of brick, four stories in height, one hundred and four feet long, and twenty-eight feet broad, containing thirty-two suites of rooms, and cost $11,991.54. This was destroyed by fire on Sunday, October 17, 1841. The fire broke out in the fourth story, in the afternoon, while the students were at church. The library of the Theological Society was burned, and very little was saved out of the building. The people of the village kindly opened their houses to the students, and College duties were not suspended for more than a single day. This building was replaced in 1842 by two new brick buildings, three stories high, — the present East and South Colleges. In the South College are the rooms of the Philologian and Philotechnian Societies, with their libraries. Here also is the Junior recitation-room, and here, on the first story, before the erection of Jackson Hall, were the rooms of the Natural History Society.

The Trustees as early as 1803 appointed a committee to petition the General Court for aid in building a chapel. In 1806 a movement was made towards this end, and also a kitchen for commons, but nothing came of these efforts. In 1826 it was determined to make an effort to raise a fund of $ 25,000, to establish a new professorship, and to erect a chapel. Through the influence and exertions of Dr. Griffin the fund was raised, and the chapel built. It stands one hundred and thirty-one rods east of the church. It was dedicated on Tuesday, September 2, 1828, when Dr. Griffin preached a sermon. It is built of brick, three stories high, and cost $ 10,000. The chapel proper, with galleries, occupies two stories of the west end. The southeast lower-story room was used as the Senior recitation-room, until the Seniors became too numerous for the space. The second story east is the conference-room, connected with many interesting and solemn associations. The third story contains the cabinet of minerals, &c., and, previous to the erection of Lawrence Hall, contained the library. The basement of the east end is the laboratory.

In 1845 a lecture-room was built east of the chapel, connected with the laboratory. Before the erection of the chapel, the laboratory was a small wooden building, which stood at the southeast corner of the East College grounds, when they were bounded south by the brow of the hill. The uses and the name of this building will now be modified by the erection of the new chapel. It would not be inappropriate to call the old edifice "Griffin Hall."

In 1836 the Astronomical Observatory was built by Professor A. Hopkins, and dedicated in 1837, — the first building erected in the country exclusively used for this object. It is of stone, consisting of a centre, with two wings, the whole being forty-eight feet in length by twenty in breadth. The central apartment is surmounted by a revolving dome thirteen feet in diameter, and each wing has an opening through the roof for meridian instruments.

Under the dome is an achromatic telescope of nine and a half feet focus. In the east wing is a transit instrument by Troughton, having a focus of fifty inches. In the same room is a compensation clock by Molineux.

East of this is the Magnetic Observatory. It is of brick and octagonal in form. In it is a large variation transit instrument for the purpose of observing the daily variations of the needle.

In 1846 Lawrence Hall was erected as a library. It is named after the late Amos Lawrence of Boston, by whose liberality it was built. It is octagonal in form, forty-eight feet in diameter, each side twenty feet, and is thirty-six feet in height. It has two stories; the lower one finished in rustic style. The second story is the library proper, containing eight alcoves separated from each other by partitions proceeding from each of the eight angles, to within twelve feet of the centre, leaving a circular space twenty-four feet in diameter. It is surmounted by a dome, supported by eight Ionic columns. It is capable of containing thirty-five thousand volumes. One of the great wants of the College is a larger and better collection of books, important alike to teacher and pupil. The partitions between the alcoves are supported by brick walls, resting upon the foundation of stone. This divides the first story into eight rooms; two of them united form the Trustees' room, one contains specimens from Nineveh, and one the daguerreotypes and photographs of the graduating classes.

Kellogg Hall was built in 1847, in the West College *garden*, south of the College. This *garden* was an acre of land purchased by Professor E. Kellogg in 1836, and given to the College for the purpose of a *garden*, to be cultivated by the students. Hence this building was named after him. It is of brick, three stories in height. The first story is divided into recitation-rooms, and the other two stories into rooms for students.

Jackson Hall was built by Nathan Jackson, Esq., of New York, for the Natural History Society of the students of the College. It is of brick, consisting of one main room, with a gallery, and a tower on the east. From this tower is obtained a fine view of the surrounding country,— one of the most beautiful valleys in the world.

The College had outgrown the largest expectations of Dr. Griffin when he built the chapel. The Senior recitation-room was too small, and better provision was needed for the Junior recitation-room and for the apparatus. The Alumni and friends of the College nobly responded to these wants, and furnished the means of building a new chapel, to be connected with such other rooms as the means and space might afford. In 1858 and 1859 the chapel was built. It is a stone building, standing on the west brow of the East College ground. It is conveniently and pleasantly located. We copy the following description of this building from the North Adams Transcript, of a date just preceding the inauguration of the Alumni Hall, August, 1859.

"The chapel walls are constructed in the most substantial manner, of bluish-gray limestone, from the quarry of John Sherman, about two miles west of Williamstown village. It is a very hard and durable stone, 'good-looking' withal, though the outside walls are 'in the rough.' The roof and tower are slated with slate of two shades of color, from Rutland County, Vt.

"The building fronts to the north, and is in a very prominent location, near all the other College structures. Its style of architecture is Gothic. The doorways are all arched, and the doors are of oak. The main building is forty-four by sixty-one feet. The vestibule is twenty-nine by eight feet, with double gable and Gothic arched doorways and windows; the flooring is of marble, laid in diamond-shaped blocks, and the plastered walls are colored in imitation of stone-work. The chapel-room is forty by sixty feet, lighted by eight pointed windows. The roof is very fine and lofty, all its timbers being shown on the inside; it is forty feet high in the centre, and sixteen feet where it joins the walls. Both the roof and railings of the seats are of oiled chestnut, — a handsome dark wood. The ends of the seats are of iron. It contains seats, arranged in four rows, for three hundred and fifty students. There are a platform and a plain desk for the officiating preacher. The tower is sixteen feet square, stands at the northeast angle of the chapel, and contains a winding staircase which leads to the Alumni Hall. The spire, which

C. Currier's Lith. E. Valois, lith. 33 Spruce St. N.Y.

COLLEGE CHAPEL.

1859.

is somewhat elaborate in architecture, is about ninety-five feet high. It contains the rich-toned bell, weighing 1,025 lbs., which was presented, last year, by Hon. Pierpont Isham of Bennington. This bell is from the foundry of Meneely and Sons, West Troy, N. Y. The tower contains comfortable rooms for the bell-ringers. Strong iron rods, with massive bolts, confine the spire to the tower walls.

"The rear building, thirty-six by fifty-six feet, contains the Alumni Hall, which is thirty-two by fifty feet, and furnished with a platform and plain desk for speakers, and settees for about three hundred persons. The roof of this hall is also a pointed arch, about thirty feet high in the centre, and twelve feet where it leaves the wall. The floor is self-supporting.

"This hall is lighted by two large and three smaller windows, and the sash is painted green. The two windows in the gable ends are of a curious shape, resembling a spear-head or the end of a clover-leaf.

"The lower story of the rear building contains the Senior and Junior recitation-rooms, each eleven feet high, with side entrances, and an apartment for apparatus adjoining the Junior room. The Senior room is thirty-two by twenty-seven feet, and lighted by three large windows. The Junior room is thirty-two by twenty-five feet, and lighted by two large windows. Each room is amply supplied with comfortable settees for the students."

Before we close this chapter we must give some

account of the libraries and apparatus. No college can be considered as well furnished without a good library. This should be an object of early and continued attention. A well-furnished library to a literary institution cannot be too highly estimated. Next to well-qualified teachers, no department of a college deserves to be more liberally fostered, as equally essential to the improvement and usefulness of teachers and pupils.

The library connected with this College cannot be considered a well-furnished one. It had a small beginning, and has had a comparatively slow increase. Since it has been kept in Lawrence Hall it has been much enlarged. Many valuable additions have been made to it within a few years. It is furnished with a tolerable supply of standard works in theology and history, but in the sciences and general literature it is deficient. Additions are now made to it from year to year. The number of books at the present time somewhat exceeds eight thousand. This number, it is hoped, will soon be so far increased that it will answer all the purposes of a well-furnished institution.

The libraries of the two literary societies contain not far from ten thousand volumes. The Mills Theological Society, perhaps. not far from twelve hundred.

The Franklin Library contains only such books as are studied in the College course. It was commenced about 1820, for the purpose of aiding needy students. The system worked so well, and the library was so much enlarged in the course of a few years, that text-books could be obtained from it for all the members of College, for one dollar a year, or four dollars for the College course. In all our libraries, we have from eighteen to twenty thousand volumes.

The philosophical apparatus had a small beginning, and it has had a slow growth. The most important additions to this department of the College course were made soon after Professor Hopkins took charge of the department of Natural Philosophy. Some additions in the department of Philosophy and Chemistry have been made from time to time since.

We do not propose to give a catalogue of the apparatus in either of the departments, but merely to say, that in Chemistry, Natural Philosophy, and Astronomy, our instruments and apparatus, though needing enlargement, are now sufficient to answer all practical purposes. Besides, with the means now at command, extensive additions to our chemical and philosophical apparatus may soon be expected.

CHAPTER XVI.

PROGRESS IN THE COLLEGE STUDIES,—ESPECIALLY IN THE NATURAL SCIENCES.

WHEN Williams College was organized, the laws adopted by the Trustees required the following course of study, "so far as it may be convenient." The first year,—"The English, Latin, Greek, and French Languages. In the second,—the several languages in part, Arithmetic, Geography, Algebra, Geometry, Mensurations, Conic Sections, Rhetoric, and Logic. In the third,—Trigonometry, Navigation, Surveying, Natural Philosophy, Astronomy, and Chemistry. In the fourth year,—Metaphysics, Ethics, History, National Law, Civil Polity, and Theology."

The original guardians of the College were men of large and enlightened views. Eight of the thirteen original Trustees were graduates of Yale College, and most of them were "men of renown." It was their intention, from the first, to have an institution of high order, one that should not be inferior to their own Alma Mater, as soon as their means should enable them to accomplish their purposes. For obvious reasons the College had a small beginning, but its advancement has been steady and manifest. If some of its days have been dark and discouraging, others have been bright and cheering. Almost as much Greek and Latin is now required for admission, as was formerly required for graduation. Geography, English Grammar, and Arithmetic formed a part of the early College course. Geography was dropped in 1831, Arithmetic in 1837, and English Grammar in 1839.

In the early provisions for imparting instruction in many branches, now considered essential to a complete liberal education, Williams College was deficient. And the same may be said of other and older institutions at that period. But this defect of the times had its advantages. It threw more labor and responsibility on the inventive powers of teachers and pupils, and stimulated the efforts of genius. There is such a thing as giving too much instruction, — of making the student's task too light and easy. It is admitted that Williams College labored long under the disadvantages of a course of instruction too circumscribed, with a corps of teachers too small, and with libraries and apparatus too limited. But "the law of progress" has here been manifest. College officers are now more numerous, our libraries are enlarged by the addition of most valuable books, our instruments and cabinets for illustration are more ample and complete, text-books have been introduced containing a wider range of subjects, a more complete subdivision of the sciences, a more natural and philosophical arrangement, more clear and precise statements, and more apt and abundant illustrations.

In the text-books of the Natural Sciences — concerning which we propose chiefly to speak in this chapter (for in these branches Williams College took an early and prominent position) — the progress has, for obvious reasons, been most marked and striking. Instead of a single volume (Enfield), containing an outline of Natural Philosophy, Astronomy, and Chemistry, meagre in its data, crude in its theories, often false in statement and inconclusive in reasoning, leaving deficiencies to be supplied by oral instruction and lectures, we now have separate, and comparatively full and well-digested text-books in each of these branches.

In the text-books of the classic authors of Greece and Rome, where, perhaps, we should least have expected it, there have been marked improvements; for example, in the substitution of English for Latin notes, and in the use of the excellent modern manuals, designed to aid the student in classic composition.

History, too, has ceased to be a mere narrative of events, — a dry digest of ill-assorted and isolated facts. It has become a system and a science, tracing everywhere the lines of cause and effect, so that we now have a philosophy of history.

Nor has advancement been confined to these branches. Mental and moral science have received valuable elucidations since the days of Locke, Berkeley, and Paley, to which the American mind has not been the least contributor.

Geology, a comparatively new science, has not improved, but introduced its text-books. The same may be said, substantially, of some other departments of Natural History.

The Natural Sciences received but little attention at Williams College previous to 1816. Prior to 1812 the College had but little philosophical, and no chemical apparatus, and anything like a regular or systematic course of experimental lectures on the Natural Sciences had not been attempted.

In 1808 Mr. Chester Dewey was elected Senior Tutor, and in 1810 was transferred to the department of Mathematics and Natural Philosophy. The course of study and instruction from the organization of the College up to this time had not been much enlarged or improved. For a few years Professor Dewey taught the Junior class Geometry, Webber's Trigonometry, Mensurations, Surveying, and Navigation, Conic Sections, and some Spherical Trigonometry, the Natural Philosophy of Enfield, embracing Mechanical Philosophy, Pneumatics, the doctrine of Fluids, Electricity and Magnetism, Optics, and Astronomy, with the calculation of Eclipses. Of course his hands were full. But so deeply convinced was he that Chemistry, with experiments, must become a part of the College course (in Yale it had already become a branch of study), that he urged the matter upon the President and

Trustees, and offered to lecture on Chemistry, as well as teach it, if they would furnish the laboratory and apparatus.

This was done. Some funds were raised, and he went to New Haven, in December, 1812, to procure the apparatus. Professor Silliman gave him all necessary directions concerning its use, and admitted him to his lectures and experiments for a week or ten days. He then returned with apparatus enough to make a beginning, and, in the small building in the southeast corner of the East College lot, commenced operations. This was in the early part of 1813. But it was soon found that this double duty was too much for him. The Trustees then appointed an additional Tutor for the Junior class, and directed Professor Dewey to deliver lectures, theoretical and practical, on Philosophy as well as Chemistry.

Some public lectures were occasionally given to all the members of College, in the chapel, directly after evening prayers; each bearing on a single point and occupying fifteen or twenty minutes in the delivery. Thus the College advanced till 1815, when President Fitch resigned, and Dr. Moore succeeded him. At the same time Professor Kellogg was chosen Professor of the Latin and Greek Languages. This was a great addition to the corps of instructors.

In the spring of 1817, lectures on Mineralogy, Geology, and Botany were given to those members of College who chose to attend, by Mr. Amos

Eaton. A new impulse was now awakened in these sciences. In consequence of Mr. Eaton's labors in the College and in the country (for he now resolved to become an itinerating lecturer), a taste was in a short time acquired for these studies in New England and New York. Men of large and liberal views were soon led to see the practical benefits which would unquestionably result from exact and extensive geological surveys, which became practicable in consequence of the training of Mr. Eaton's pupils.

The following communication from Professor A. Hopkins will be read, in this connection, with interest.

"Professor Eaton was one of the first to popularize science in the Northern States. For this task he had some special qualifications. He had an easy flow of language, a popular address, and a generous enthusiasm in matters of science, which easily communicated itself to his pupils. I well remember attending a lecture of his in my native town, the first scientific lecture I ever attended, and, if I may judge by the sharp outline of it still in my mind, one of the most interesting and impressive. Perhaps the 'leafy month of June,' the subject of the lecture, *Flowers*, and the presence of a large number of interesting young persons, may have added something to the charm; but making all due allowances, I am sure that the lecture itself must have had a good deal of intrinsic merit.

"Professor Eaton was at this time (1817, I think)

nearly in his prime. His person was quite striking,—a large frame, somewhat portly and dignified, though entirely free from what is commonly called *starch.* His face was highly intellectual,— the forehead high and somewhat retreating, locality strongly marked, and the organs of observation and comparison well developed. His hair at that time was black, and being combed back, rendered his fine physiognomy still more striking. I well recollect the flowers, which I believe his young pupil Emmons had been employed to collect for the occasion. They were, in the first place, the common lilac, which I had probably seen before; however this may be, the small floret, with its salver-form corolla and long tubular throat, into which the Professor dexterously inserted his penknife, with no murderous intent, but to give us a view of the organs which the great Linnæus had selected as the basis of his classification,— this little floret, I say, is the first I now recollect to have seen; and seen it was, and still is, with great distinctness. Then followed the pedicularis and some plants more difficult in their analysis. In the analysis of these plants Professor Eaton made use of his manual, descriptive of plants in the vicinity of Williams College, a book which, with some imperfections, was highly valuable as a pioneer work.

"Professor Eaton was among the first in this country to study Nature *in the field* with his classes. In pursuance of this idea, he used to make an annual excursion with the Rensselaer School; sometimes leading these expeditions in person, at others deputing some competent teacher to take the lead.

"The cause of Natural History in Williams College owes, undoubtedly, a good deal to Professor Eaton. I think his zeal in the department of Botany led Professor Dewey to direct his discriminating mind to the study of plants, — a study which he pursued farther than Professor Eaton had done, in certain lines, particularly in Caricography, which was then a kind of *terra incognita*, and still is, except to the initiated. At this time, also, as has been hinted, Dr. Emmons took the field. In fact, Natural History came in on a spring tide, and has never lost the impulse since!"

In the spring of 1819, while I was a member of Lenox Academy, Mr. Eaton came there, at the request of Hon. H. W. Bishop, and delivered a short course of lectures on Botany. And I retain a vivid recollection of his manly appearance, his constantly flowing conversation, and his instructive lectures. As Mr. Eaton was an Alumnus of this College, and his name has become so identified with unwearied and self-denying labors in the cultivation of the Natural Sciences, no apology will be needed for giving him more than a passing notice on these pages and in this connection.

Amos Eaton (son of Abel and Azuba Hurd Eaton) was a native of Chatham, Columbia County, N. Y., and was born May 17, 1776. His father was a farmer, in comfortable circumstances, a highly respected citizen, and a deacon of the church.

Young Eaton early manifested superior abilities, and his aspirations were for a wide field of action. He was selected to deliver an oration on the 4th of July, 1790, when but fourteen years of age, which was a creditable performance. About this time, having acted as chain-bearer in surveying some land, he resolved on learning the surveyor's art. But how shall he obtain the requisite instruments? He soon interested a skilful blacksmith in his behalf, who agreed to work for him at night, if he would "blow and strike" by day. An accurately constructed needle (magnetized from kitchen tongs) and a good working chain were the result of several weeks' work. This circumstance in his life doubtless gave rise to the remark, found in Silliman's Journal, that "in 1791 he was an apprenticed blacksmith." The bottom of an old pewter plate, well smoothed, polished, and graduated, made a pretty good compass case; so that Eaton, when sixteen years old, was in the field with his home-made instruments, doing little jobs of surveying in the neighborhood. But he aspired to higher attainments, a wider sphere of action. Encouraged by his parents, he fitted for college with the late Rev. Dr. David Porter, of Catskill, then of Spencertown, N. Y., and was graduated at Williams College in 1799, with high reputation for his scientific attainments. He commenced the study of law in Spencertown, with Hon. Elisha Williams, September 13, 1799, and subsequently continued his studies in New York, with the Hon. Josiah Ogden Hoffman.

It was at this period, and under the instructions of Dr. David Hosack and Dr. Samuel L. Mitchell, that Mr. Eaton first became especially interested in the study of Botany and other Natural Sciences. While in New York, in 1802, he borrowed Kirwan's Mineralogy, then a scarce book, and made a manuscript copy of the entire work. He was admitted attorney of the Supreme Court of the State of New York, at Albany, October 30, 1802, and soon after established himself as a lawyer and land-agent in Catskill, N. Y. Here he remained several years; his position affording him good opportunities for cultivating his growing taste for the Natural Sciences. In May, 1810, he made, in Catskill, it is believed, the first attempt in this country at a popular course of lectures on Botany (compiling for the use of his class a small elementary treatise), for which he was highly complimented by his former teacher, Dr. Hosack, as "first in the field," saying, "you have adopted the true system of education, and very properly address yourself to the senses and the memory." Here we find Mr. Eaton, at this early day, adopting that mode of instruction which he perfected in after life, and which rendered him so pre-eminently successful in inspiring young men with that enthusiasm which assures success.

Owing to a concurrence of circumstances, which our limits will not allow us to explain, Mr. Eaton now found his love for the details of his profession diminishing, and his interest in the Natural Sciences fast growing upon him; he therefore resolved to abandon the practice of law, and to prepare himself to become an efficient laborer in the more congenial pursuits of science. With this end in view he went to New Haven, in 1815, to avail himself of the advantages of Yale College. Here he placed himself under the instruction of Professor Silliman, who threw open to him his lectures on Chemistry, Geology, and Mineralogy, as also his own library and the cabinet of minerals of that institution. Here, also, he found a good botanist in Dr. Eli Ives, Professor of Botany and Materia Medica in the Medical Department of the college, who had accumulated a good library, to which he gave Mr. Eaton free access. With these advantages, and Mr. Eaton's already advanced acquirements, he made such rapid progress that he was soon well qualified to take the field as an explorer, and the desk as a teacher. He now turned towards his own Alma Mater, with whose honorable indorsement, as a competent teacher, he desired to go forth into the world. He therefore came to Williamstown in March, 1817, and was most cordially received by the Faculty of the College, especially by Professor Dewey, and gave courses of lectures on Botany, Mineralogy, and Geology, to volunteer classes of the students. His influence in the College was remarkable. He awakened a lively interest in the Natural Sciences, which has never died out. With few books adapted to his department, he accomplished wonders. The graduates of that day who were among his pupils always speak of him in terms of the most affectionate interest and gratitude. They published, in 1817, the first edition of his Manual of Botany, a 12mo of 164 pages, which "gave (as the late Dr. Lewis C. Beck wrote in 1852) an impulse to the study of Botany in New England and New York, as the only descriptive work which was then current was that of Pursh, an expensive one, with Latin descriptions." This work, improved by repeated revisions and additions, became, in the eighth edition, published in 1840, a large octavo volume of 625 pages, entitled "North American Botany," and contained a description of 5,267 species of plants. In this edition Mr. Eaton was assisted by the late Dr. John Wright. Mr. Eaton always aimed to render scientific principles and facts useful; still, he loved science, though it brought no pecuniary gain. To him knowledge was in itself a good; which idea he carried through all the editions of his Manual from the fifth, by introducing as a motto the following sentence of Linnæus: "That existence is surely contemptible which regards only the gratification of instinctive wants, and the preservation of a body made to perish."

The patronage and encouragement which Mr. Eaton received at this time from the Faculty and students of Williams College determined him to give courses of popular lectures, accompanied with practical instructions, to such classes as he might be able to organize in several of the larger towns of New England and New York. The aid he thus received he gratefully acknowledged in 1818, by inscribing the second edition of his Manual of Botany to the President and Professors, saying to them, "The science of Botany is indebted to you for its first introduction into the interior of the Northern States: and I am indebted to you for a passport into the scientific world." To Professor Dewey he was warmly attached, and through life regarded him as a successful fellow-laborer; and his friendship and co-operation were warmly reciprocated. From Williamstown he went first to Northampton, where Governor Strong, the Hon. E. H. Mills, and others, patronized and encouraged him. He gave popular scientific lectures, and practical instructions in many places, with great success. In the course of two or three years he diffused a great amount of knowledge on these interesting subjects; and so far excited the curiosity and enthusiasm of many young students, that there sprung up, as the result of his labors, an army of botanists and geologists.

In 1818, in compliance with a special invitation from Governor De Witt Clinton, he went to Albany, and there gave a course of lectures before the members of the Legislature. Here he became acquainted with many of the leading men of the State, interesting them especially in Geology, and its application, by means of surveys, to agriculture. There and then were set in operation a train of causes which resulted in giving to the world that great work, "The Natural History of New York," so creditable to the State and to those scientific gentlemen who executed it, — several of whom had been Professor Eaton's pupils. In this year he published the first edition of his Index to the Geology of the Northern States, which "was the first attempt at a general arrangement of the geological strata in North America." Although this and his subsequent works on Geology have been found to contain some errors, still, it is universally conceded that great credit is due him for his early and successful labors in developing the Geology of America.

He afterwards delivered several courses of lectures in the Medical College at Castleton, Vt., in which he was appointed Professor of Natural History in 1820. Professor Eaton's lectures and practical instructions in Troy produced a most happy impression, where, through his efforts, seconded by many of the most distinguished gentlemen of that city, such as Drs. Barrett, Robbins, and Hall, there was established a Lyceum of Natural History, which for many years did much service to the cause of Natural Science. In the fall of 1818 Troy could boast of a more extensive collection of American geological specimens than could be found at any literary institution in this country. In 1820 and 1821 Mr. Eaton, with the assistance of Drs. T. Romeyn and Lewis C. Beck, made, at the expense and under the patronage of the Hon. Stephen Van Rensselaer of Albany, N. Y., Geological and

Agricultural Surveys of Albany and Rensselaer Counties, reports of which were published. This, it is believed, was the beginning of such surveys in this country, of which Professor Silliman in his Journal remarked, "The attempt is novel in this country;" adding, "We are not aware of any attempt on so extensive and systematic a scale, to make them (such surveys) subservient to the important interests of agriculture."

The Hon. Stephen Van Rensselaer, for many years one of the Trustees in Williams College, — the generous patron of merit, — employed Professor Eaton to make a Geological Survey of the District adjoining the Erie Canal, and the result was published, in 1824, in a Report of 160 octavo pages, addressed to his patron, with a profile section of rock formations, from the Atlantic Ocean, across the States of Massachusetts and New York, to Lake Erie.

Of this work of Professor Eaton, Governor Seward, in his Introduction to the Natural History of New York, said: "This publication marked an era in the progress of Geology in this country. It is, in some respects, inaccurate, but it must be remembered that its talented and indefatigable author was without a guide in exploring the older formations, and that he described rocks which no geologist had, at that time, attempted to classify. Rocks were then classified chiefly by their mineralogical characters, and the aid which the science has since learned to derive from fossils in determining the chronology and classification of rocks was scarcely known here, and had only just begun to be appreciated in Europe. We are indebted, nevertheless, to Professor Eaton for the commencement of that independence of European classification, which has been found indispensable in describing the New York system." For, he adds, "After examining our rocks with as much care and accuracy as I am capable of doing, I venture to say that we have, at least, five distinct and continuous strata, neither of which can with propriety take any name hitherto given and defined in any European treatise which has reached this country. Professor Eaton enumerated nearly all the rocks in Western New York, in their order of succession, and his enumeration has, with one or two exceptions, proved correct. It is a matter of surprise that he recognized, at so early a period, the old red sandstone on the Catskill Mountains, a discovery, the reality of which has since been proved by fossil tests."

In 1824 the Hon. Mr. Van Rensselaer established at Troy, N. Y. a school of science called the Rensselaer School, placing Mr. Eaton at its head as "Senior Professor." Here he continued his labors through the remainder of his life, publishing, at different times, several scientific works, required for his own pupils, as well as for the general advancement of science. Among them, a Philosophical Instructor, several editions of the Manual of Botany, Chemical Instructor, Zoölogical Text-Book, Geological Text-Book, Botanical Grammar and Dictionary, Art without Science, &c., &c. In this school Professor Eaton was enabled to perfect and carry out, to a high degree of success, his favorite plan of teaching classes by making his pupils experimenters and workers, in every department of science where it was practicable; substituting, also, lectures by the pupils to each other, in place of the usual system of recitations. This method of giving instruction, and of preparing young men to become successful teachers, has here succeeded most admirably, and has been, in some of its features, introduced into other schools of science. The Rensselaer Institute still exists, with only a slight change of name; its course of study, though modified and extended, still retains the characteristic features impressed upon it by its first Senior Professor. As a school for practical science, it occupies the very highest rank; and its graduates are to be found in every State of the Union.

It will thus be perceived that, in developing the Botany and Geology of the Northern States, Professor Eaton rightfully ranks among the pioneers of the new era of the Natural Sciences in this country. His efforts in the various departments of Natural History were a rich gift to New England, New York, and even to the whole country, for which the country owes him a debt of gratitude. Many of his pupils have been for years among the most justly distinguished scientific men of the country. As an educator and an active laborer in the general cause of Natural History in America, his memory will long be cherished. The history of Natural Science on this continent can never be faithfully written, without giving the name of Amos Eaton an honorable place. It was he, more than any other individual in the United States, who, finding the Natural Sciences in the hands of the learned few, by means of his popular lectures, simplified text-books, and practical instructions, threw them broadcast to the many. He aimed at a general diffusion of the Natural Sciences, and nobly and successfully did he accomplish his mission.

Professor Eaton was a kind-hearted and courteous gentleman. His vast acquirements and simple habits induced a distinguished lady, who knew him well, to speak of him as AMOS EATON, THE REPUBLICAN PHILOSOPHER. He died in Troy, N. Y., May 6, 1842, in the sixty-sixth year of his age, saying, "I submit to my Heavenly Father's will." His remains are interred in the new cemetery at Troy, N. Y., where, we regret to state, no suitable monument has yet (1860) been erected to mark their resting-place.*

---

* Three of Professor Eaton's sons, who were educated by their father to follow him in the walks of science, died young. H. Hulbert Eaton, Assistant Professor of Chemistry in Transylvania University, a scholar of great promise, died at the age of twenty-three. Another son, Major A. B. Eaton, resides in New Haven, Conn., was graduated at West Point in 1826, is an officer in the United States Army, a man of scientific taste, and has no small knowledge of Botany. A daughter of Professor Eaton, Miss Sara C. Eaton, is a teacher of the Natural Sciences and the Modern Languages in the flourishing Female Seminary at Monticello, Illinois. Daniel Cady Eaton, a son of Major Eaton,

As early as 1815 a cabinet of minerals was commenced in Williams College, and before Professor Dewey left Williamstown a respectable collection of geological specimens, for that day, had been made, which, with the exception of the shelves on which they were placed, cost the College no money. From this cabinet Professor Dewey was able to give much valuable instruction in connection with the course in Chemistry. Still, this was the day of small things with the cabinet, compared with the extensive, rare, and splendid additions which were made to it, twenty years afterwards, by Professor Emmons.

As early as 1816 and 1817 Professor Dewey began to teach Botany, Mineralogy, and Geology, in connection with Chemistry. From this time forward the Natural Sciences have maintained a steady

---

was graduated at Yale College in 1857, and is probably unsurpassed in his knowledge of Botany by any one of his age in this country.

Professor Eaton published an Elementary Treatise on Botany, 1810; Manual of Botany, 1817; Botanical Dictionary, 1817; Botanical Exercises, 1820; Botanical Grammar and Dictionary, 1828; Chemical Note-Book, 1821; Chemical Instructor, 1822; Zoölogical Syllabus and Note-Book, 1822; Cuvier's Grand Division, 1822; Art without Science, 1800; Philosophical Instructor, 1824; Directions for Surveying and Engineering, 1838; Index to the Geology of the Northern States, 1818; Geological and Agricultural Survey of the County of Albany, N. Y., 1820; Geological and Agricultural Survey of Rensselaer County, N. Y., 1822; Geological Nomenclature of North America, 1822; Geological and Agricultural Survey of the District adjoining the Erie Canal, 1824; Geological Text-Book, prepared for popular lectures on North American Geology, 1830; Geological Note-Book, for Troy Class, 1841. Of most of these works, a number of different editions were published.

and growing interest in this College. After Mr. Eaton left Williamstown, Professor Dewey pursued an independent course, and, unaided except by a few pupils, began an investigation of the Geology of Berkshire, and the neighboring counties. Journeys were made for the purpose of tracing out the formations, which, after a few years, furnished a stock of materials for a full elucidation of the Geology and Mineralogy of Berkshire County. The full results were published by the Rev. Dr. Field, in his History of Berkshire County. Several important communications were likewise made to the American Journal of Science. And probably these communications embraced all the leading points respecting the Geology of Berkshire, as well as the adjacent counties in Vermont, and a large portion of the old county of Hampshire.

In the earliest period of Professor Dewey's career in Natural History, his earnest attention was turned to the study of Botany; and the results of his investigations in this department have been eminently successful and honorable, especially in the department of Caricography, — a difficult branch of investigation, in which he has few if any superiors. Some of the valuable results of his investigations in this department were published as early as 1824, with plates, in Silliman's Journal.

It was about this time that the late Professor Olmstead of Yale College, made a geological survey of North Carolina, the results of which were published in 1825. Regarding the study of Natural History as receiving a new and practical impulse, about the year 1816 (it was at this time that Professor Cleveland of Bowdoin College published his treatise on Mineralogy and Geology), without wishing to detract from other individuals or institutions in the least, we may safely say that Williams College had a large share in the initiatory work. Much was here done to open and prepare the way for those further investigations and discoveries which have since been made. Professor Hitchcock was employed to make a geological survey of the State of Massachusetts, and his report was published in 1839, in two quarto volumes. The survey of New York was commenced in 1836, and one of Professor Dewey's pupils, Professor Emmons, to whom we have already alluded, was appointed one of the principal geologists of that State. He was connected with that survey until 1851, when he was appointed by the Governor of North Carolina to take charge of a similar work there, in which he is still engaged. Besides the five annual reports made by Professor Emmons, five quarto volumes have issued from his pen, and three reports in an octavo form have been made by him since the Carolina enterprise was undertaken.

Professor Emmons was also appointed a commissioner on the Zoölogy of Massachusetts, by Governor Everett, and published one report on the mammals of the State.

In 1825 Professor Emmons published a Manual of Mineralogy, which was adopted as a text-book in the Renssalaer Institute. A second edition of this work was published 1832, both of which are now out of print.

Professor Emmons is now engaged in the preparation of a work on American Geology, of which several numbers have already appeared. In this work will be embraced the results of his researches in the various fields, which he has personally examined.*

In the department of Natural Science Professor Dewey made an early and excellent beginning. What he accomplished was of vast consequence to the College and to the country. A very low estimate had previously been placed on such studies. In a great measure he had to be his own teacher. Very few books had, up to his time, been published on these subjects in this country. But circumstances have changed. Original investigations have placed Natural History and its collateral branches on a new footing. Every part of our country has been explored, and almost every subject has been elucidated; and information on these subjects, instead of being confined to a few learned

* Professor Ebenezer Emmons was a native of Middlefield, fitted for college with the Rev. Mr. Perkins of Amherst and the Rev. Mr. Hallock of Plainfield; was graduated at Williams College in 1818, with high attainments in the department of Natural History. His class has long been regarded as one of the best the College has produced. Among its prominent members are Barnard, Bartlett, Benedict, Danforth, Emmons, Esterbrook, and Porter, to mention no others. It is not often that more than one third of a class make their mark in the world.

men, has become, as it were, like the light and air which surround us, — common property.

Professor Dewey resigned his post in Williams College in 1827; but Natural History maintained its advanced position, and still continued to be cultivated with spirit and success. The Trustees and Faculty have uniformly given these studies their hearty approbation and efficient support, having early seen their importance in an educational point of view. It is especially due to Professor Albert Hopkins to say that a species of enthusiasm prevailed in consequence of his own early example, and the lead which he took in exploring expeditions. What College in this country sent out a large scientific expedition prior to 1835? It is unnecessary to state in detail all the facts respecting the progress of Natural History in this institution. It is sufficient if we refer to the causes of its eminent success, which have become obvious to the public in consequence of the organization of a society for its special cultivation; the erection of a large hall by Mr. Jackson (and we never know which to admire most, the aspirations which called for it, or the benevolence which caused its erection), the collections which have been made, and the numerous scientific journeys which have been undertaken, some of which were formidable and expensive from their extent, and the difficulties attending their execution.

The ground of success to which we have alluded has been no doubt due to the practical turn which these sciences have taken under the guidance of its teachers, and the original investigations which have been encouraged from the first. The fruits of these special encouragements are seen in the published works of many of the graduates, especially in the production of the Rev. Moses Ashley Curtis, D. D., of Hillsborough, North Carolina, a native of Stockbridge, and a graduate of Williams College in 1827. His work on Cryptogamian Botany is of great value. His labors have by no means been confined to this interesting family of the vegetable kingdom.

Nor must we pass over the works of Professor John Darby, a native of Adams, and a graduate of Williams College in 1831. He has published an elaborate and valuable work on Southern Botany, and is still zealously and successfully engaged in its perfection, by personal explorations in all parts of the Southern States.

Professor Edward Lasell, a native of Schoharie, N. Y., and a graduate of Williams College in 1828; cut down in early life, he did not publish any work on this subject, yet had made more than ordinary attainments in the department of Chemistry. He was extremely happy in the presentation of a subject to an audience, and accompanied his lectures with very beautiful experiments.

Mr. David A. Wells, of the class of 1847, also acquired a taste for Natural History while here. Instead, however, of confining himself to one department, he has pursued a more general course, which led him, in connection with another individual, to project the plan of a Scientific Manual, of which he is now the sole proprietor. This work has a wide circulation in this country and Europe. His various publications amount to twenty-seven volumes.

Professor Paul A. Chadbourn, a native of Great Falls, N. H., and a graduate of Williams College in 1848, is successfully devoting his time to the study of Botany, and though he has not published anything more than some fugitive articles on his favorite department, yet as a teacher and lecturer he is as accomplished and successful as those we have named, and is fast rising to distinction.

We feel it due also, in this connection, to mention the name of Samuel Hubbard Scudder, a native of Boston, and a member of the class of 1857. He is devoting his time entirely to the study of Natural History, and gives promise of future eminence, having already distinguished himself for his exact knowledge and extensive attainments in the science of Entomology.

We may err in our views respecting the causes which have imparted so much interest to this branch of education in this College. The course pursued here has been such, to a great extent, as to enkindle a love for Natural Science, — a love which, in many instances, verged upon enthusiasm, if it did not really become so. Let the pupil adopt a different course. Let him suffer himself to be content with his text-books, or with the mere hearing of lectures, and his feelings are not sufficiently interested and enlisted to lead him to make any marked or useful attainments. Now let him wander over regions of beauty and magnificence, where everything is suggestive and is inviting to thought and improvement; let him study nature in the field, under the guidance of competent Christian teachers, and thoughts and feelings are awakened "that shall perish never."

But in addition to the advantages named, Natural History is regarded, in Williams College, as a part of a system of education, designed and adopted more especially to improve and strengthen *the observing powers.* Some students acquire a taste for Botany, others for Zoölogy, others still for Mineralogy and Geology. Now it matters but little to which the student directs his attention, so far as his improvement is concerned. Patient investigation is indispensable to the study of Natural History. A knowledge of external nature, if acquired by personal application, is of unspeakable importance in a system of education. In connection with Natural History, the study of Anatomy is pursued in this College as an introduction to the study of the intellectual and moral man. The study of external nature, in her varied forms, the structure and composition of man's physical organization, and of comparative anatomy, open and prepare the way for the investigation of man's higher nature, — his relations to law, to government, and to God.

"I will mention one idea more," says Dr. Hopkins, in his Jubilee Address,* "which we have of late attempted, in this College, to realize. It is that of making the College studies have the impression and effect of a system on the mind of the student. Laying the power of expression, whether by writing or speaking, and of the question, we divide our course into the Languages, Mathematics, Physical Science, and Man, as he is in himself, and in his relations to his fellow-creatures, and to God. Pursuing Mathematics and the Languages in the manner already spoken of, we take up the *physical man*, and endeavor to give, as by the aid of the admirable preparation of Auzoux we are able to do, an idea of every organ and tissue of the body. We then take up the *intellectual man*, and investigate, first, and classify his several faculties; then the grounds of belief and the processes of the mind in the pursuit of truth, with an explanation of the inductive and the deductive logic; then the *moral nature*, together with individual and political morality, comprising a knowledge of constitutional history, and of the rights and duties of American citizens; then the emotive nature, as taste and the principles of the fine arts; then natural theology and the analogy of the natural to the moral government of God. Perhaps other and better systems have been adopted elsewhere; but I know that formerly, here, the studies were pursued as

* Miscellaneous Discourses, p. 297.

separate and isolated, and there is reason to suppose that the idea of system, of the communication of one great organized body of knowledge answering, in unity as well as diversity, to the universe of God, is too little regarded."

CHAPTER XVII.

SCENERY OF WILLIAMSTOWN, AND PLACES OF INTEREST IN ITS VICINITY.

THE location of Williams College, if we regard the pleasures and advantages of natural and romantic scenery, is perhaps unsurpassed by that of any other college in the country. Environed as it is by some of the loftiest mountains in New England, in a region replete with scenes of historic interest, and abounding in wild and picturesque views, the surrounding country, as might be expected, presents many objects well worthy of the attention of the tourist and geologist, and which, by numerous and delightful associations, have become hallowed in the memory of every graduate. The climate is not as cold as has been generally supposed. The average temperature here, during the winter months, is higher than in towns many miles south. The average temperature for some years past has been 46° Fahrenheit. The prevailing opinion respecting the elevation of Williamstown has been very erroneous. Stockbridge village is 827 feet above Hudson River at Albany. Pittsfield, 1,035. Williamstown, where the College chapel stands, is only

730. The giant mountains which surround this place, muffled in their winter drapery, protect it from the bleak winds which howl in vain for admittance. However, we have breezes enough to ventilate the valley, and to refresh and invigorate our bodies. The weather in summer is not so warm as to be enfeebling. On the whole, the climate may be called salubrious. It is easy of access. The Troy and Boston Railroad, now in successful operation from Troy to Adams, passing within half a mile of the College, joins us to the net-work of railroads, which now pervade our country.* We cannot but regard the situation of Williams College as most fortunate,—as calculated to awaken those finer feelings in the heart of every student, which arise from a frequent contemplation of the sublime and beautiful, and the influence of which may, in some measure, account for the ardent and cherished attachment which has ever characterized the Alumni of this institution. In this chapter we propose to accompany our reader to some of the most interesting places, and point out, as well as we are able, the distinctive features and history of each.

The first place of note which we propose to visit

---

* FIRST TRAIN FROM TROY!—On Thursday morning, December 30, 1858, a locomotive and two freight cars entered North Adams from the West, and were greeted by a crowd of spectators. They came to obtain bridge timber, which was required in Pownal, and on the way received several passengers. This train carried back a lot of warps from S. Johnson & Co. to R. Carpenter & Co. of Pownal,—the first business freight over the road.

is the site of Fort Massachusetts, situated about three miles from the College, on the road to North Adams, and interesting both from the historical associations connected with it, as well as from the few scattered relics that yet remain upon the ground. "The plough has passed over its rude lines, but what scenes of humble heroism and almost forgotten valor are associated with its name. It was the bulwark of the frontier in the day of its infancy. The trembling mother, on the banks of the Connecticut in the heart of the Commonwealth, clasped her babes closer, at an idle rumor that Fort Massachusetts had given way. A hundred villages reposed in the strength of this stout guardian of New England's Thermopylæ, through which, for two generations, the French and Canadian foe strove to burst into the colonies."

This fort was built in 1741 – 42, and was part of the line of defence erected to protect the northern and western settlements of New England against French and Indian hostilities. It was at that time the most extreme northern outpost, in the very centre of the wilderness, the nearest settlements being Albany and Springfield. The enemy directed their principal movements towards Connecticut River, but some came down the Hudson, and, proceeding eastward up the Hoosac, appeared, at intervals, in the neighborhood of this fort, beneath whose walls many bloody skirmishes took place.

The first action of any importance occurred on

the 20th of August, 1746, when an attack was made by upwards of nine hundred French and Indians, under General Vaudreuil. The garrison at that time consisted of thirty-three persons, including women and children; of this number twenty-two only were effective men, who were miserably supplied with ammunition. Notwithstanding these unfortunate circumstances, the fort was most bravely defended for forty-eight hours, when they were compelled to surrender, the means of defence being wholly exhausted. The terms of capitulation stipulated that none of the prisoners should be delivered into the hands of the Indians; but this condition was most shamefully violated on the succeeding day, on the plea that there was danger of mutiny in the army, — the Indians being irritated because they they were cut off from the profits of the conquest. One half were accordingly delivered up, the sick and infirm immediately butchered, and the remainder carried captive to Canada. The enemy lost forty-five men, a portion of whom, from the quantity of bones discovered, during the summer of 1846, in the rear of the Magnetic Observatory, possibly were buried in that place. The fort, which was destroyed, was rebuilt the succeeding summer by Colonel Williams, who was attacked on the 25th of May, 1747, by a large party of the enemy, who came with the design of hindering the undertaking, but were repulsed with considerable loss. In 1748 another action took place. Colonel

Williams was compelled to retire, after some sharp fighting, within the walls.

After the death of Colonel Williams, the command of the fort devolved on one Captain Wyman. The last attack was in June, 1756, when the enemy killed a few men whom they unexpectedly surprised in the fields.

The Rev. Stephen West, afterwards Dr. West, and first Vice-President of the College, was stationed at this fort, as chaplain, from 1755 to 1757.

The following incident is said to have occurred in 1746. It was the daily custom of an old Indian to come upon a ledge of rocks (by the side of which the present road now passes), in full sight of the garrison, and provoke them with insulting gestures and taunting exclamations. The old fellow had cautiously calculated the intervening distance, and safe beyond the reach of shot from the fort, would calmly await any attempt to approach him, when he would retire to the adjoining woods, where, on account of the numbers and strength of the enemy scouting in the vicinity, it was highly imprudent to follow. This scene was daily repeated for some time, and what measures to take the garrison were for a time at a loss to know. To submit to these repeated outrages was not to be thought of by the stern old settlers for an instant.

Among the various topics that formed the subject of conversation at that time, the merits of a famous long gun, celebrated along the borders for its power to send a ball to a great distance, held a prominent place. This gun was owned in Springfield, and without delay a messenger was despatched on the long and perilous journey of seventy-five miles, through a trackless wilderness, to obtain it. In five days, the man, fortunately escaping the enemy's outposts, returned, having effected his object, and when the unsuspecting Indian again made his appearance, a sure and fatal shot prevented him from ever repeating the performance. So the story runs, as narrated by Israel Jones, one of the early Trustees. That the shot was a long one, any one who will take the trouble to examine the distance will not for a moment doubt.

The locality of this fort is still indicated by the print of the cellar, and by horse-radish, which was planted by the soldiers, and still grows upon the spot. Beneath an apple-tree, a short distance from the road, are two rude monumental stones, one of which bears the following inscription: —

1746,
JUNE 26,
ELISHA NIMS.

The inscription upon the other, with the exception of the date, 1748, and a few other rude characters, is nearly obliterated. Tradition having asserted that the *gallant Nims* was shot in the back by the Indian above referred to, while carrying water to the garrison (from the spring which still bubbles at the foot of the hill), a party of students, a few years since, while making some explorations in the vicinity, opened the grave designated by the stone as his. A skeleton was there found, with a bullet imbedded in one of the vertebræ; having been undisturbed and in a good state of preservation for nearly a hundred years. The vertebræ containing the ball is still to be seen in the Museum of the Lyceum of Natural History. The foundations of the chimneys, together with some traces of the walls, were at the same time discovered.

It was probably while stationed at this fort (from 1747 to 1755), that the mind of Colonel Williams, foreseeing that brighter days were yet to dawn upon the infant settlement, and that the little groups of log-cabins, the smoke from whose chimneys had just began to curl up amid the lonely and mysterious woods, would soon give place to prosperous and thriving villages, resolved thus early to devote his property to the cause of future education, the result of which, fifty years afterwards, was the establishment of Williams College.

Leaving Fort Massachusetts, and proceeding about a mile across the fields, towards the eastern extremity of Saddle Mountain, you enter a wild and beautiful gorge, which is well worthy the attention of all lovers of romantic scenery. Following the mountain stream, that rushes in miniature cascades along the narrow bottom of the ravine, now half concealed by the thick foliage, and at times apparently lost amid the huge boulders and broken trunks that are scattered in every direction, you come at last to a beautiful waterfall, falling, by a series of successive leaps, a distance of about sixty feet over the opposing precipice into a circular rock basin, whose placid and mirror-like surface presents a pleasing contrast with the turbulence and foam of the stream above. The scenery around is of the wildest and most romantic character.

The steep moss-covered rocks that rise on either side, the lofty and primeval forests that crown their summits and hang over the gulf, the accumulated rocky masses below, all remain unmodified by the hand of man, just as the mighty agencies of nature have left them. This spot, although so near the College, is so effectually concealed among the recesses of the mountains that its very existence was comparatively unknown until about 1840. In honor of the generous benefactor of the College, this place has received the name of LAWRENCE GORGE.

Two miles east of Fort Massachusetts, situated in the town of Adams, is a natural bridge. A small stream, flowing over the soft white limestone, has excavated for itself a deep chasm, from fifteen to twenty feet wide and thirty rods in length. The rocks terminate on the south in a steep precipice, over which the waters of the brook once fell; but finding in some places natural fissures, and wearing away the rocks themselves in others, the present stream now flows far below its former bed, leaving two masses of rock, which connect the opposing sides and form natural bridges. The upper bridge is now much broken; the lower one, which is yet perfect, is beautifully arched, and spans the stream now flowing fifty feet below. Singular and grotesque cavities, of different figures and dimensions, worn by the action of the water, appear on either side of the precipice, while the adjoining rocks, even in some places that appear inaccessible, are covered with the names and initials of numerous visitors. The scenery about the bridge is very fine, and the place itself is well worthy of a visit.

But the principal object of attraction in the vicinity of the College is Saddle Mountain; so called from the appearance which its summits have been fancied to have, at a distance, though we think it would be somewhat difficult to trace the resemblance. This mountain, properly speaking, does not belong to either of the three great ranges that traverse the State in various directions, but is in fact an insulated eminence, connected at its southern extremity with the Taconic, and at the northern with the Hoosac, ranges of mountains, running diagonally between them, and surrounded by valleys. This mountain, with the exception of some peaks of the White Mountains, is the most elevated point in New England, rising by barometrical measurement 3,600 feet above the tide-water of the ocean, and 2,800 feet above the situation of the Colleges. It is chiefly the insulated character of this mountain that renders it so striking an object in the surrounding scenery; and seen from the adjoining towns, to the south and east, it presents a grand and imposing appearance. The highest peak has received the more poetical designation of Greylock, from the singular and fantastic appearance of the frost, which, wreathing itself, during the winter months, along the dark evergreens, and extending for a great distance in an apparently horizontal line, it needs no great effort of the imagination to regard as the gray locks of the venerable mountain. This distinct line of congelation, sinking lower and lower as the cold increases, and covering more of the mountain with its gray and sparkling mantle, and exhibiting a contrary result from an increase of temperature, is a most interesting and beautiful phenomenon.

Greylock is to the student in his rambles what Mecca is to the Mahometan; and a pilgrimage to the summit is considered necessary, at least once during the collegiate course. There is an ancient and time-honored custom which has existed from the establishment of the College, of granting to the students, once a year, a certain day of relaxation and amusement, known by the name of "Mountain Day." It usually occurs about the middle of June, when the weather is most favorable for excursions to the mountains and other places of interest in the vicinity. It is customary on this, and other occasions during the summer, for parties to pass the night upon the summit, both for the novelty of the thing, and also to enjoy the unrivalled prospect at sunrise next morning. We invite our readers to accompany us upon one of these excursions; for we think that the general features of the mountain can be better described in this way than in any other. The summit of Greylock is accessible by various routes; but the one usually preferred by students is to pass directly over the nearest point (called Prospect Mountain), and descending the other side, join the main road that comes up the Hopper.

We will suppose our party, each amply supplied with provisions and a huge pile of blankets, to leave the College about the middle of the afternoon. After proceeding about a mile over the adjoining fields, we arrive at the base of Prospect Mountain; and here our labor properly begins. The elevation to be overcome is about 1,800 feet. The sides of the mountain are extremely steep, and covered with a thick growth of trees and underbrush. After toiling up the lower part of the mountain, which to some extent has been cleared, and stopping here and there to refresh yourself with the wild berries, which, in tempting profusion, flourish on every side, or to admire the green valley below, you pass from the broad, clear sunlight, to the thick gloom of the almost impenetrable woods. And now for the ascent: "Hic labor, hoc opus, est," as every one will readily say who has experienced it. Now clambering over the trunks of fallen trees, catching at this and that twig to assist us; now stopping to dislodge from the bed, where the last deluge had left it, some nicely poised boulder, and send it crashing down the precipitous side; now resting, and then pushing forward with renewed zeal, we at last, weary, and ready to sink with exhaustion, reach the summit. The view which unexpectedly bursts upon you here is surpassingly beautiful. Below you is a valley, completely encircled by a huge wall of mountains, with two silver-like streams crossing it in opposite directions. In the centre is the village of Williamstown, and on an eminence in the midst stand the Colleges and the Astronomical Observatory. On your right, the vast slope of the Hoosac Mountains, stretching far away into Vermont; on the left, the Taconic range, stretching northerly still farther, while in the far-off horizon you witness peak after peak towering one above another, until blended in the distance. Behind you Greylock rises in silent grandeur, and the vast gulf of the Hopper is a thousand feet below you. The view from Greylock may have more of sublimity and grandeur, but that from Prospect Mountain we regard as by far the most beautiful.

But our time is short, and the way is yet long; so once more resuming our bundles, we again commence our march, by descending the southern slope, which is divested of trees, and is comparatively a gentle declivity. On reaching the bottom we again commence the ascent, but now by a carriage road, which was constructed with great labor, some years since, by the contributions of the inhabitants of the adjoining towns. The ascent is moderate, the road circuitous and winding, — now descending amid seemingly impenetrable thickets of evergreens and the decayed accumulations of centuries, and now mounting up and catching a faint glimpse of the world beneath. In about three hours after leaving the Colleges, we reach the summit. Here, in the midst of a cleared space of about an acre, was once a wooden building of two stories, from the top of which arose a tower, with an elevation of about fifty feet from the ground, erected partly for meteorological purposes, and partly in order to afford to visitors a more uninterrupted view of the surrounding country. The second story formerly contained an ingenious apparatus for registering the strength and direction of the wind, together with some other instruments; but the apartment was forcibly entered, and the whole machinery shamefully destroyed or carried away by some persons unknown. The tower and building, which have suffered considerably from the action of the elements, and still more from the destructive propensities of visitors, is yet in a tolerable state of preservation.

On reaching the summit, a huge fire is speedily kindled, spruce boughs are collected for beds, and fuel for the fire during the night. After performing these duties, and witnessing the gorgeous spectacle at sunset, the party proceed to supper with an appetite not a little heightened by their long and fatiguing walk. The evening is generally spent in merriment and conversation around the fire (for, although the heat in the valley below may be most oppressive, there are few times in the course of the season when a fire on Greylock is at all uncomfortable), or in enjoying the singular appearance of the sentinel-like peaks below you, seen through the thick gloom of the evening. One of the most impressive circumstances at this time and spot, if the air be clear and the winds at rest, is the solemn stillness which pervades the whole place, and the feeling of solitude which invariably steals over you. Not a light can be seen from any human habitation, not a sound breaks in upon the serene quiet which there reigns, while the appearance of the surrounding forest, so wild and unreclaimed from a state of nature, greatly heightens the sublimity of the scene. As the evening advances the circle around the fire by degrees breaks up, and each, wrapping himself in his blanket and selecting the most comfortable place among the spruce boughs, lays himself away for a night's rest.

The scene at sunrise, from the top of the tower, is unequalled, and any description would fail of giving any adequate idea of the magnificence of the spectacle. "I know of no place," says President Hitchcock, in the Geological Survey of the State, "where the mind is so forcibly impressed with the idea of vastness, and even of immensity, as when the eye ranges abroad from this eminence. Towards the south, you have a view, more or less interrupted by spurs from the Taconic and Hoosac ranges of mountains, of that fertile valley that crosses the whole of Berkshire County. On your right and left you look down upon, or rather overlook mountains, which, from the valley beneath, seemed of towering height and grandeur." In the distance, is the Hudson, winding majestically through a region of country thick with countless towns and villages, while far beyond, standing in bold relief against the western sky, the blue peaks of the Catskills are distinctly visible. In another direction, the principal towns of Berkshire, interspersed here and there with some beautiful sheets of water, are spread out before you as upon a map; while farther to the east, the eye wanders over the valley of the Connecticut, checkered with cultivated fields and forests, the view being limited by Mount Tom in one direction, and Monadnock at the farthest extremity, on the other. As the sun rises, the scene becomes changed. The mist, gradually rising and filling the whole valley, presents the appearance of a vast sea of vapor,

> " Where vales and mountains round
> Stand motionless, in solemn silence bound;
> Like leaning masts of stranded ships appear
> The pines that near the coast their summits rear;
> Of mountains, woods, and plains, a pleasant shore,
> Bound calm and clear the chaos still and hoar."

This mist, by a refraction of the sun-rays, assumes, at times, a beautiful golden appearance, as if the beauties of the landscape below, resolved by some magic power, had risen in vast and gorgeous exhalations around us.

Descending the mountain by a different route, and following the naked summit of Bald Mountain (the southwest peak of Saddle Mountain) nearly to its extremity, you find yourself upon the edge of a gulf, at least a thousand feet deep, the four sides of which apparently converge to a point at the bottom. This place, from its peculiar form, is called the Hopper. The sides, which are extremely steep, are covered, for the most part, with bright patches of evergreens and other trees of various species; but in some places the rocks are left bare for hundreds of feet, exhibiting the strata, in some instances, to the very base. On the northern side may be seen traces of several avalanches, by which the trees and loose soil have been swept away, in some cases from a height of sixteen hundred feet, and of considerable width. The most remarkable of these slides occurred in 1784, when a vast accumulation of earth, trees, and rocks, descending from an elevation of fourteen hundred feet, produced a sudden deluge in the narrow valley of the Hopper below, destroying, in its course, a dwelling-house, the inmates of which barely escaped with their lives. A similar slide took place in 1823, and several smaller ones have since occurred, the paths of which are yet destitute of vegetation. Vestiges of earlier avalanches may be perceived in other places, through the stunted growth or the peculiar character of the trees that have sprung up since. Traces of diluvial action, seen in furrows and scratches on the rocks, occur in various places on Bald Mountain. There are some other places of interest connected with Saddle Mountain, and an excursion there in the summer will not fail to furnish ample gratification.

To the north of the College, on the road leading to Bennington, is a curious geological phenomenon, called the "Weeping Rock." The water exuding from the limestone cliff, heavily impregnated with calcareous matter, drops continually upon a mass of sand and gravel, which it has cemented into a firm and solid rock. Specimens of conglomerate may be obtained here, most singular in their aspect, and sometimes beautiful in their appearance.

There is a legend about these gray old rocks, which runs as follows: That as the last Indian, standing here, bade adieu to the homes and the graves of his forefathers, to his rivers and mountains, and recounting his tale of oppression and wrong, turned away from them forever, the rocks wept, and since that time, through sympathy, have continued to pour out fountains of tears. Hence the name "weeping rocks."

A few miles farther north, upon the summit of a neighboring mountain, is a natural curiosity, known by the name of "SNOW HOLE." Here, in a huge crevice or fissure, of unfathomable depth, the snows that accumulate during the winter are preserved unwasted and in all their original purity throughout the year. This place is considerably resorted to during the summer months, on account of the beautiful prospect to be obtained from the summit, as well as to enjoy the novelty of snow-balling during the months of July or August. The mountain is situated in New York, and forms a portion of the manor of Van Rensselaer.

In an adjoining valley, near the route by which you ascend the mountain, is a stone monument, marking the three corners of the three States of New York, Massachusetts, and Vermont, which at this place intersect with one another; one side of the stone being in New York, another in Massachusetts, and a third in Vermont. The curious may here gratify themselves by visiting, in a short space of time, three different towns, each situated in different counties and States.

There is a mineral spring in this town, about one mile northwest from the College, — a few rods from the road that leads to Pownal. It is a place to which the students often resort. It greatly resembles the waters at Lebanon, N. Y. It is warm, contains very little saline matter, is very soft to the skin, and has a very favorable influence on several cutaneous diseases. If some enterprising individual would here provide suitable accommodations, this might be made a place of much resort.

The battle-field of Bennington, to which excursions are sometimes made, is situated fourteen miles to the north of the Colleges.

In preparing this sketch of a few of the numerous and beautiful places of resort in the vicinity of Williams College, we have of necessity been obliged to omit many, which some may deem more worthy of a place than those we have mentioned; but we think it sufficient to say, in closing, that if wild and romantic scenery, the sharp bold mountain, the craggy and precipitous cliff, the beautiful cascade, or the gently winding river, can add anything of attraction or interest to a place, then surely the country in the vicinity of Williams College possesses these attractions.

> "Scenes of such beauty, varying in the light
> Of living nature, cannot be portrayed
> By words, nor by the pencil's silent skill,
> But is the property of him alone
> Who hath beheld it, noted it with care,
> And in his mind recorded it with love."

APPENDIX.

APPENDIX.

No. I.

PRESIDENTS AND ORATORS OF THE SOCIETY OF ALUMNI.

THE following is a catalogue of those who have been elected Presidents and Orators of the Society of Alumni. It is impossible to ascertain just how many of the Orators have fulfilled their appointments; some have failed.

	PRESIDENTS.	ORATORS.
1821.	Asa Burbank, M. D.	
1822.	Rev. Ebenezer Jennings.	Hon. Elisha H. Mills.
1823.	Rev. Jared Curtis.	Rev. John Woodbridge, D. D.
1824.	Rev. Isaac Knapp.	Hon. Samuel Howe.
1825.	Hon. William P. Walker.	Rev. Ezra Fisk, D. D.
1826.	Hon. Elisha Mack.	Hon. James McKown.
1827.	Professor G. S. Olds.	Hon. John K. Paige.
1828.	Rev. Ezra Fisk, D. D.	Rev. Justin Edwards, D. D.
1829.	Rev. Ezra Fisk, D. D.	Rev. Darius O. Griswold.
1830.	Hon. David Buel, Jr.	Rev. Azariah G. Orton, D. D.
1831.	Hon. David Buel, Jr.	Hon. William Porter.
1832.	Hon. David Buel, Jr.	Rev. Justin Edwards, D. D.
1833.	Hon. William P. Walker.	Hon. Henry W. Bishop.
1834.	Rev. Sylvester Burt.	Hon. David Buel, Jr.
1835.	Professor Chester Dewey.	William H. Dillingham, Esq.
1836.	Dr. H. H. Childs.	Dr. Henry H. Childs.
1837.	Hon. Samuel R. Betts.	Hon. Julius Rockwell.
1838.	Hon. Henry W. Bishop.	Rev. Orville Dewey, D. D.
1839.	Rev. Emerson Davis, D. D.	Hon. Timothy Childs.
1840.	Rev. Thomas Robbins, D. D.	Hon. E. C. Benedict.
1841.	Hon. Oliver B. Morris.	Hon. Elisha H. Allen.

	PRESIDENTS.	ORATORS.
1842.	Hon. Oliver B. Morris.	Rev. Nicholas Murry, D. D.
1843.	Hon. Samuel R. Betts.	Rev. Mark Hopkins, D. D. Rev. Thomas Robbins, D. D.
1844.	Hon. Homer Bartlett.	Hon. D. D. Barnard.
1845.	Dr. Ebenezer Emmons.	Hon. Emory Washburn.
1846.	Rev. Emerson Davis, D. D.	Hon. James M. Howard.
1847.	Hon. Charles A. Dewey.	Rev. Jonathan E. Woodbridge.
1848.	Hon. Henry W. Bishop.	Rev. Aaron W. Leland, D. D.
1849.	Joseph Hyde, Esq.	Rev. Professor Tatlock.
1850.	Hon. Homer Bartlett.	Hon. David Dudley Field.
1851.	Hon. Oliver B. Morris.	Hon. Homer Bartlett.
1852.	Hon. Charles K. Williams.	Hon. Harvey Rice, Poem.
1853.	Hon. Martin I. Townsend.	Rev. Joshua N. Danforth, D. D.
1854.	His Excel. Gov. Washburn.	William Pitt Palmer, Poem.
1855.	Hon. Patrick Boise.	Hon. Joseph White. E. W. B. Canning, Poem.
1856.	Hon. David Dudley Field.	Professor Albert Hopkins.
1857.	Hon. William C. Kittredge.	Rev. Willis Lord, D. D.
1858.	Hon. Abraham Olin.	Rev. John Morgan, D. D.
1859.	Hon. Henry H. Childs.	Hon. Martin I. Townsend. Rev. Amos D. Wheeler, Poem.
1860.	Hon. James D. Colt, President elect.	Rev. Parsons Cook, D. D., Orator elect. Charles N. Emmerson, Esq., Poet elect.

No. II.

We have concluded to insert the will of Colonel Williams; the Petition of the Trustees to the Legislature for permission to remove the College; the Remonstrance of the town of Williamstown against the measure; and the Report of the Committee of the Legislature on that subject; presuming they will be objects of interest to our readers in general, and of curiosity to the antiquarian in particular.

THE WILL OF COLONEL WILLIAMS.

In the name of God, Amen. I, Ephraim Williams, of Hatfield, in the County of Hampshire, in New England, now at Albany, in the province of New York, on my march in the expedition against Crown Point, being of sound and perfect mind and memory (blessed be God therefor), but not knowing how God in his providence may dispose of my life, and remembering the uncertainty of it at all times, I do therefore make, and publish this, my last Will and Testament, in the following manner: —

First, I give my soul into the hands of God that gave it, and my body to the dust, from whence it was taken, humbly hoping for pardon, acceptance, and a resurrection to immortal glory, through the merits and mediation of a glorious Redeemer; and as touching such worldly estate, wherewith it has pleased God to bless me in this life, I give, bequeath, and dispose of the same, in manner and form following, that is to say: —

Item. It is my will and desire, that my just debts and funeral charges be first paid and discharged by my Executors, hereafter named, out of my estate.

Item. It is my will and desire that the deed I gave my brother Elijah Williams, of my house and homestead at Stockbridge, and my note of hand, payable for one hundred pounds, in twelve months after my parents' decease, as also his mortgage deed and his bond to me, be destroyed, and made of none effect.

Item. I give and bequeath unto my beloved brothers, Josiah Williams and Elijah Williams, and the heirs of their bodies, my homestead at Stockbridge, with all the buildings and appurtenances thereunto belonging, with all the stock of cattle, and negro servants now upon the place, to be equally divided between them, upon the following conditions, and not otherwise, viz.: That they pay annually to my honored mother, for her support, twenty-six pounds thirteen shillings and four pence, and also, provided they fulfil the obligations I laid myself under, in a certain bond to my honored parents, for their support, and decent interment, exclusive of the money I then obliged myself annually to pay her; provided also, that they pay unto my sister Judith Williams, or the heirs of her body, the sum of one hundred pounds, and to the heirs of my sister Abigail Dwight, born of her body, the sum of one hundred pounds, to be paid them severally, within twelve months after my honored mother's decease. In case my sisters, Judith or Elizabeth should come to die without heirs, then it is my will that her, or their part or parts shall devolve to the heirs of my sister Abigail Dwight.

Item. It is my will, that in case one of my aforesaid brothers die without issue, then the whole of the above bequest revert to the survivor, and the heirs of his body, provided he fulfil the above obligations laid on them both; but in case my said brothers die without issue, then my will is that the above-mentioned estate be sold, and the money be put out to interest, and that the said interest shall be used for some pious or charitable purposes, as the propagating Christianity, the support of the poor in the County of Hampshire, or for schools on the frontier, in the county aforesaid, to be at the direction of my Executors, hereinafter named, and after their decease to be at the direction of the justices of the sessions for the county aforesaid; but in case my brother, Elijah Williams, should deny, or refuse to destroy the above-mentioned writings, as above directed, then it is my will he pay to my honored mother, annually, for her support, twenty-six pounds thirteen shillings and four pence, and also the sum of thirteen pounds six shillings and eight pence, to my brother Josiah Williams, annually, until my honored mother's decease, after which, to pay to my sisters, and the heirs of my sister Abigail Dwight, as above directed, and that, within one twelve months after my honored mother's decease; also to pay to my brother Josiah Williams, or the heirs of his body, the sum of four hundred pounds, and in case my said brother Josiah should die without issue, then it is my will that my brother Elijah shall pay the said sum of four hundred pounds to my Executors, to be appropriated by them to some, or all the public uses above mentioned.

Item. I give and bequeath unto my beloved brother, Thomas Williams, one hundred pounds, to be paid him out of my bonds; but in case of his decease in the present expedition, to be equally divided amongst his five daughters, viz.: Elizabeth, Anne, Cynthia, Mary, and Martha.

Item. I give and bequeath to my beloved cousin, Thomas Williams, son to my brother, Thomas Williams, nine hundred dollars of land, known by the name of the Equivalent, and joining upon the township of Stockbridge; and in case he dies without issue, I give it to my beloved cousins, Erastus Sergeant and John Sergeant, to be equally divided between them; but in case one dies without issue, the whole to go to the survivor; if they both die without issue, the whole to be appropriated to the public uses, as before mentioned.

Item. I give and bequeath to my loving cousins, Elijah Graves, Moses Graves, John Graves, and Martha Graves, children of Moses and Martha Graves, the sum of one hundred pounds, to be equally divided between them; in case any dies without issue, then the whole to go to the survivor or survivors; and in case they all die without issue, then the said hundred pounds to be appropriated to the public uses, as above directed, the said money to be taken out of Moses Graves's and Elisha Chapin's joint bond, and to be put on interest until the children come of age.

Item. I give and bequeath to my beloved cousins, James and John Gray, sons of James and Sarah Gray, fifty acres of land lying north of the great pond, in Stockbridge, so called, bounded upon land of their father, James Gray, on the east, by Josiah Jones's land on the west, by the great pond on the south, and the town line on the north, to be equally divided between them; but in case they die without issue, then the said land to be disposed of for public uses, as aforesaid.

Item. I give and bequeath to my loving cousins, William Williams and Israel Williams, sons of Israel Williams, Esq., and Sarah, his wife, two lots of meadow land in Hatfield, Great Meadow, the contents of which, and the bounds, may be seen in a deed given to me of the same, by Moses Graves, of Hatfield. The lot lying nearest to Pine Bridge, I give to William, and the other to Israel, and in case one of them dies without issue, then both lots to go to the survivor; if they both die without issue, then the lots to be disposed of for public uses, as above directed.

Item. I give and bequeath to my beloved cousins, Eunice Williams, Jerusha, Elizabeth, and Lucretia Williams, daughters of Israel Williams, Esq., and Sarah his wife, the sum of twenty pounds each. In case any of them die without issue, their part to be equally divided among the survivors; and in case they all should die without issue, the money to be disposed of for public uses as aforesaid.

Item. I give and bequeath to my loving cousin, Elizabeth Williams, over and above the twenty pounds above mentioned, my silver cream-pot and teaspoons.

Item. I give and bequeath unto my loving brother, Thomas Williams, all my wearing apparel, and my shoe-buckles; but in case my said brother should die, I then give them to my surviving brothers, to be equally divided among them.

Item. I give to my beloved friend and kinsman, Israel Williams, Esq., of Hatfield, my sorrel mare, now at Northampton, and my bald colt, now at Sheffield.

Item. I give to my trusty and well-beloved friend, John Worthington, Esq., of Springfield, my Chambers's Dictionary, with the whole of Pope's works, and some other books that came in the same box, now in his hands; and also my French firearm, my case of pistols and hanger, in case the French don't get them; but if he dies without issue, then the above articles to be given to the eldest male heir in Colonel Israel Williams's family.

Item. I give and bequeath to my beloved brother, Thomas Williams, my firearm, now in possession.

Item. I give the remaining part of my library, not yet disposed of (excepting my large Bible and Ridgley's Body of Divinity), to my beloved brothers, Thomas and Elijah Williams, to be equally divided between them; but in case my brother Thomas dies, his part to go to his son Thomas; and in case my brother Elijah dies without issue, then his part to be given to my cousins, William and Israel Williams, to be equally divided between them, over and above the lots of land bequeathed them above; and it is my will and desire, further, that my cousin William Williams, above mentioned, shall have the perusal of the books hereby given to my brothers, Thomas and Elijah, any reasonable time upon his desire.

Item. I give and bequeath unto my brother Thomas Williams's two eldest daughters, three silver spoons, now at Hatfield, and a silver tankard now at Stockbridge, and what silver may be bequeathed me by my aunt Cooke in New Town.

Item. I give to my brother Josiah, my large Bible and Ridgley's Body of Divinity.

Item. I give to Solomon and Israel Stoddard, sons of my great benefactor, John Stoddard, deceased, my two colts now at Northampton.

Item. I give and devise and remit to the poor, distressed, and imprudent Captain Elisha Chapin, the sum of one hundred pounds, to be deducted out of the bond given jointly by Moses Graves and said Elisha Chapin; the said hundred pounds to be remitted out of said Chapin's part.

Item. It is my will and pleasure and desire that the remaining part of lands not yet disposed of shall be sold at the direction of my Executors, within five years after an established peace, and the interest of the money, and also the interest of my money arising by my bonds and notes, shall be appropriated towards the support and maintenance of a free school (in a township west of Fort Massachusetts, commonly called the West Township), forever, provided the said township fall within the jurisdiction of the Province of the Massachusetts Bay, and, provided also, that the Governor and General Court give the said township the name of WILLIAMSTOWN; and it is my further will and desire that if there should remain any moneys of the above donation, for the said school, it be given towards the support of a school in the East Township, where the fort now stands; but in case the above provisos are not complied with, then it is my will and desire that the interest of the above-mentioned moneys be appropriated to some pious and charitable uses, in manner and form as directed in the former of this, my last Will and Testament.

Lastly. I nominate and appoint my trusty and well-beloved friends, Israel Williams, Esq., of Hatfield, and John Worthington, Esq., of Springfield, in the County of Hampshire, and Province of Massachusetts Bay, of New England, to be Executors of this my last Will and Testament, and thereby revoke, disannul, and make void all former Wills and Testaments by me heretofore made, done, or executed; and I do hereby confirm and allow this, and no other, to be my last Will and Testament, and desire it may be observed as such.

In witness whereof, I hereunto set my hand and seal, the twenty-second day of July, in the twenty-ninth year of his Majesty's reign, and in the year of our Lord one thousand seven hundred and fifty-five.

Signed, sealed, published, pronounced, and declared, by the said Ephraim Williams, as his last Will and Testament (the erasure at the word Hatfield, being first made), in the presence of us, who were present at the signing.

EPHRAIM WILLIAMS (Seal).

WILLIAM WILLIAMS, JR.
NOAH BELDING.
RICHARD CARTWRIGHT.

The following letter has recently come to light: —

ALBANY, July 21, 1755.

DEAR SIR: —

Enclosed I send you my last Will and Testament, and desire you to consult with Mr. Worthington whether it be legal, — if it is not, please to write one that is, — send it up and I will execute it. I have altered my mind since I left your house, for reasons, as to what I designed to give (which should have been handsome) to one very near to you; have given a small matter to others, as near to you, whose conduct to me has rendered themselves most amiable. Also since I left your house, for reasons, I have altered my mind, as to what I designed to give to the children of my great benefactor; have given but a small matter to two of them only. You will perceive I have given something for the benefit of those unborn, and for the sake of those poor creatures I am mostly concerned, for fear my will should be broke. I believe, sir, it would have been more agreeable to you if I had given it for an academy at Hadley. I turned the affair over and over in my mind, found so many difficulties, I thought it was better to give it in another shape. I desire that you and Mr. Worthington would inquire into the affair of the Stockbridge Indians, which my Honored [manuscript torn] . . . . . left in charge; by no means let them be . . . . . I desire you to pay £ 20 to your nieces, at a venture upon . . . . . know that I owe them one quarter of it, but for fear I do, I will put enough in. Also please to pay the following persons whose names are hereafter mentioned, if they are to be found, being soldiers under my command. I received the money out of the treasury, but never could find the men; have paid all but these: Daniel Wood, £ 4 10*s.* 8*d.*; Jonathan Comally, £ 1 13*s.* 6*d.*; Nathaniel Sawyer, £ 2 12*s.*; William Williston, £ 1 16*s.*, lives near Rehoboth. These things above mentioned are most material. I shall conclude by recommending myself to your prayers, and you and your dear family to the Divine protection.

I am, with great esteem, your honored,
Most humble, and most obliged servant,
EPHRAIM WILLIAMS.

To Israel Williams, Esq.

P. S. In my will you will find I ordered some money for the benefit of the lost town. I don't know that it will be enough for the will, but so far as it goes will pay well, and then some good will come out of it.
E. W.

P. S. 2d. Let no one but yourself and John Worthington know what my will contains.

No. III.

PETITION OF THE PRESIDENT AND TRUSTEES TO REMOVE THE COLLEGE TO NORTHAMPTON.

To the Honorable, the Senate and House of Representatives of the Commonwealth of Massachusetts, in General Court assembled: —

The President and Trustees of Williams College respectfully represent, that Williams College was incorporated and established at Williamstown, in the County of Berkshire, in the year of our Lord one thousand seven hundred and ninety-three. That at that time there was no similar institution in operation in the State of Vermont, and none in the State of New York, except in the city, and said College was designed by its founders and patrons for the parts of those states adjacent to Williamstown, as well as for the western counties of this Commonwealth, and was expected to derive from them, in a very considerable degree, its support, and did, for a number of years after its establishment, receive a considerable proportion of students from those States. That by the establishment of other colleges since that time in the State of Vermont, and in the State of New York, one of them less than fifty miles from Williamstown, Williams College receives much less support from the inhabitants of those states than it formerly did. That for several years past Williams College has been resorted to almost entirely by students from the four western counties of the Commonwealth, and is now almost wholly dependent on those counties for support and usefulness. That the College is now at Williamstown, remote from the greater part of the population which supports it, and far less convenient of access than it would be in another situation. That its removal to some place on or near Connecticut River, has long been considered a desirable object. That your petitioners have taken such measures as to them seemed most proper for determining to what place the College may be removed with most advantage to the institution, and most satisfaction to the western section of the Commonwealth, and those measures have led to the selection of Northampton, in the County of Hampshire, as the future site of the College; and that such subscriptions in aid of the College have been made, on condition of its removal to Northampton; fifty thousand dollars having been already subscribed for that object, and such are the expectations of future assistance, if it is placed there, that in the opinion of your petitioners the removal will very much conduce to the prosperity of the institution.

Your petitioners further represent, that a college in the western part of the Commonwealth will promote the interests both of religion and literature in the western counties. They are too distant from the principal institution in the Commonwealth to share conveniently, and in full measure its advantages. Opportunities not unsuitable to the present state of education in this country may be enjoyed by them at a college placed at Northampton, at a less expense than they can at the University at Cambridge, or at the institutions of neighboring States.

Williams College has repeatedly experienced the favor and liberality of the Legislature in grants of money and lands. But the Trustees are concerned to state, that the funds of the institution are very small and inadequate, and do not permit them to make any enlargement of the number of instructors, or material addition to the other means and helps of education at the College. They are therefore of opinion, that the College in its present situation cannot be made to serve effectually the interests of the western parts of the Commonwealth. At Northampton it would both be more central and more convenient of access to them, and might be expected to receive such assistance from a generous and enlightened public as would perpetuate its reputation and usefulness.

Your petitioners, therefore, humbly pray your honorable body, that they may be permitted to remove Williams College to Northampton, with such of its funds and other property as it shall be found lawful and expedient to remove, without affecting, however, the right in law and equity of the inhabitants of Williamstown to any moneys or other property derived to them by the late Colonel Ephraim Williams, for the support of a free school in said town of Williamstown. And as in duty bound, &c.

By order, and in behalf of the Trustees,

ZEPH. SWIFT MOORE, *President.*

WILLIAMSTOWN, *November* 2, 1819.

House of Representatives, *January* 17, 1820. — Read and committed to Messrs. Sullivan of Boston, Lewis of Gorham, Mosely of Newburyport, Williams of New Bedford, with such as the Honorable Senate may join, to consider and report. Sent up for concurrence.

TIMOTHY BIGELOW, *Speaker.*

In Senate, *January* 17, 1820. — Read and concurred, and the Hon. Messrs. Gay, Hobart, and Adams are joined.

JOHN PHILLIPS, *President.*

No. IV.

THE REMONSTRANCE OF THE TOWN OF WILLIAMSTOWN AGAINST THE REMOVAL OF THE COLLEGE.*

To the Honorable, the Senate and House of Representatives of the Commonwealth of Massachusetts, in General Court assembled: —

The memorial of the inhabitants of the town of Williamstown, in legal town meeting assembled, respectfully showeth: —

That they have witnessed with no small degree of surprise, the various proceedings of the President and Trustees of Williams College, having for their object the removal of that institution to the County of Hampshire; proceedings highly important in their consequences to the public, and deeply affecting the rights and privileges of the inhabitants of this town and its vicinity.

Constituted as the Trustees of Williams College were, the guardians of a literary institution, located in the town of Williamstown, and vested only with powers to superintend its interests in this place, to us it has ever seemed that in the various steps hitherto taken by the Trustees in relation to this subject, they were transcending the powers granted them, and usurping those which belong exclusively to the Legislature. But whatever measures may have been adopted in relation to this object, by the Trustees, your memorialists feel the most perfect confidence that those proceedings will never receive the sanction of your honorable body, until a full and impartial investigation shall have produced in your minds a decided conviction of the expediency and justice of them. With these views of the principles which would guide the Legislature in deciding the question of the removal of Williams College were we to await in silence your decision, we are well satisfied that the result would not be otherwise than favorable to the continuance of the College in its present location; but lest silence as to our claims should be mistaken for indifference, lest the neglecting to expose the fallacy of the arguments urged in favor of removal should be construed into an admission of the reasonableness of them, we have deemed it proper to submit to you the reasons which lead us to declare that the

* This paper, it is said, was drawn up by the Hon. Charles A. Dewey.

proposed removal is alike inexpedient as regards the public, and unjust as respects the inhabitants of this town.

Why has the agitation in relation to Williams College taken place? Why are you at this time called upon to change the location of an institution established in this town by an act of the Legislature more than twenty-six years since? Has the College failed of success in its present location? Can it no longer progress at Williamstown upon the plan contemplated by the Legislature at the time of its establishment?

These are questions worthy the serious consideration of your honorable body, and the answer to each of them will, it is believed, be found highly favorable to the continuance of the College in its present location.

So far as we can understand the petition and other public documents of the Trustees, the avowed arguments in favor of removal rest wholly on three points.

1. That since the erection of Williams College, the establishment of two colleges in the State of Vermont, and of two others in the State of New York, has so far interfered with its operations that it receives much less support from those States than it formerly did.

2. That it is not in the local centre of that part of the Commonwealth upon which it is, in a considerable measure, to depend for its support and usefulness.

3. That the funds of the institution are small, and its resources such that it must be removed or soon become extinct.

In regard to the first of these positions, we have to remark, that, however much plausibility it may carry on the face of it, it is perfectly unsatisfactory to those acquainted with all the circumstances. It is indeed true that the number of colleges to the north and west have somewhat increased since the incorporation of the College in this place, though it is not true to the extent stated by the advocates of removal. Burlington College, in the State of Vermont, was founded 1791, two years earlier than Williams, and Union College was established in 1794, only one year later than Williams. With the exception of Hamilton College, an institution established one hundred and fifty miles to the west, all those institutions, the establishment of which are now for the first time discovered to have an important bearing upon the prosperity of Williams College, and which are said to render its immediate removal absolutely necessary, have been established twenty years or more. Ten years after all these institutions were in successful operation Williams College enjoyed its full share of prosperity. If at a subsequent time it partially declined, the late increase of its members, and the bright and animating prospects which had attended it for the last three years, furnish conclusive evidence that its diminution of numbers a few years since was not to be attributed to its local situation.

It seems to us that it is only necessary to bear in mind that Burlington College was established two years earlier than Williams, Union College, in the State of New York, the year succeeding, Middlebury, twenty years since, and that Hamilton College is one hundred and fifty miles distant, to satisfy any candid mind that these are not the moving causes of the present agitation about removal, however formidable a shape they may be made to assume on paper.

But suppose the number of students in Williams College has been somewhat lessened in consequence of the influence of other colleges in the adjoining States. How will you remedy the difficulty by removal? The farther you place the College to the east or south, instead of lessening, you greatly increase the evil by approaching more important seminaries than you withdraw from.

Place Williams College in the vicinity of Harvard and Yale, and will they be less likely to take students from it than Union and Middlebury now are? And if it were possible, would it be expedient to make Williams College a great and splendid institution at the expense of our University at Cambridge? We know indeed that this is a favorite plan with many of those who are the zealous advocates of removal, but to us it seems such an object is as improper as it would be impracticable.

In answer to the argument that Williams College is not located in the centre of the western part of the Commonwealth, and ought therefore to be removed, the first objection which naturally presents itself would be as to the time of originating this point. To us we confess it appears not a little singular that this circumstance is called in to aid the present attempt at removal, when the local situation of the College has in no respect changed, as regards the people of the Commonwealth since it was first established. The Legislature of 1793, which established Williams College well knew that Williamstown was not the local centre of the western section of the State, but finding many powerful inducements to erect a College in Williamstown, they did not deem the circumstance of its not being a local centre a sufficient one to prevent them from establishing it in this place. Much less will your honorable body, after the establishment and successful operation of the College twenty-six years, deem the want of a local centre a sufficient cause for removal.

It is further urged that the resources of the College are small, and therefore it must be removed. It is true that the funds of this College, like most other country institutions, are small; but small as they are, they are fully adequate with the present number of students to support a very respectable college establishment, and leave a decent surplus for the purpose of increasing the advantages of education.

But how are the funds to be increased by the proposed removal? We are told, indeed, that the people of Northampton and its vicinity believing that the removal "would advance the pecuniary interest of the town," have offered to the Trustees a subscription of thirty-five thousand dollars, and a bond for the sum of fifteen thousand dollars, payable in ten years hence, with interest, with this condition annexed: "unless they shall in the mean time procure said sum for said Trustees, by subscription, donation, grant, endowment, or otherwise." It must appear obvious to your honorable body that hopes are entertained that you will be disposed to grant the last sum out of the public funds in the course of a few years, and if so we can hardly conceive why it should be less burdensome to the treasury to endow the College at Williamstown than at Northampton.

But if this call is never made on the Legislature, and the whole sum of fifty thousand dollars is paid by the subscriptions, and the signers of the bond, we would ask what sacrifices are to be made to obtain this proffered bounty? The Trustees have at Williamstown two large and commodious brick edifices, one containing thirty-two rooms for students, and the other twenty-eight rooms for students, and a chapel, two dwelling-houses for the President and a Professor, with several acres of land connected with the same, and also a building for a Laboratory. They have a cash fund they received from our Academy, of more than nine thousand dollars, and subscriptions for the benefit of the College in case of its continuance in Williamstown, for the sum of eighteen thousand dollars.

The real estate owned by the Trustees (and which must be almost entirely sacrificed in case of removal), could not be replaced in Northampton at less than thirty-four thousand dollars. This with the funds of our Academy, which must remain at Williamstown, and the subscriptions for the benefit of the institution at that place, will amount to sixty-one thousand dollars, leaving the Trustees, in case of removal, with eleven thousand dollars less than they now have. If you deduct from this sum three thousand dollars, which is the highest estimate that can be made on the avails of the real estate left at Williamstown, in case of removal, the Trustees still suffer a loss by removal of eight thousand dollars. In reference to this part of the subject, we ought to say that there has been a material change in the situation of the institution since the meeting of the Trustees, and one which it is believed has not been without its effects in changing the views of many gentlemen as to the general question of removal.

As connected with the resources of the institution, we may here with propriety call the attention of the Legislature to the reports which have been circulated with some degree of zeal, of the rapid diminution of students, and the necessity of taking immediate measures to prevent the College from becoming extinct. A few facts will enable you to judge what foundation there is for these reports. Williams College has now eighty-seven students, a greater number than Hamilton, Burlington, or Bowdoin College, and about the same as Middlebury. It has its President and Professor of Divinity, Professor of Mathematics and Natural Philosophy, a Lecturer on Chemistry, Professor of Languages, and the necessary Tutors; and all these the present funds, with the income from the term bills, will honorably support. It has given a complete collegiate course to 512 students, averaging 20 graduates each year since its first establishment. For the last ten years the average number exceeds this. The number of candidates for the first degree at the ensuing Commencement is now 21. In view of these facts, we ask whether the reasons assigned for the proposed removal are not unsatisfactory, and such as become insignificant when compared with the evils to be sustained by the measure? Will the advantages arising to the students from a more central and populous place bear any comparison with the injury which they must suffer from increasing the expenses of their education, and the greater exposure of their morals? Will the treasury of the College be enriched by the positive loss of more than eight thousand dollars. Why then abandon the certain prospect of usefulness here to enter upon untrodden ground? Why put at hazard so much, when you have so little, when, indeed, you have nothing to gain?

In the view we have thus far taken of this subject, we have considered it as though it were fully open for discussion, but we apprehend that we have rights which are not to be unnecessarily sacrificed, — rights which your honorable body will readily recognize when you shall have attentively considered the facts on which they rest.

Colonel Ephraim Williams, a gentleman whose name will long be remembered with gratitude by the inhabitants of this town, gave by will a liberal donation to be expended in Williamstown for the purposes of education. By the generous donations of the inhabitants of this town and vicinity, and the aid of a lottery granted by the Legislature, the donation of Colonel Williams was considerably increased, and we were enabled to build a large and commodious brick edifice, and make all necessary arrangements for a large public school. Our institution commenced under the most favorable auspices. The cheapness of education, the good habits of our citizens, and the few temptations to vice that our local situation presented, soon gave it a high reputation. So bright were its prospects, such the promise it gave of being an ornament to our County and State, that its friends became solicitous, that an institution rivalling in usefulness the established seminaries, should receive a more appropriate name, and enjoy those privileges which peculiarly belong to incorporated colleges. The Legislature, coinciding in these views, and deeply impressed with the importance of giving the institution its full aid and support, granted a charter for a college, and at the same time vested all the funds of our Academy, as well those received from the donation of Colonel Williams, as those received by the generous subscriptions of the people of this town and vicinity, and also those procured by the aid of a lottery (the profits of which were realized almost solely from the sale of tickets in this and the adjoining towns, and which was therefore in its operation a tax of so much upon the inhabitants), in the hands of a Corporation by the name of the President and Trustees of Williams College. Subscription papers, which were then in circulation to procure further funds for the Academy, were immediately withdrawn that others might be substituted for the benefit of the College. Lands were generously given for the erection of a second college edifice, and a house for the President.

The inference to be drawn from these facts is too plain to be misunderstood. The Academy and College now became one and the same. Can your honorable body for a moment doubt but that the Legislature when they established a College in this town, and transferred to it our *private funds*, gave a most solemn pledge that the institution should be permanent here? Can it be supposed that the inhabitants of this town who gave so liberally of their money and their lands, gave upon any other principle than this? Would they have parted thus freely with their property to endow an institution which was to be temporary as to its location among them? Are you ready to sacrifice our rights and privileges, in fact in a degree to impoverish us, merely to enrich another town, or for the less worthy purpose of aiding the designs of those who have other objects at heart than the mere propagation of literature and science, or the pure principles of our holy religion? Is a measure which originated in the selfish and illiberal views of a few individuals, but which was wholly undesired by the great body of the people, worthy of your countenance and support?

We have the most perfect confidence that you will not hesitate to declare that neither justice or expediency will permit the proposed removal of Williams College. Before you come to a different result we entreat you to weigh well the consequences. Recollect the injury you are inflicting upon that portion of the community who have done so much towards originating, supporting, and establishing the institution; but more particularly bear in mind the disastrous effects of such a measure upon the people, as regards their loss of confidence in the public authorities of the land.

The views we have presented you are not the views of this town only. We carry with us the entire County of Berkshire, and, as is believed, a very decided majority of the people of the four western counties of the Commonwealth. To this we add, that there are feelings of no small interest in the adjoining counties of the States of New York and Vermont.

We are gratified to have the pleasure of stating that the public expressions which have been made in favor of the continuance of the College at Williamstown have been accompanied with the most satisfactory evidence of their sincerity. Subscription papers bearing the names of respectable gentlemen for the amount of eighteen thousand dollars, for the use of the College in this town, have already been placed in the hands of the Treasurer of the College.

With this exposition of our views and feelings, we leave the subject with your Honorable body, renewing the expression of our perfect confidence that when you shall have attentively considered all the facts which have a bearing in relation to this subject you will not hesitate in deciding that Williams College shall remain in its present location.

At a legal meeting of the inhabitants of Williamstown, holden December 27th, 1819, It was *unanimously* voted that the foregoing memorial be presented to the General Court as expressive of the feelings of the inhabitants of this town in relation to the removal of Williams College.

Attest: STEPHEN HOSFORD, *Town Clerk.*

House of Representatives, *January* 17, 1820. — Read and committed to Messrs. Sullivan of Boston, Lewis of Gorham, Mosely of Newburyport, Williams of New Bedford, with such as the Honorable Senate may join. Sent up for concurrence.

TIMOTHY BIGELOW, *Speaker.*

In Senate, *January* 17, 1820. — Read and concurred, and the Hon. Messrs. Gay, Hobart, and Adams are joined.

JOHN PHILLIPS, *President.*

No. V.

THE REPORT OF THE COMMITTEE OF BOTH BRANCHES OF THE LEGISLATURE ON THE SUBJECT OF THE REMOVAL OF THE COLLEGE TO NORTHAMPTON.

Commonwealth of Massachusetts.

In the year of our Lord one thousand eight hundred and twenty.

The joint committee to whom was referred the petition of the President and Trustees of Williams College, pray leave, respectfully to state that the petition has been supported and opposed before them with great ability, and with the most commendable candor.

That the committee have diligently attended to all that either party have seen fit to offer, and hope that they do not assume too much in saying, that in hearing, deliberating, and in deciding, they have sought only to understand *rightly*, and to judge with *fidelity*, as well in relation to the interested parties as to the Commonwealth.

It appeared to your committee that in the year 1755, Ephraim Williams, Esq., made his last Will and Testament, and therein devised as follows, viz.: — "*Item.* It is my will, desire, and pleasure, that the remaining part of the lands not yet disposed of, shall be sold at the discretion of my Executors within five years after an established peace, and the interest of the money, and also the interest of my bonds and notes shall be appropriated towards the support and maintenance of a free school, in a township west of Fort Massachusetts, commonly called the West Township, forever, provided the said township shall fall within the jurisdiction of the province of Massachusetts Bay, and provided also the Governor and General Court give the said township the name of 'Williamstown,' and it is my further will and desire, that if there should remain any moneys of the above donation for the school, it be given towards the school in the East Township, where the fort now stands; but in case the above provisos are not complied with, then it is my will and choice that the interest of the above-mentioned moneys be appropriated to some pious and charitable uses, in manner and form as above directed in the former part of this my last Will and Testament."

That in the year 1785, the Executors of the said Ephraim Williams, Esq., represented to the General Court that such devise had been made, and prayed legislative aid to carry the will of the testator into effect.

That on the 8th day of March, 1785, an act was passed, declaring that the donation made in the before recited clause of the said testator's will ought to be applied to the use and maintenance of a free school in Williamstown, and that if the annual interest of the donation should be more than sufficient to support such school, that the surplus should be appropriated to the support and maintenance of a free school in the town of Adams; and in and by the same act, a body politic was erected to be a corporation, forever, by the name of "The Trustees of the Donation of Ephraim Williams, Esq., for maintaining a free school in Williamstown," and by the same act Trustees were appointed.

The said corporation was placed under the visitation and direction of the Supreme Judicial Court. The possession, management, and disposition of the whole interest and estate, real and personal, which was given and devised by the aforesaid clause of said will, was vested in said Trustees, and their successors, forever; to erect and maintain a free school within the town of Williamstown, for the instruction of youth in such manner as most effectually to answer the pious, generous, and charitable intention of the Testator.

In pursuance of the said will, and of said act of the Legislature, the said Executors delivered over property to said Trustees amounting to the sum of $ 9,157.

On the 11th of February, 1789, the Legislature authorized the Trustees of Williamstown Free School to raise by lottery £ 1,200, for the purpose of erecting a building for the accommodation of the scholars. From this lottery $ 3,459.68 were realized, and to this sum was added, by subscriptions, for the above purpose $ 903.58, making $ 4,363.26, which sum was applied to the purpose intended.

The Williams Free School being thus founded at Williamstown, it continued until the 22d day of June, 1793, when an act was passed establishing Williams College, and erecting a corporation to conduct and manage this institution.

The ninth section of this act is in these words: "The Legislature of this Commonwealth may grant any further powers to, or alter, annul, limit, or restrain any of the powers by this act vested in the corporation, as shall be judged necessary to promote the best interests of the College; and may appoint overseers or visitors, with all necessary powers and authorities for the better aid, preservation, and government thereof."

The tenth section is in these words: — that all the property, real and personal, belonging to the Trustees of the Williams Free School, be, and the same hereby is, vested in the corporation which by this act is created.

The eleventh section gives £1,200 out of the treasury to Williams College. The College being thus established, several donations were made thereto, and among others, one from Woodbridge Little, Esq., of Pittsfield, in the month of May, 1811, as follows, viz.: —

"And it is always to be understood that the principal of the above sum, together with such further sum as I have it in contemplation to leave to said College, by my last will and testament, shall constitute a fund separate from the ordinary funds of said institution, to be called 'Woodbridge Little's Charitable Fund,' the principal of which shall forever remain in the hands of the President and Trustees of said College, not to be expended, and the annual interest thereof shall be from year to year applied in the manner following, viz.: The President of said College, for the time being, with two other persons whom the corporation of said College may appoint a committee for that purpose, shall select from the members of said College, such persons as said committee or a majority of them shall consider suitable objects of charitable aid and assistance, and such as intend to prepare themselves by their education for the ministry; who shall always be persons of good moral character, and whose talents promise eminent usefulness in the profession for which they are designed; and those members of said College who shall be thus selected by said committee shall be entitled to receive such portions of the annual income of said donation as said committee shall from time to time determine; not less in ordinary cases to any one student than at the rate of twenty-five dollars *per annum*, nor more than fifty dollars; but it shall be in the discretion of said committee in cases of peculiar need of such pecuniary assistance, and of characters highly deserving and meritorious, to increase the allowance to such student or students, to a sum not exceeding one hundred dollars *per annum*, and if in any one year the whole income of said donation shall not be applied as aforesaid, the interest shall be added to the principal, to increase the fund hereby established, or, at the discretion of the said committee, it may be applied to similar appropriations in the manner aforesaid, in subsequent years. Whenever the corporation of said College shall accept the above donation, on the terms above mentioned, this deed to have full and complete effect."

Donations of land were made to the College Corporation, whereon the College buildings are erected; and sums of money were subscribed and paid by persons in Williamstown and its vicinity, and some by persons in Vermont, and in the State of New York.

Four townships of land have been granted to Williams College, and it has an interest in a certain gore of land. It has also its three sixteenths of the bank tax, as expressed in the act making the apportionment thereof.

The College edifices are two brick buildings (one of which was the original Free School building), containing fifty-four rooms, a house for the President, a house for a professor, a chapel, and a laboratory.

The whole number of students which have been graduated is five hundred and twelve; the number resident has varied at different times; in the year 1815, the number was *fifty-eight;* in 1819 the number was *eighty-seven.*

In the year 1815 a project for removal commenced, and subsided. In 1818 the proposal was revived, in consequence of an application of certain gentlemen, members of the academic association at Amherst; a proposal was made about the same time to remove the institution to Northampton; a committee, consisting of highly respectable individuals, was empowered to decide on *location* in case of removal; they decided that Northampton was the preferable place. Nine out of twelve of the present Trustees are decidedly of opinion that the interests of the College would be greatly promoted by removal, and that it will languish and expire in its present location; three of the twelve are as decidedly of opinion that the College may, and will be maintained, as well as it has been where it now is.

In contemplation of removal, subscriptions have been made to the amount of fifty thousand dollars, and on the final and permanent fixing of the college in its present place, subscriptions have been made payable to the amount of fourteen thousand and five hundred dollars.

The committee herewith present a statement which contains, as they believe, a view admitted or proved by parties interested as to funds, viz.: —

Condition of the College if it retain its Location at Williamstown.

Net balance of disposable property, . . .		$ 28,432.55
Net amount of subscriptions, to take effect if the institution be fixed at Williamstown, . . .		17,681.65
		$ 46,114.20
Whole expense annually at the present establishment,		$ 4,100.00
To meet which, —		
1. Interest on $ 46,114.20, . . .	$ 2,766.85	
2. Income from term bills, room-rent, back tuition, ...	2,396.00	
		5,162.85
Leaving a balance in favor of the institution of . .		$ 1,062.85

Condition of the College if removed to Northampton.

From the amount disposable funds, viz.		$ 28,432.55
Deduct the Williams Free School fund, . . .		9,157.00
		$ 19,274.89
Subscription on condition of removal, ...		$ 50,000.00
Net proceeds of real estate belonging to the College at Williamstown, ...		2,500.00
		$ 71,774.89
Expense of land, buildings, &c., at Northampton, viz.: —		
2 Colleges, ...	$ 24,000	
6 Acres of land, ...	3,000	
2 Houses, ...	6,500	
Laboratory, ...	500	
		34,000.00
Balance, ...		$ 37,774.89
Annual income of balance, ...	$ 2,266.49	
Income from tuition, room-rent, quarter bills, &c., of course, *contingent.*		

The committee apprehend that this petition must be decided upon principles of *great importance*, and they have attended to the duty assigned to them with no small anxiety. They experience, however, a welcome relief in the fact that a revision of their doings by both branches of the Legislature remains to the interested parties.

Two questions seem to the committee to arise out of the facts and arguments which have been presented for their consideration.

First. — Has the Legislature *power* to grant the prayer of the petition? If it has,

Secondly. — Is it expedient to exercise their power in the manner prayed for?

The committee assume that every corporation created by Legislative authority is *that*, and *that only*, which the act of its creation makes it to be; or after its creation it is *that* which the Legislature, *with its consent*, enacts it to be.

That when a donation for charitable purposes has been made, and the Legislature is petitioned to for a grant of power to use and apply such donation, the Legislature can grant no other power than such as is consistent with the original intention of the donor.

That no power exists in or out of the Legislature to appropriate any charitable donation to any other purpose than that which the donor intended, *without his consent*. By the act of the 8th of March, 1785, Trustees were incorporated to apply the funds which were given by Ephraim Williams, Esq.

In the creation of this corporation, the Legislature appears to have done not more nor less than was necessary to give effect to his known intention. The individuals incorporated were William Williams, Theodore Sedgwick, Woodbridge Little, John Bacon, Thompson J. Skinner, Seth Swift, Daniel Collins, Israel Jones, and David Noble.

On the 22d of June, 1793, this corporation existed, and was in the full exercise of all the faculties which the Legislature had conferred. On the last-mentioned day, a new corporation was created. The natural persons on whom the corporate powers were conferred, were the nine persons who were incorporated in 1785, together with Stephen West and Elijah Williams, and the President of the institution *ex officio*.

The *first* mentioned corporation was not expressly *dissolved* by the act which created the *second*, but all the estate, real and personal, which had been vested in the first corporation was transferred to the second; and from that time the first corporation ceased to act under the law of 1785.

From these facts one of *three* consequences necessarily arises:—

First. The corporation of 1785 and that of 1793 are still existing; or,

Secondly. The corporation of 1785 was by its own consent, and by consent of the natural persons, incorporated in 1793, and by consent of the State *dissolved*; or,

Thirdly. The act of 1793 was a new charter to the corporation erected in 1785, enlarging its faculties and giving it a new name, which were by that corporation *accepted*.

The committee reject the *first* supposition, and are of opinion that there are not now in existence *two* corporations.

The committee reject also the *second* supposition, and are of opinion that the act of 1793 did not dissolve the original corporation.

They adopt the third supposition, because the act of 1793 was either an exercise of power not delegated to the Legislature, whereby the Williams fund was perverted from the uses intended by the donor; or it was a confirmation of faculties already given to use that donation consistently with the donor's intention.

The committee think it must be understood to be the latter, *because* the act of 1793 arose out of the petition of the Trustees of the Williams fund; *because* it must then have appeared to the Legislature that this fund, together with other funds which had been acquired, and those which the Legislature had it in view to grant, would justify the erection of a collegiate establishment on the foundation of the Williams Free School; *because* the Legislature in the act of 1793, seems, by the *name* and *location* of the *new institution* to have had in view the original donor, and the place which he had selected for the application of his charity *forever; because* the Justices of the Supreme Judicial Court, who were made the visitors of the corporation first erected, must be presumed to have assented to the act of 1793, although they are not made visitors of the new institution; *because*,

The second Corporation seems to have considered itself a continuation of the first one; the records of the second are kept in the same book with those of the first; the funds of the first institution have been applied and used jointly and indiscriminately with those of the second, and no separate and distinct accounts between the one and the other have been shown to the committee.

If the first corporation, and the natural persons who were made a corporation in 1793, and the *State*, jointly assented to the present institution, as appears to the committee to have been the fact, it seems to follow, as an unavoidable consequence, that there was an assent of these parties to the establishment of it at Williamstown.

By what process, in what form, and by what parties, is that assent to be now annulled, and the Williams fund separated from the College fund, and the latter transferred to be used in another place?

The petitioners admit that the Williams fund cannot be removed; but what natural or political body now exists to act in separating these funds? And if the Williams fund, after the lapse of six and twenty years, can be distinguished and set apart from all others, who is to receive and apply that fund according to the original intention of the donor, after the present corporation shall have been removed to another place? If a new corporation must be created to receive and apply the Williams fund before the proposed separation can be made, there are not now before the Legislature any petitioners who seek to be invested with this authority.

The committee consider the act of 1793, creating the College at Williamstown, not as changing the destination of the funds of Williamstown Free School (for that would necessarily imply an illegal exercise of power in the Legislature), but as extending its powers, and increasing its capacity; that it was promotive of the views of the beneficent Testator as well respecting the *general* object, viz. the dissemination of learning, as the *particular one*, the location at Williamstown.

That, in short, the Williamstown Free School fund was at all times to be considered as the stock, located and rooted *there*, on which public and private munificence might be occasionally engrafted.

This construction is strengthened by the fact that the residuary legatees of Colonel Williams have never claimed these funds as forfeited by any supposed illegal interference of the Legislature by the act of 1793, and by the complete and absolute amalgamation of the funds of the Free School, with those of the College, and the absolutely undistinguishable manner of their appropriation to a common object, all which seems necessarily to imply *a single institution.*

And this is a construction in which the contingent claimants under the will of Colonel Williams unquestionably acquiesce. The committee respectfully submit that the Williams fund cannot be lawfully separated (even if it were practicable to do so) from the other funds of Williams College. That the Legislature, and all parties interested, and lapse of time, have concurred in making the original donation the vital principle of this corporation. And that the Legislature, after having first raised the *Free School* to be a *College*, and after having sanctioned its existence so long in the latter relation to the public, and to the *memory* of the *founder*, cannot now break up this connection and transfer the College to another place, and leave the *Free School* to the contingencies of the future.

The committee have supposed it to be their duty to notice that Woodbridge Little, Esq., of Pittsfield, and some persons in Williamstown, and some in Vermont, and some in the State of New York, have made donations to Williams College, and the committee suppose that they ought not to disregard the presumption that the *location* of this seminary constituted *some part* of the motives to this *bounty*, and the committee cannot but doubt the *justice* of removing, and consequently the power to remove this seminary to any place not contemplated by such donors, to be the site of the future use of their charities.

The committee have expressed this opinion on the law with the most unaffected diffidence. But they have thought it their duty to express some opinion hereon, because the two Houses must judge of, and decide upon, the legal principles which arise on this petition, since this is not a case, as the committee believe, in which the opinion of the Supreme Judicial Court may be required. The constitution authorizes the aid of such opinions *only* in *cases where no private rights are involved.* It is apparent that this subject relates to parties who may, hereafter, possibly become *suitors* in that court, and whose rights cannot be judged of until they are *first* heard.

The committee, however, have this grateful certainty, that if they have erred in opinion, they may safely rely on those to whom they report, to save the interested from the evil of this error.

The *second* inquiry is on the *expediency* of the proposed removal.

The committee admit that if the question were *now*, whether a College should be established at Northampton or at Williamstown, well informed and honest men might fairly differ in opinion. The principal arguments urged in this behalf were grounded (on the one side) on the central position of Northampton, on the mass of industrious, moral, wealthy, well-informed, and truly respectable population of the counties which are traversed by *the Connecticut*, and on the superior facilities of access, and the attractions which arise from the aggregation of educated men. These considerations were resisted (on the other side) by arguments intended to show that seclusion is favorable to literary proficiency, and to purity of morals; and that the advantages of comparatively smaller expenditure in the process of education were more attainable in Williamstown than in Northampton.

The committee beg leave to state, with great deference, and in the sincere hope that they shall not prejudice either party in the future consideration of this subject, and in conformity also with their conclusions on the first *great question* in this case, that they are of opinion that so important a measure as the removal of Williams College ought not to take place without a *reasonable* and *unembarrassed conviction that some great benefit will result therefrom not attainable in the present location.* The committee are by no means satisfied that *mere location* determines the degree of estimation and respect in which any literary institution may be held. It is *reputation* which constitutes the *attraction*, and this is founded on the modes and means of instruction; and although it might be a very interesting question whether fifty thousand or a hundred thousand dollars should be *originally* expended at Northampton or at Williamstown, yet considering the length of time which has elapsed since the establishment of Williams College in the place where it is, that a considerable part of its funds were given in contemplation of its permanency there, and considering too that no change of very imposing cast is likely to be effected *immediately*, or before the lapse of some years, in the future usefulness of this institution, if at all, by removal, the committee have come to the result that it is *inexpedient* to remove Williams College to Northampton.

In concluding, the committee pray leave to state that they do most highly appreciate, and most profoundly respect the motives of the petitioners; these are *unquestionably* founded in a truly honorable and elevated desire, to extend the usefulness of this respectable College in promoting learning, virtue, piety, and religion; and, under these impressions, the committee feel the most sincere regret that their perception of duty compels them to submit to the two Houses, that it is neither *lawful* nor *expedient* to grant the prayer of the petition; and for these reasons, respectfully *report*, that the petitioners have leave to withdraw their petition. All which is respectfully submitted.

EBEN. GAY, *per order.*

February 1, 1820.

In Senate, *February* 8, 1820. — Read and accepted. Sent down for concurrence.

JOHN PHILLIPS, *President.*

House of Representatives, *February* 14, 1820. — Read and concurred.

E. H. MILLS, *Speaker pro tem.*

GENERAL INDEX.

THE END.

ERRATA.

Page 115, *for* "1805," *read* "1806," *in three instances.*
" 239, 7th line from bottom, *for* "Electa Williams, a half-sister," *read* "Electa Sergeant, a niece" of Ephraim Williams.
" 244, line 15, *for* "our generation," *read* "another generation."
" 245, " 7, *for* "Lecture," *read* "Two Lectures."
" 264, " 24, *for* "Mr. Amos Lawrence," *read* "Mrs. Amos Lawrence."
" 378, " 7, *for* "Great Falls, N. H.," *read* "North Berwick, Me."
" 380, " 7, *for* "and," *read* "out."

www.ingramcontent.com/pod-product-compliance
Lightning Source LLC
LaVergne TN
LVHW021136110826
845150LV00005B/1044

* 9 7 8 1 4 2 5 5 4 9 4 1 1 *